HIGH-PERFORMING FAMILIES: CAUSES, CONSEQUENCES, AND CLINICAL SOLUTIONS

Edited by
Bryan E. Robinson and Nancy D. Chase

THE FAMILY PSYCHOLOGY AND COUNSELING SERIES

■ ■ ■

Developed Collaboratively by the American Counseling Association and
the International Association of Marriage and Family Counselors

HIGH-PERFORMING FAMILIES: CAUSES, CONSEQUENCES, AND CLINICAL SOLUTIONS

10 9 8 7 6 5 4 3 2 1

American Counseling Association
5999 Stevenson Avenue
Alexandria, VA 22304

Director of Publications
Carolyn C. Baker

Production Manager
Bonny Gaston

Copy Editor
Elaine Dunn

Cover design by Martha Woolsey

Library of Congress Cataloging-in-Publication Data

High-performing families: causes, consequences, and clinical
solutions / edited by Bryan E. Robinson and Nancy D. Chase.
    p. cm. (The family psychology and counseling series)
    Includes bibliographical references.
    ISBN 1-55620-183-4 (alk. paper)
    1. Work and family—United States. 2. Workaholics—United
States. 3. Children of working parents—United States. 4. Family
psychotherapy—United States. I. Robinson, Bryan E. II. Chase,
Nancy D.

HD4904.25.H54 2000
362.82—dc21   00-040156

The Family Psychology and Counseling Series

Counseling the Aging and Their Families
Irene Deitch, PhD, and Candace Ward Howell, MS

Counseling Asian Families From a Systems Perspective
Kit S. Ng, PhD

Counseling Families With Chronic Illness
Susan McDaniel, PhD

Ethical Casebook for the Practice of Marriage and Family Counseling
Patricia Stevens, PhD

Feminist Family Therapy
Kathleen M. May, PhD

High-Performing Families: Causes, Consequences, and Clinical Solutions
Bryan E. Robinson, PhD, and Nancy D. Chase, PhD

Mid-Life Divorce Counseling
Lita Linzer Schwartz, PhD

Social Construction in Couple and Family Counseling
John D. West, EdD, Donald L. Bubenzer, PhD, and James Robert Bitter, EdD

Techniques in Marriage and Family Counseling, Volume One
Richard E. Watts, PhD

Transitioning From Individual to Family Counseling
Charles Huber, PhD

Understanding Stepfamilies: Implications for Assessment and Treatment
Debra Huntley, PhD

In Preparation

African American Family Counseling
Jo-Ann Lipford Sanders, PhD, and Carla Bradley, PhD

Integrative and Biopsychosocial Therapy
Len T. Sperry, MD, PhD

Practical Approaches for School Counselors: Integrating Family Counseling in School Settings
Lynn D. Miller, PhD

Techniques in Marriage and Family Counseling, Volume Two
Richard E. Watts, PhD

Advisory Board

■ ■ ■

THE FAMILY PSYCHOLOGY AND COUNSELING SERIES

Table of Contents

From the Series Editor

Did they develop this monograph just for me? The volume editors Robinson and Chase are like the boy in the story of the Emperor's New Clothes. They, along with their co-contributors, clearly expose how overwork and overdedication to career are unhealthy and how family life and marriage are compromised and children frequently sacrifice their own needs for those of their parents. They show how mental health workers are blind and do not see this as a problem and therefore misdiagnose and provide treatment incorrectly.

As I read these chapters, I can see some of the negative impacts of my workaholism and wonder what I have lost or missed. Success has had a severe price tag, and the contributors to this monograph help us to identify patterns and how to prevent their continuation. Learning how to balance work and life is probably what most of us desire. I discussed this in a January 1997 editorial statement for *The Family Journal*.

> Recently I completed a 5K run at the American Psychological Associations annual convention. The race has been called the Rat Race. I have been able to run this race for several years, however, this year it was different. Before giving us the official go ahead, the starter told a little story about the only problem with winning the Rat Race is that when it is over, you are still a rat. For some reason, I couldn't get this thought out of my mind. It was déjà vu and I was back in the 1960's. Again, I was

thinking more and more about dropping out of the Rat Race. Do I have the courage? My two oldest children are in their 20's and are making decisions upon values. My wife and I did the same thing at their age when we sold our house and all of our possessions and went to Hawaii with two dozen boxes, mainly books, two children and a car. What happened? How did I get off of that track and on to this new one? When did I lose control and rejoin the rat race. I know I didn't do it consciously. What do I do now? I like what I do, at least I think I do, however, I am confident that I meet the definition of the word workaholic. Can I give myself permission to provide for more of my family's emotional needs and fewer material ones? Would I know how to do it over time? Being a systems theorist, I wonder if my wife and family would want a closer relationship. Families of origins dictate who we are and what distance is comfortable. (p. 3)

In Suzanne Levine's book (2000), *Father Courage*, she describes the challenges that men have trying to put families first. She describes many of the reasons causing the stress felt by fathers and mothers trying to find effective roles in today's world. It is easy to see as I read these two books how careers can zoom while marriages and friendships crumble.

I urge that you read *High-Performing Families* carefully. There are a lot of case examples and practical suggestions that allow the reader to see just how it is possible to create harmony and balance in our lives. My applause and admiration go to Bryan Robinson, Nancy Chase, and their co-contributors.

—*Jon Carlson, PsyD, EdD*
Series Editor

Reference

Levine, S. B. (2000). *Father Courage: What happens when men put family first.* New York: Harcourt.

Preface

The director-actor Penny Marshall, confessing to being a workaholic in a *People* magazine interview, said that when she is working, she is obsessively working and that she loses all concept of what day it is. Her devotion to work means that she puts her personal life second. Throngs of high performers openly admit their obsession for work while concealing the darker side of their obsessive drive. They testify to their passion for work and take pride in their nonstop schedules—both of which reflect their artistic temperament and present them in a favorable light. They fail, however, to mention their episodes of depression, anxiety, and chronic fatigue that almost always occur as a side effect of binge working for days on end. High performers are extolled by a society that honors their accomplishments while turning a deaf ear to the accompanying family discord, brittle marital relationships, and problems with children.

This monograph is a befitting one for the new millennium, given the fact that for the past 30 years, the mental health and family psychology fields have kept their heads in the sand regarding the debilitating effects of high performance, workaholism, and parentification on the family system. Throughout the years, the mental health profession has co-conspired to aid and abet this problem by extolling the positive features of high performance while failing to cite the negative effects on the individual, children, and the family. Clinicians have minimized or downplayed the problems endemic in high-performing families to the extent that we believe it has become one of the best-dressed mental health problems of the past century. Some professionals have looked on these problems much like society views caffeine or prescription drugs—as harmless, even beneficial. Instead of citing the problems of compulsive high performance on individuals and families, well-meaning clinicians often prescribe work immersion as a solution to a problem rather than the cause of one.

As early as 1971, Wayne Oates coined the term *workaholism* and elucidated its deleterious effects on family relationships and child development. Despite this warning and almost 30 years later, workaholism still has not been accepted into the official psychiatric and psychological nomenclature (Pietropinto, 1986). Moreover, concepts and clinical assumptions still lack clarification, definition, and empirical testing. In the late 1990s, however, there was indication that a trend toward greater research interest and activity in this area was beginning to take form. Although few studies exist on the impact of workaholism and high performance on family functioning, the first study to examine the relationship between workaholism and marital adjustment was completed at the end of the last millennium (Robinson, Carroll, & Flowers, in press). Findings from the study indicated a pattern of marital estrangement, fewer positive feelings toward spouses, and more external locus of control among spouses of workaholics compared with spouses of nonworkaholics (Robinson et al., in press).

It is important to emphasize that the contributing authors to this volume are not denouncing high performance, career success, or achievement per se. On the contrary, the goal is to present the downside of compulsive overperformance, which is frequently overshadowed by the accomplishments that high performance brings. This volume seeks to help family counselors begin to look behind the attractive facade of high performance and to identify the dysfunction extant in these families. We call it the Tao of high work performance. The United States was built on hard work. It landed us on the moon and gave us vaccines for polio and other devastating diseases. Hard work is necessary for a happy and healthy standard of living and for our survival as a country and a species. However, when achieving, performing, and productivity become imbalanced, marital and family relationships suffer. Healthy high performance (e.g., hard work) becomes compulsive high performance or workaholism when two conditions prevail: (a) when overfunctioning by one or more family members negatively affects the healthy functioning of other family members in the family system and (b) when change in one aspect of the family constellation promotes unhealthy overfunctioning in one or more family members, as when a child is expected to fulfill the role of an absent workaholic parent. Thus, a high performer could be a parent, spouse, or child. Typically, compulsive high performance becomes problematic in one or a combination of the following conditions:

- the high performer works to the exclusion of other life activities;
- the high performer abdicates his or her parenting role in favor of working, thereby creating parentification among one or more children;
- the parental bond becomes stronger than the marital bond as a result of high performance; or
- high performance interferes with marital communication and contributes to a breakdown of the marital bond and leads to spousal alienation.

Our goal for this volume was to bring together several diverse bodies of research to further clarify the familial problems that masquerade behind the masks of high performance, workaholism (e.g., compulsive overworking), and *parentification*—the process in which children, because of the family's roles and functioning, are required to forfeit their own needs for attention, comfort, and guidance to accommodate and care for the emotional needs and pursuits of adult family members. In merging these diverse bodies of research, we hope to clarify the distinctions between healthy and dysfunctional patterns of high performance, workaholism, and parentification. Moreover, we have sought to present the causes, consequences, and clinical solutions to these grossly understudied and misunderstood family problems.

This book is composed of three parts. Part I examines high performance, workaholism, and family relationships. Chapters 1 and 2 provide a sociocultural and familial context of the hurried and harried society within which families function in the 21st century. The impact of high performance and workaholism on family functioning is presented through theoretical frameworks, reviews of research, case studies of the contributors' clinical experiences, and suggestions for family intervention and counseling.

Part II further exposes the problems due to compulsive high performance and workaholism by addressing the intersect between high performance in the workplace and family patterns and relationships. Chapter 3 focuses on the relationship problems of workaholics as they are manifested on the job, and chapter 4 explores the professional careers of attorneys vis-à-vis high performance and family relationships.

Part III highlights the relationship between high performance and parentification outcomes in families. Chapters 5, 6, and 7 focus on the detrimental aspects of high performance on children and the diverse pathways in which pathological parentification can emerge. Adult legacies of psychological maladjustment due to parentification, case examples, and recommendations for clinical interventions for family counselors who deal with parentification are presented.

We wish to extend our appreciation to all the contributors to this volume whose expertise has made it such a unique collection. It is our hope that this book will fill a gap in the family literature, become a valuable resource for family practitioners, and support the essential and important work that they perform.

—Bryan E. Robinson, PhD, and Nancy D. Chase, PhD, MSW

References

Oates, W. (1971). *Confessions of a workaholic.* New York: World Publishing.

Pietropinto, A. (1986). The workaholic spouse. *Medical Aspects of Human Sexuality, 20,* 89–96.

Robinson, B. E., Carroll, J. J., & Flowers, C. (in press). Marital estrangement, positive affect, and locus of control among spouses of workaholics and spouses of nonworkaholics: A national study. *American Journal of Family Therapy.*

Biographies

Bryan E. Robinson, PhD, is a professor of counseling, special education, and child development in the College of Education at the University of North Carolina at Charlotte. He maintains a private psychotherapy practice in Charlotte, North Carolina, and has authored numerous books and research publications on family functioning. He is a member of the American Counseling Association (ACA), the International Association of Marriage and Family Counselors, and a clinical member of the American Association of Marriage and Family Therapists. He is distinguished for his groundbreaking research on work addiction and the family, for which he received ACA's 1998 Extended Research Award. His research has appeared in *The Family Journal, Journal of Counseling and Development, American Journal of Family Therapy, Journal of Family Psychotherapy, Psychotherapy,* and many others. His most recent books are *Chained to the Desk: A Guide for Workaholics, Their Partners and Children, and the Clinicians Who Treat Them* (New York University Press, 1998) and *Don't Let Your Mind Stunt Your Growth* (New Harbinger, 2000).

Nancy D. Chase, PhD, MSW, is an associate professor in the Department of English at Georgia State University, Atlanta, Georgia. She is also a licensed social worker and former clinical associate at the Atlanta Area Child Guidance Clinic, where she worked primarily with adolescents and adults. She is editor and contributing author of *Burdened Children: Theory, Research, and Treat-*

ment of Parentification (Sage, 1999). She has published numerous articles on variables affecting young adults' adjustment to college, including family alcoholism, parentification, literary tasks, and reader responses to text. Her work has been published in *Alcoholism Treatment Quarterly, American Journal of Family Therapy, Journal of Reading Behavior,* and *Journal of Developmental Education.*

Jon Carlson, PsyD, EdD, is distinguished professor at Governors State University in University Park, Illinois, and director of the Lake Geneva Wellness Clinic in Wisconsin. He is the founding editor of *The Family Journal: Counseling and Therapy for Couples and Families* and has served as president of the International Association of Marriage and Family Counselors. Dr. Carlson holds a diplomate in family psychology from the American Board of Professional Psychology. He is a fellow of the American Psychological Association and a certified sex therapist by the American Association of Sex Educators, Counselors, and Therapists. He has authored over 25 books and 125 professional articles. He has received numerous awards for his professional contributions from major professional organizations, including the American Counseling Association, the Association for Counselor Education and Supervision, and the American Psychological Association. Dr. Carlson and his spouse of 32 years, Laura, are the parents of five children and grandparents of two.

Contributors

Jane J. Carroll, PhD, is an assistant professor in the Department of Counseling, Special Education, and Child Development, University of North Carolina at Charlotte, Charlotte, North Carolina.

Sean Casey, MEd, is a graduate student in the Department of Psychology, Georgia State University, Atlanta, Georgia.

Nancy D. Chase, PhD, MSW, is an associate professor in the Department of English, Georgia State University, Atlanta, Georgia.

Clarence Hibbs, PhD, is a professor of psychology in the Social Sciences Division, Pepperdine University, Malibu, California.

Gregory J. Jurkovic, PhD, is an associate professor in the Department of Psychology, Georgia State University, Atlanta, Georgia.

Robert Miller, EdD, is associate director and director of training at the Thomas E. Cook Counseling Center, Virginia Technical Institute, Blacksburg, Virginia.

Richard Morrell, JD, is vice president of the Meridian Educational Resource Group, Inc., a nonprofit community-based outreach program for children and families, and a doctoral student in the Department of Psychology, Georgia State University, Atlanta, Georgia.

Gayle Porter, PhD, is an associate professor in the School of Business, Rutgers, The State University of New Jersey.

Bryan E. Robinson, PhD, is a professor in the Department of Counseling, Special Education, and Child Development, University of North Carolina at Charlotte, Charlotte, North Carolina.

Marolyn Wells, PhD, is a professor of counseling and psychological services at the Counseling Center, Georgia State University, Atlanta, Georgia.

PART I

HIGH PERFORMANCE, WORKAHOLISM, AND FAMILY RELATIONSHIPS

Workaholism and Family Functioning: A Psychological Profile of Family Members

Bryan E. Robinson, PhD

Over the past three decades, alarming reports on the effects of alcoholism on the alcoholic's spouse, children, and family interactions appeared in the literature (e.g., Jacob, Favorini, Meisel, & Anderson, 1978). A vast body of empirically based literature has evolved on adult children of alcoholics, showing how young children carry their legacies into adulthood where they continue to be at risk in terms of psychosocial adjustment and intimate relationships (e.g., Kelly & Myers, 1996; Post & Robinson, 1998; Post, Webb, & Robinson, 1991; Robinson & Rhoden, 1998; Tweed & Ryff, 1991). Parental alcoholism has been linked to low self-esteem, external locus of control, higher levels of depression, and greater anxiety among children, just to name a few of the variables that have been studied.

Three decades ago it was also suggested that workaholism may negatively affect the development of children, although little attention has been paid to this important topic since Wayne Oates (1971) first coined the term *workaholism*. During the late 1980s, workaholism was identified as a serious and legitimate type of compulsive disorder that created family dysfunction and harmed marriages (Pietropinto, 1986; Robinson, 1989). During that decade, psychiatrist Anthony Pietropinto (1986) declared that family conflict is inevitable in workaholic families. Although the term *workaholism* became a household word in the 1990s, it still has not been accepted into the official psychiatric and psychological nomenclatures as we enter the 21st century.

Recent reports, however, indicate that while attempting to medicate emotional pain by overworking, workaholics suffer some of the same symptoms as alcoholics (Robinson, 1997a, 1997b, 1998a). They have similar denial systems, reality distortion, need to control, and highs and lows. Careers take off while marriages and friendships crumble as workaholics get adrenaline highs from their work binges and experience hangovers as they ultimately start to come down. The downward swing is often accompanied by withdrawal, irritability, anxiety, and depression. It would follow that if children of workaholics live in similar symptomatic families, they would experience similar coping problems to those of children of alcoholics.

Indeed, recent studies suggest that workaholism, like alcoholism, takes its toll on other family members living in this condition and that mental health risks may exist for children and spouses of workaholics. The structural and dynamic characteristics of the workaholic family indicate that all family members are negatively affected by workaholism and that they may develop a set of mental health problems of their own (Robinson, 1998a, 1998b, 1998c). The structure of the workaholic family system is such that spouses and children become extensions of the workaholic's ego, inevitably leading to family conflict (Robinson, 1996a, 1996b).

This chapter reviews the body of literature on the workaholic, the workaholic family system, and its influence on the psychological outcomes of its members, followed by implications for counselors in clinical practice.

The Workaholic: A Psychological Profile

Although the term has been variously described and categorized, *workaholism*—which is used interchangeably with *work addiction* in this chapter—is defined as "an obsessive–compulsive disorder that manifests itself through self-imposed demands, an inability to regulate work habits, and an overindulgence in work to the exclusion of most other life activities" (Robinson, 1998a, p. 7). Workaholism is an addiction in the same way that alcoholism is an addiction.

Progressive in nature, it is an unconscious attempt to resolve unmet psychological needs that have roots in the family of origin and can lead to an unmanageable life, family disintegration, serious health problems, and even death.

Similar to alcoholics, workaholics have rigid thinking patterns that feed their addiction. Because of their self-absorption with work, workaholics often do not notice signals, such as physical aches and pains or reduced ability to function, that can be warnings of serious health problems. Workaholism damages the mental and physical health of the workaholic. It is physiological and chemical in nature and can lead to anxiety, depression, and even suicidal ideation. Work highs, reminiscent of the alcoholic euphoria, run a cycle of adrenaline-charged binge working, followed by a downward swing. Euphoria eventually gives way to work hangovers characterized by withdrawal, depression, irritability, and anxiety. Like other addictions, there is a point at which workaholics hit bottom, some before they can admit they have a problem and get the help they need. Finding themselves alone, unable to feel, and cut off from everyone they care about, some workaholics become so depressed they cannot get out of bed. Widespread in its devastation, health problems hit crisis proportions and marriages crumble (Robinson, 1998a). These personal problems are often carried into the workplace where they lead to inefficiency and erode trust throughout the organization (Porter, 1998).

Workaholism has many faces. Robinson (in press) developed a typology of workaholics based on their level of work initiation in proportion to their work completion. The stereotyped workaholics that Oates (1971) referred to as dyed-in-the-wool were classified as *relentless workaholics*—those who are high work initiators and high in work completion and who work compulsively and constantly day and night, holidays, and weekends with no let up and no periods of downtime. They are hurried and relentless in meeting deadlines, often weeks ahead of schedule. *The bulimic workaholic*, who is low in work initiation and high in work completion, has extreme work patterns that vacillate from bingeing to purging. This is the procrastinating workaholic whom Fassel (1990) called the work anorexic. *Attention deficit workaholics* are adrenaline-seeking workaholics who are easily bored and constantly seeking stimulation. They are high work initiators but low in work completion. They have difficulty keeping their focus on the task before them, get bored, and jump ahead to the next item on the agenda, leaving many projects unfinished. *Savoring workaholics* are slow, deliberate, and methodical. Consummate perfectionists, they are afraid that the finished project is not going to be good enough. They savor their work just as alcoholics would savor a shot of bourbon. They are low in work initiation and low in work completion because they prolong and create additional work when they realize they are nearly finished with a project. They are nitpickers who overanalyze, get bogged down in detail, and reexamine tasks to the point that it impedes their ability to initiate and complete work in a timely fashion.

Early research on workaholism indicated that workaholics had significantly higher scores on depression, anxiety, and anger than nonworkaholics (Haymon, 1992/1993). These findings confirm earlier anecdotal reports that work addiction has severely negative consequences including depression, anxiety, and anger (Fassel, 1990; Oates, 1971; Robinson, 1989) and that underneath obsessive work habits are the workaholic's inferiority feelings, fear of failure, and defense against unresolved anxiety (Pietropinto, 1986; Spruell, 1987). Haymon (1992/1993) concluded,

> Other maladaptive behaviors such as an inability to say no, and/ or limit the amount of time committed to others, accepting work that "others won't do," and maintaining a hurried, frenzied pace by over-committing and overdoing, may reflect anxiety, in the form of excessive functioning and mania as exemplified in continuous goal-directed animations accompanied by an exaggerated concept of one's abilities. (p. 45)

The first national study on workaholism in the United States assessed work addiction as defined by high scores on measurements the researchers termed "work involvement and driveness" and low scores on a measure of "enjoyment of work" (Spence & Robbins, 1992). Work addiction was contrasted with *work enthusiasm*, which was defined as high work involvement and enjoyment and low drivenness.

Women were found to show significantly higher scores on the Driven, Enjoyment, Job Stress, Job Involvement, and Time Commitment scales, whereas there was no difference by gender on the Work Involvement, Perfectionism, and Nondelegation scales. Reports of health complaints among the respondents increased with greater scores on Job Stress, Perfectionism, Nondelegation, and Driven scales. A negative correlation was reported between enjoyment of work scores and health complaints. A major difference between work enthusiasts and workaholics was that workaholics perceived themselves as having more job stress, perfectionism, and unwillingness to delegate job responsibilities to others. Moreover, workaholics of both sexes reported a greater number of health complaints than did work enthusiasts. A replication of this study with Japanese workers reported a significant impact of workaholism on health complaints and job stress among Japanese male employees (Kanai, Wakabayashi, & Fling, 1996).

These large-scale studies, similar to Haymon's (1992/1993) study, also confirmed many of the early clinical reports (e.g., Oates, 1971; Pietropinto, 1986; Robinson, 1989) by suggesting that workaholics, compared with nonworkaholics, have more difficulty delegating, feel more stress from the job, tend to be perfectionists, and have more health complaints. Workaholism and health complaints also were significantly associated in a positive direction in a study of 121 full-time university employees in the southeastern United States (Fogus, 1998). These findings are further congruent with Haymon's (1992/1993) conclusions that workaholics have greater anxiety, anger, and depression than nonworkaholics. Spence and Robbins (1992) concluded, "It is likely that the workaholics and others elevated on the Job Stress scale of our study tend to be more generally anxious than others" (p. 177). Other investigators have established that chronic trait anxiety increases vulnerability to physical illness (Taylor, 1990) and that work addiction is directly related to stress proneness and burnout (Nagy, 1985; Pace & Suojanem, 1988). Figure 1.1 shows a profile of the workaholic.

FIGURE 1.1
A Profile of the Workaholic

The handful of studies that have been conducted on workaholics indicate that, compared with nonworkaholics, workaholics tend to have more

- health complaints
- difficulty delegating
- stress from the job
- perfectionism
- anxiety
- anger
- depression
- difficulty feeling than thinking
- hours at work per week
- families that they perceive as dysfunctional
- difficulty with intimacy
- self-inadequacy
- impaired social functioning

According to social scientist Uehata (1993), in Japan it is widely known that chronic, excessive work habits and work-related stress can result in various mental, physical, and interpersonal problems, including death from overworking. Although Japan enjoys an international reputation for strong work ethics, various medical and psychosocial problems have surfaced associated with workaholism. According to Ishiyama and Kitayama (1994), helping professionals and social critics stress the necessity for improvements and reevaluation of how individuals, employers, society, and the government deal with workaholism and job stress.

Researchers Haraguchi, Tsuda, and Ozeki (1991) asserted that workaholism is closely associated with high work stress reactions such as depression, anxiety, anger, and irritability, as well as behaviors such as absenteeism, withdrawal, low productivity, mistakes, and accident proneness on the job. They reported that workers with these high stress reactions tended to work more hours per week (over 70 hours) and more overtime (50 hours per month) than workers with low stress reactions.

In fact, because death from overworking has become so common in their culture, the Japanese coined a name for it. Known as *karoshi*, it refers to the 10,000 workers a year who drop dead at their desks from 60- to 70-hour workweeks. *Karoshi* among corporate workers in their 40s and 50s has become so common that the Japanese workplace has been dubbed "a killing field" (Ishiyama & Kitayama, 1994).

The Workaholic Family: An Overview

Over time, family members build a pattern of responses to their loved one's work addiction (Robinson, 1998c). Spouses, not unlike alcoholic spouses, become consumed with trying to get workaholics to curb their compulsive behaviors and spend more time in the relationship. Spouses and children of workaholics report feeling lonely, unloved, isolated, and emotionally and physically abandoned (Robinson, 1998b, 1998c). They may habitually complain or become cynical about the workaholic's abusive work habits. A common refrain is that even when workaholics are physically present, they are emotionally unavailable and disconnected from the family. Spouses of workaholics may have single-handedly raised the children and complain of having the major portion of parenting responsibilities dumped on them. Filled with resentment of this one-sided arrangement, they tend to react with anger and complaining. Some workaholics then use the verbal complaints as justification for their physical and emotional aloofness. Thus, circularity often occurs when workaholics assert, "I wouldn't work so much if you wouldn't nag me all the time" whereupon spouses retort, "I wouldn't bug you so much if you didn't work all the time."

In Japanese families, workaholic men are often referred to as "7–11 husbands"—a term for marginal fathers who work from dawn to dusk, have extricated themselves from family life, and live on the fringes of their families (Ishiyama & Kitayama, 1994). In both Japan (Ishiyama & Kitayama, 1994) and the United States (Robinson, 1998a), once family alliances become solidified in the workaholic father's absence, spouses resent having their turfs violated when workaholics do try to become more actively involved in their families. Older children too often rebuff the workaholic's attempts to reconnect with the family because they feel the reentry is too little, too late. Japanese wives use the derogatory term *nure-ochiba* (a wet fallen leaf stuck to the bottom of their shoes) to refer to retired workaholic husbands who do not know what to do with themselves when they are not working and who hang around the house expecting their wives to be in charge of their spare time (Ishiyama & Kitayama, 1994).

A national study conducted in the United States provides evidence suggesting that workaholism can lead to brittle family relationships, contribute to marital conflict, and create dysfunction within the family (Robinson & Post, 1995, 1997). The investigators administered a battery of instruments to 107 participants from Workaholics Anonymous across the United States and Canada. Workaholism was significantly correlated with current family functioning. The higher the work addiction scores, the higher the degree of perceived dysfunction in one's current family. Greater work addiction was related to less effective problem solving, lower communication, less clearly established family roles, fewer affective responses, less affective involvement, and lower general functioning in families. On the basis of the work addiction scores, three groups were established from the sample: low, medium, and high risk for work addiction. Individuals in the high-risk group were more likely to rate their families as having problems in communication or in the exchange of information among family members than those in the low- or medium-risk categories. They were more likely to rate their families as having unclearly defined family roles and believed their families were less likely to have established behavior patterns for handling repetitive family functions than those in the other groups. They also said their families were less likely to appropriately express feelings in response to various events that occurred in the family. High-risk adults said their families were less likely to be interested in and value each other's activities and concerns. High-risk individuals also were perceived to more likely have problems in the general functioning and overall health and pathology of their families than individuals at low or medium risk for work addiction.

Although spouses and children were not directly targeted in this study, one could predict from its findings and from other empirical research that both spouses and offspring of workaholics may be at risk for certain psychological outcomes, not unlike those of family members of alcoholics.

Spouses of Workaholics: A Psychological Profile

Most of the information that is available on marital relationships of workaholics comes from magazine surveys (Herbst, 1996; Weeks, 1995), a poll assessing the perspectives of physicians (Pietropinto, 1986), and case study reports (Robinson, 1998a).

A survey by the American Academy of Matrimonial Lawyers cited preoccupation with work as one of the top four causes of divorce (Robinson, 1998a). *Exec Magazine* surveyed the work habits of 3,000 men in which one third reported having been accused of having an affair because of the long hours they had put into their jobs (Weeks, 1995). Eighty-six percent of those surveyed said their personal relationships were marred by work-related stress. Similar findings were reported in a survey by *McCall's Magazine*, in which 80% of the readers said their husbands worked too much (Herbst, 1996).

A group of 400 physicians were polled regarding their observations of workaholics as marital spouses (Pietropinto, 1986). Results indicated that workaholics devote an inordinate amount of time to work as opposed to marriage and they have higher than normal expectations for marital satisfaction. They are more demanding of achievement in their children than nonworkaholics, and their typical approach to leisure time is to fill it with work activities. The workaholic's usual style in marital disagreements is to avoid confrontation or use passive–aggressive maneuvers such as silence and sulking. Physicians as a group generally agreed that these combined factors wreak havoc on the family unit. A 10-point profile, developed from hundreds of case studies from spouses of workaholics, is shown in Figure 1.2 (Robinson, 1998a, 1998b).

FIGURE 1.2
A Profile of Spouses of Workaholics

- Feel ignored, neglected, closed out, unloved, and unappreciated because of the workaholic's physical and emotional remoteness.
- Believe they are carrying the emotional burdens of the marriage and parenting, which brings feelings of loneliness and aloneness in the marriage.
- View themselves as second choice behind work because family time is dictated by work schedules and demands that come first.
- Perceive themselves as extensions of the workaholic who must be the center of attention.
- View themselves as controlled, manipulated, and sometimes rushed by their partners who "call the shots."
- Use attention-seeking measures to get their partners to see them or give in to conversations and activities around work in order to connect with them.
- View the relationship as serious and intense with a minimum of carefree time or fun.
- Harbor guilt for wanting more in the relationship while their partners are applauded by colleagues and society for their accomplishments.
- Have low self-esteem and feel defective in some way that they cannot measure up to their partners, who are often put on a pedestal.
- Question their own gratitude and sanity when faced with the accolades bestowed on their workaholic spouse.

The first and only study to directly investigate the marital relationships of workaholics indicated that women married to workaholic men were at higher risk for marital problems than women married to men who carry an average workload (Robinson, Carroll, & Flowers, in press). A random national sample of 326 women, drawn from the membership list of the American Counseling Association, was surveyed. Spouses of workaholics reported feeling more estranged from their husbands, had less positive feelings toward them, and felt in less control of their lives than a comparison group of women married to nonworkaholics.

Children of Workaholics: A Psychological Profile

Case studies of children of workaholics indicate that offspring of workaholics become resentful of their parents' emotional absence

(Oates, 1971; Robinson, 1992, 1998a). Psychologically unavailable to their offspring, workaholics generally do not take an active role in their children's development. When they do, it is often to make sure that their children are mastering their perfectionist standards. Expectations are often out of reach for children of workaholics who internalize their failure as self-inadequacy. The anecdotal literature suggests that many children of workaholics carry the same legacy as their workaholic parents: They become other-directed and approval seeking to meet adult expectations (Robinson, 1998a).

Unlike alcoholic families in which children can point to the bottle as a source of their discontent, in workaholic families there is no visible cause for the confusion, frustration, and self-inadequacy because the Puritan work ethic prevents work addiction from being viewed as a viable compulsive disorder. It is, in fact, an addiction that gets rewarded and encouraged in U.S. society (Porter, 1996).

Oates (1971) identified four symptoms from his conversations with several children of workaholics. *Preoccupation* was the most significant symptom cited by children of workaholics whose parents always had something else on their minds. The second symptom was *haste*—their parents were always rushing around. *Irritability* was pronounced as when parents were so deeply involved in their work that it made them cross and cranky. Related to the fact that the children felt their workaholic parents took work too seriously and lacked humor was the fourth symptom identified by children, which was parental *depression* about work.

It has been argued that in workaholic-headed families the generation lines that typically insulate children from the parental adult world get violated or blurred and these children become what family therapists call *parentified* (Robinson, 1998a, 1999). *Parentified children* by definition are parents to their own parents and sacrifice their own needs for attention, comfort, and guidance in order to accommodate and care for the emotional needs and pursuits of parents or another family member (Chase, 1999; Jurkovic, 1997). Workaholics who were parentified as children often pass their own parentification onto their offspring, who are chosen to be emotional surrogates for the missing workaholic parent (see chapters 5, 6, and 7 of this monograph). A typical example is the child who is elevated into an adult position within the family system to accommodate a parent's emotional need for intimacy by becoming the adult of the house during the workaholic parent's physical or emotional absence (Robinson, 1998c). Another scenario exists when the nonworkaholic spouse is consumed in the single-parent role during the workaholic's absence, and children (usually the oldest) become parentified when required to become overly responsible at a young age before they are fully emotionally constructed themselves. Examples include assuming household chores or caretaking responsibilities for young siblings to bring homeostasis to the family system. The gap of having to forfeit childhood—leaving youngsters void of feelings of approval, reassurance, love, and the comfort and protection from adult pressures—shows up years later as an oft-described "empty hole inside" (Robinson, 1998a, 1999). See Figure 1.3 for a profile of children of workaholics.

The first empirical study on children of workaholics indicated that family-of-origin dysfunction may get passed on to offspring. In the study, 211 young adults were asked to rate their parents on their workaholism (Robinson & Kelley, 1998). On the basis of their ratings, parents were grouped as either workaholic (scores of one standard deviation above the mean) or nonworkaholic. Then the young adults (mean age = 24 years) were given a battery of tests that measured depression, anxiety, self-concept, and locus of control. Results indicated that adult children of workaholic fathers suffered greater depression, anxiety, and external locus of control than the comparison group of adults of nonworkaholic fathers. The findings corroborate similar findings among children of alcoholic popula-

FIGURE 1.3
A Psychological Profile of Children of Workaholics

Children of workaholics tend to be

- extrinsically motivated and outwardly focused
- obsessive–compulsive
- self-critical
- self-disparaging people who feel unworthy for not being able to meet others' expectations
- depression-prone
- approval seekers to make up for self-inadequacy
- performance-driven perfectionists who judge themselves by their accomplishments, rather than by their inherent worth
- overly serious people who have difficulty having fun
- angry and resentful
- prone to generalized and performance anxiety
- parentified as children
- unsuccessful in adult intimate relationships
- chameleons with an undeveloped sense of self

tions compared with adult children of nonalcoholics (Robinson & Rhoden, 1998). There were no differences on self-concept, and children of workaholic mothers scored no differently than children of nonworkaholic mothers.

A second empirical study compared young adults who grew up in workaholic families with those who grew up in alcoholic families (Carroll & Robinson, in press). In that study, 207 young adults (mean age = 25 years) were classified into one of four categories: (a) adult children of workaholics, (b) adult children of alcoholics, (c) one parent was either workaholic or alcoholic, and (d) neither parent was workaholic or alcoholic. The results indicated that adult children of workaholics had higher scores on depression and parentification than any of the other groups. In a third study, 121 professional nurses rated their parents in terms of their workaholism (Navarrette, 1998). Findings indicated that adult children of workaholics scored significantly higher than adult children of nonworkaholics on anxiety, obsessive–compulsive tendencies, and extrinsic motivation.

Although research in this area is still embryonic, results of these studies suggest that children are affected by parental work addiction in negative ways that are mentally unhealthy and can cause problems well into young adulthood. Other clinical accounts also suggest that children of workaholics often become workaholics themselves—using performance as a measure of their self-worth (Robinson, 1998a). They are described as self-critical, perfectionistic, overly self-demanding, and chameleons in adult relationships—eager to forfeit the self for the approval of others.

A Case Study: The Stewart Family

Beth, 65 years old, came to therapy because of a lingering unhappiness in her 30-year marriage to her then-retired husband, Paul. She even had begun to question if she had ever loved him as she looked back over their marriage. For as long as she could remember, Paul had been unwilling to participate in family talks and casual pastimes, consumed instead by his engineering job, which provided them with a comfortable living and sent all three children to college. Paul had withdrawn from family relationships.

When the children were small and they took them on picnics, Beth carried the blanket and picnic basket while Paul carried his briefcase. Beth was angry that Paul was constantly preoccupied with work. She felt like a single mother rearing children who were angry at their father for not letting them get close to him. Although today the three children are successful adults, they admitted to Beth that they never believed they could do anything good enough to please their father.

Beth was remorseful that in her marriage Paul was a "no show" and she was "left holding the bag" when it came to child rearing, managing the house, and attending social gatherings where Paul would fail to keep his promise to be present. The family's tone and activities revolved around Paul's moods and whims. Everybody postponed their plans, hoping that by chance they would grab some time with him. The children learned they could have these special times with their dad by photocopying documents for him or going to his engineering office on Saturdays and playing in an adjacent room while Paul worked.

On vacations Beth complained that Paul, lugging his briefcase across Europe, worked constantly and of how lonely it was on trips when she would frequent the museums alone while he holed up in their hotel working. Even when they took the children on long weekends to their mountain retreat in the Adirondacks, Paul felt compelled to carry a portable phone with him on the fishing boat. He maintained direct and constant contact with the other colleagues in his New York City firm.

On those rare occasions when Paul tried to take an active role in his family, he said he felt rebuffed by his wife who felt that he was intruding on her turf. Still today when Paul's now-grown children visit, they complain to Beth about their father sequestering himself in his workshop instead of sitting around and interacting with the family. Beth, in turn, finds herself relaying the annoyances to her husband and feeling her resentment rise along with that of her children. She started to realize that a large portion of time with her grownup kids was spent ganging up on and complaining about their father. Unknowingly, for a lifetime she had been caught in the middle between Paul and their disenchanted children, trying to mediate, keep the peace, and patch the brittle father–child relationships. Tired and weary from carrying the family burden for so long, Beth wept tears for the guilt she felt in creating the family divide and for not being able to repair it. She cried for the pain she saw in Paul's confused face when he asked why the kids never seemed to want to hug, kiss, or spend time with him. She grieved for the hurt and resentment her children still carried, evidenced by their stiffness and awkwardness when giving their father obligatory goodbye hugs. But most of all she mourned the loss of an image of a family that never was and would never be.

During the course of couples therapy, the concept of workaholism was introduced to Beth, which helped her see Paul in a different light. "Workaholic huh? That sounds as if my husband's a sick man. That gives me a whole new way of looking at him—with more compassion and understanding."

Suggestions for Clinical Practice

Counselors can provide effective counseling for couples whose marriages have been damaged by workaholism. By helping couples identify and express their feelings about the problem, counselors can reduce tension and reactivity and set the stage for change in the structural patterns and behaviors of the workaholic family members.

The Intake Process

Clinicians can screen for workaholism in families of all clients during the intake process, just as they do for alcoholism and other addictions. The identification of familial workaholism provides pertinent information that can be used in implementing a therapeutic plan for the client and family. Counselors need to ascertain family dynamics, structure, and interaction patterns that have been established. Is there a tacit family contract that encourages workaholism? Is the spouse unwittingly enabling the addiction? Are there unspoken expectations of children that place them into parentified roles that could cause them long-term emotional problems? Bringing these patterns into the light can help families restructure dysfunctional interaction patterns.

Enabling and Restructuring Family Patterns

Clinicians can inform family members of the potential damage of joining in the compulsive work habits out of desperation to spend time with their workaholic loved ones and of bringing them work to do when they go to bed sick. Family members can refuse to make alibis for the workaholic's absenteeism or lateness at parties or family get-togethers and let the workaholic be responsible for explanations. They can stress the importance of not enabling workaholics by refusing to assume their household chores, return phone calls, fulfill family obligations, or "cover" for them in a business meeting or social gathering. It is important for family members to understand that building their lives around the workaholic's busy schedule only sets them up for further hurt and disappointment.

Expectations of change in workaholics require that family members, who have built a pattern of reactions to their loved one's workaholism, be prepared to change as well. Spouses sometimes fall into the habit of complaining or being cynical about the workaholic's absence. Clinicians who work with workaholic couples must be prepared for resistance on both sides. Triangles across generations can occur when spouses become competitive and the parental bond becomes more valued than the marital bond. The mother, for example, may align with a child against the father because of his emotional absence. The father is excluded, and thus the mother–child bond is strengthened at the expense of the marital bond. This boundary violation can exacerbate the child's resentment of the absent workaholic father and escalate the tension between them. A mother who single-handedly raised the children may become resentful when suddenly her workaholic spouse decides to take a more active role in parenting. Change in family structure can evoke anger and resentment on the part of spouses and grown children who feel it is too little too late (Robinson, 1998a). As emotions surface between father and offspring, the mother may intercede on the child's behalf, further eroding the marital bond while solidifying the parental bond.

Part of the restructuring of family patterns includes helping families negotiate boundaries around the amount of time they spend working together and talking about work. They can be helped to learn that work does not have to dominate their conversations but that they can discuss work frustrations and successes as all healthy couples and families do. Additional goals that have emerged from the empirical research on workaholic families are the need to work on effective family roles, greater affective responses, more affective involvement, and higher general functioning—all of which characterize the workaholic family system (Robinson & Post, 1995).

Twelve Steps and Referral to Support Groups

In conjunction with individual counseling, workaholics benefit from support groups composed of other members struggling with various addictive behaviors. In group therapy, members help one another to see past denials and distractions that prevent them from taking responsibility for their actions and putting more balance in their lives. Most large cities have support groups such as Workaholics

Anonymous that can provide literature and weekly meetings for workaholics. Clinicians can apprise themselves and inform clients of Twelve Step programs such as Workaholics Anonymous or Al-Anon, the family adjunct to Alcoholics Anonymous, to complement their individual therapy plans.

The Twelve Steps have worked for millions of people with a variety of addictions, including alcohol and other drugs, food, gambling, and shopping. Continuing in the Twelve Step tradition, Workaholics Anonymous provides a setting that is accepting, anonymous, and safe in which workaholics share their experience, strength, courage, and hope. They follow the Twelve Steps and work with other recovering workaholics and sponsors with solid programs of personal growth who mentor newcomers. Under the guidance of their sponsors, members are encouraged to develop their own self-care plan of work moderation. Abstinence from compulsive working on a physical level is encouraged as well as development of a positive attitude by surrendering to a Higher Power. The work plan is a guide to daily work that provides healthy boundaries and moves workaholics toward a more balanced way of living. Elizabeth described how she benefited from Workaholics Anonymous.

> Workaholics Anonymous gives me the opportunity to go and sit down with other people like me, with anonymity. I don't have to worry if I don't want the world to know about me, that what I say will go out of that room. It gives me an opportunity to share with others and to hear myself for an hour. It gives me a chance to calm down. It's very soothing to be with other people just like you who understand and know what you feel. At the same time, listening to them and what they've done to change their behavior helps you realize what you can do because they share their experience, strength, and hope. They don't give advice.

For more information on Workaholics Anonymous and its locations and contact persons across the United States, write to Workaholics Anonymous, P.O. Box 289, Menlo Park, CA 94026-0289.

Support for Family Members

Helping families break the cycle of workaholism is important. Protecting children from out-of-reach aspirations, unreasonable expectations, and parental perfectionism can prevent the development of Type A behaviors and the intergenerational transmission of workaholism. Children of workaholics often mask low self-esteem, anxiety, depression, and parentification with high performance, resiliency, overresponsibility, and self-reliance to the point that it may be difficult for them to ask for help. Clinicians can look underneath the veneer to see if young and adult children of workaholics are driving themselves for approval.

Family members often need help expressing their feelings of emotional abandonment, guilt, inadequacy, anger, resentment, and hurt to their workaholic loved one. Spouses especially need help in developing constructive outlets for their feelings, such as journaling, support groups, or individual therapy. Family members often benefit from understanding that they did not cause, cannot cure, and cannot control the workaholic's problem and that workaholism is often a cover for low self-esteem, past hurt and fears, and difficulties with intimacy.

Presenting the disease concept of workaholism to families can be a great relief and can help families reframe the problem from seeing it as personal rejection to seeing it more as the complex condition that it really is. The disease concept also is useful for family members to understand how they are affected in subtle ways of which they are not aware. The disease concept allows clinicians to use a Twelve Step approach and many of the principles of Alcoholics Anonymous and Al-Anon that have been extrapolated to treating workaholics.

An organization called WorkAnon was founded in suburban New York at the same time Workaholics Anonymous started. WorkAnon serves spouses, family, and friends of workaholics in the same way Al-Anon serves as a family adjunct to Alcoholics Anonymous. Like Al-Anon, WorkAnon helps spouses and family members deal with their personal feelings about work addiction, not cure their workaholic partners.

Family members who cannot find a WorkAnon or Workaholics Anonymous group in their area can attend Al-Anon, which addresses issues similar to those that emerge in living with someone with work addiction. Clinicians can establish structured support groups for partners of workaholics similar to Al-Anon or WorkAnon. These special groups can help spouses cope with their own bruised self-esteem, guilt, stress, and isolation. It can be a comfort for many families who feel alone and hopeless and who fear that their coming forth will be greeted with accusations and insults aimed at them for their lack of gratitude. These groups can support spouses, help them feel connected to others who understand, and give them constructive actions they can take to face the workaholism and change their lives.

Conclusion

In conclusion, the findings presented in this chapter fit with increasing information that workaholism, like alcoholism, may take its toll on family members as well as on the workaholic. Despite these problems and because of society's lack of understanding, clinicians often do not recognize the serious impact workaholism has on today's families. It is imperative that counselors assess for workaholism and the possibility of hidden problems in the family interaction patterns. Increased clinical awareness and support for families are essential as our fast-paced society increases its demands on today's families.

References

Carroll, J., & Robinson, B. E. (in press). Depression and parentification among adults as related to parental workaholism and alcoholism. *The Family Journal*.

Chase, N. (Ed.). (1999). *Burdened children: Theory, research, and treatment of parentification*. Thousand Oaks, CA: Sage.

Fassel, D. (1990). *Working ourselves to death*. Center City, MO: Hazelden.

Fogus, J. L. (1998). *Relationships among flow, work addiction, and health*. Unpublished master's thesis, Middle Tennessee State University, Murphresboro, Tennessee.

Haraguchi, M., Tsuda, A., & Ozeki, Y. (1991). The current status of stress among information-related industry workers. In M. Tanaka & A. Tsuda (Eds.), *L'espirit d'aujourdhui [The spirit of today]: No. 290: Stress and karoshi* (pp. 75–86). Tokyo: Shibundo.

Haymon, S. (1993). The relationship of work addiction and depression, anxiety, and anger in college males (Doctoral dissertation, Florida State University, 1992). *Dissertation Abstracts International, 53*, 5401-B.

Herbst, A. C. (1996, November). Married to the job. *McCall's Magazine*, 130–134.

Ishiyama, F. I., & Kitayama, A. (1994). Overwork and career self-validation among the Japanese: Psychosocial issues and counselling implications. *International Journal for the Advancement of Counselling, 17*, 167–182.

Jacob, T., Favorini, A., Meisel, S., & Anderson, C. (1978). The alcoholic's spouse, children, and family interactions: Substantive findings and methodological issues. *Journal of Studies on Alcohol, 39*, 1231–1251.

Jurkovic, G. (1997). *Lost childhood: The plight of the parentified child.* New York: Brunner-Mazel.

Kanai, A., Wakabayashi, M., & Fling, S. (1996). Workaholism among employees in Japanese corporations: An examination based on the Japanese version of the Workaholism Scales. *Japanese Psychological Research, 38*, 192–203.

Kelly, V. A., & Myers, J. E. (1996). Parental alcoholism and coping: A comparison of female children of alcoholics with female children of nonalcoholics. *Journal of Counseling and Development, 74*, 501–504.

Nagy, S. (1985). Burnout: A comparative analysis of personality and environmental variables. *Psychological Reports, 57*, 1319–1326.

Navarrette, S. (1998). *An empirical study of adult children of workaholics: Psychological functioning and intergenerational transmission.* Unpublished doctoral dissertation, California Graduate Institute.

Oates, W. (1971). *Confessions of a workaholic.* New York: World Publishing.

Pace, L., & Suojanem, W. W. (1988). Addictive Type A behavior undermines employee involvement. *Personnel Journal, 67*, 36–42.

Pietropinto, A. (1986). The workaholic spouse. *Medical Aspects of Human Sexuality, 20*, 89–96.

Porter, G. (1996). Organizational impact of workaholism: Suggestions for researching the negative outcomes of excessive work. *Journal of Occupational Health Psychology, 1*, 70–84.

Porter, G. (1998). Can you trust a workaholic? How work addiction erodes trust throughout the organization. *Journal of Contemporary Business Issues, 6*, 48–57.

Post, P., & Robinson, B. E. (1998). A comparison of school-age children of alcoholic and nonalcoholic parents on self-esteem, anxiety, and locus of control. *Professional School Counseling, 1*, 36–40.

Post, P., Webb, W., & Robinson, B. (1991). Relationship between self-concept, anxiety, and knowledge of alcoholism by gender and age among adult children of alcoholics. *Alcoholism Treatment Quarterly, 8*, 91–95.

Robinson, B. E. (1989). *Work addiction.* Deerfield Beach, FL: Health Communications.

Robinson, B. E. (1992). *Overdoing it: How to slow down and take care of yourself.* Deerfield Beach, FL: Health Communications.

Robinson, B. E. (1996a). The psychosocial and familial dimensions of work addiction: Preliminary perspectives and hypotheses. *Journal of Counseling and Development, 74*, 447–452.

Robinson, B. E. (1996b). Relationship between work addiction and family functioning: Clinical implications for marriage and family therapists. *Journal of Family Psychotherapy, 7*, 13–29.

Robinson, B. E. (1997a). Work addiction and the family: Conceptual and research considerations. *Early Child Development and Care, 137*, 77–92.

Robinson, B. E. (1997b). Work addiction: Implications for EAP counseling and research. *Employee Assistance Quarterly, 12*, 1–13.

Robinson, B. E. (1998a). *Chained to the desk: A guidebook for workaholics, their partners and children, and the clinicians who treat them.* New York: New York University Press.

Robinson, B. E. (1998b). Spouses of workaholics: Clinical implications for psychotherapy. *Psychotherapy, 35*, 260–268.

Robinson, B. E. (1998c). The workaholic family: A clinical perspective. *American Journal of Family Therapy, 26*, 65–75.

Robinson, B. E. (1999). Workaholic children: One method of fulfilling the parentification role. In N. Chase (Ed.), *Burdened children: Theory, research, and treatment of parentification* (pp. 56–74). Thousand Oaks, CA: Sage.

Robinson, B. E. (in press). A typology of workaholism with implications for counselors. *Journal of Addictions and Offender Counseling.*

Robinson, B .E., Carroll, J. J., & Flowers, C. (in press). Marital estrangement, positive affect, and locus of control among spouses of workaholics and spouses of nonworkaholics: A national study. *American Journal of Family Therapy.*

Robinson, B. E., & Kelley, L. (1998). Adult children of workaholics: Self-concept, anxiety, depression, and locus of control. *American Journal of Family Therapy, 26*, 223–238.

Robinson, B. E., & Post, P. (1995). Work addiction as a function of family of origin and its influence on current family functioning. *The Family Journal, 3*, 200–206.

Robinson, B. E., & Post, P. (1997). Risk of work addiction to family functioning. *Psychological Reports, 81*, 91–95.

Robinson, B. E., & Rhoden, L. (1998). *Working with children of alcoholics: The practitioner's handbook* (2nd. ed.). Thousand Oaks, CA: Sage.

Spence, J. T., & Robbins, A. S. (1992). Workaholics: Definition, measurement, and preliminary results. *Journal of Personality Assessment, 58*, 160–178.

Spruell, G. (1987). Work fever. *Training and Development Journal, 2*, 47.

Taylor, S. E. (1990). Health psychology: The science and the field. *American Psychologist, 45*, 40–50.

Tweed, S. H., & Ryff, C. D. (1991). Adult children of alcoholics: Profiles of wellness amid distress. *Journal of Studies on Alcohol, 52*, 133–141.

Uehata, T. (1993). *Karoshi no kenkyu* [Research on karoshi]. Tokyo, Japan: Nihon Planning Center.

Weeks, D. (1995, June). Cooling off your office affair. *Northwest Airlines World Traveler Magazine*, 59–62.

■ ■ ■

2

Spouses of High-Performing Men: A Profile of Marital Adjustment and Psychological Outcomes

Jane J. Carroll, PhD

Having pride in being productive in one's work can mitigate against self-perceived mediocrity or inferiority (Carroll, 1998). A compulsive approach to achieving work-related goals, however, can override the attraction, interest, and consideration partners in relationships otherwise might have for their spouses. This chapter addresses the following questions: What might be the nature of relationships in which male partners' work patterns disguise or compensate for self-perceived inferiority? What psychological burdens might performance-oriented men and their spouses allow to pervade and corrupt their relationships? In what ways is marital quality influenced and wives' satisfaction with marriage affected by their husbands' compulsive work behavior? How can counselors help the spouses of high performers?

To understand why some men become compulsive high performers, it helps to be aware of the context in which such behavior may originate for two reasons. First, high achievement is highly prized among the male population, so young boys are socialized to be competitive and accomplished. Research indicates that from an early age boys are encouraged more than girls to engage in Type A behavior (Robinson, 1996). Second, in threatening circumstances, children often have difficulty coping—as when peers reject or ridicule them and when parents separate or divorce or become dependent on alcohol or other drugs. These children think they are insignificant and that they lack the wherewithal to achieve the purposes or goals they construct for themselves. They devise ways, therefore, to survive their disturbing thoughts and subsequent fears by creating psychological escape plans to counter emotional chaos (Kefir, 1981). One way children and, then later, adults survive feelings of inadequacy and inferiority is to engage in behavior that could be considered compulsive. For example, being copiously productive is a way for boys to say to the world and to themselves, "I matter."

Seeds planted in childhood blossom fully in behavioral patterns of adulthood. The psychological needs of both partners presumably go unmet in many relationships where one partner is a compulsive high performer. The present chapter focuses on the effects on women who are in relationships with high-performing men. To the extent that it is possible to isolate and explain only one partner's thoughts, feelings, and behaviors, this chapter discloses what is currently known about the difficulties these female spouses often experience. The emphasis here is on contextualist perspectives regarding spousal interactions. That is, the focus is mainly on what has been written about the social and cultural influences on relationships rather than on what has been written about the inherent differences between men and women. Suggestions are presented for clinicians to help the frustrated spouses of high-performing men.

Spouses of workaholic men, a subset of high-performing men, frequently seek professional counseling during which they present a dismal picture, often describing their lives as joyless and lonely. They complain of being addicted to alcohol or other drugs, of feeling depressed and anxious, and of being worried about the increasing frailty of their spousal relationships. Their relationships are organized around their husband's questionable work patterns. In such cases the women often feel lonely and disappointed because they think they have been abandoned and betrayed (Miles, Krell, & Lin, 1975; Nichols & Rohrbaugh, 1998; Pietropinto, 1986; Robinson, 1998; Sakinofsky, 1980). The only empirical study ever to measure marital adjustment among wives of workaholics indicated that, compared with wives of nonworkaholics, they felt more estranged from their workaholic husbands, had fewer positive feelings toward them, and had greater external locus of control (Robinson, Carroll, & Flowers, in press).

After watching an American Broadcasting Company (ABC) *20/20* segment on workaholism, a viewer wrote the following message:

> I was raised with an alcoholic, and because of that I stayed away from alcohol, but I ended up with a workaholic. At least when they [alcoholics] are not drinking they are nice. The workaholic is never off. After 20 years and three kids, I am ready to divorce him because it is hurting me too much. He tends to manipulate everyone around him so that he can be a workaholic. I stayed at home and did all the repairs on the home while raising my children. In his eyes I was lucky. My husband makes the man [workaholic] on the television show look like he is father of the year.

Family Structure and Development

In the United States, *family* is often thought of as people who are related either through heredity or by way of custom or law. For example, adults may be legally married or they may be unmarried spouses in other types of committed relationships. In either case, they may perceive themselves as family partners who are "challenged to balance their basic needs for belonging . . . with that of striving for individuality" (Curtis, 1999, p. 54) while being influenced by the circumstances and behaviors of their spouses.

As with individuals and larger family units, couples establish internal boundaries (between themselves) and external boundaries (outside themselves). Setting boundaries helps couples define their identity early in the partnership's existence when each person has expectations of the other and for the relationship. They establish their internal and external peripheries and develop beliefs about the partnership that are fundamental to how the couple will function (Steinglass, 1987). They agree on individual responsibility for tasks, how to define their personal and physical spaces, the nature of their sexual behavior, and the character of outside friendships. Each partner's behavior is viewed in its context with attention to the rules and understandings the couple has developed. When these "tacit family contracts" change, it creates dissension in relationships such as Betsy, the spouse of a workaholic husband, described.

> The first year and a half of our marriage is the only time I can remember a time of happiness and joy being present in our

relationship—that was the "honeymoon period." We worked happily together building up a small business. We both worked long hours 7 days a week back then, and I didn't see anything unusual or wrong about that. I believed, as my husband did, that if the business was going to grow and be successful, that kind of dedication and hard work were what it would take. I did expect though, as the business grew and became successful, we would begin to take time off. Soon, when I became pregnant, I started to cut back and work more normal hours, but Michael kept working 18–20-hour days.

Over time, couples acting alone or as part of an expanding family create an environment that either nurtures or stifles growth. Growth is nurtured by people who are emotionally mature and stable. They have flexible views, are able to compromise, and are earnest supporters of their relationship. A couple or family whose growth is "arrested," however, do not communicate well, are rigid in their opinions, and blame others for their problems. They have few problem-solving skills (Curtis, 1999, p. 61). Betsy described how she reacted when it became apparent that her marriage was not what she had hoped it would be.

By the time we had been married 5 years and had two daughters, [Michael's] work habits were still the same. I continued to vent my frustration and dissatisfaction about the hours he worked. There were often tearful outbursts, and each time, he listened and seemed to feel badly, but he kept right on working those long hours and days. I felt like a single parent, married yet without a husband. It felt like Michael was an outsider, in many ways a stranger to us. I felt as if he didn't know us, his own family.

Research findings suggest that mental health counselors and family therapists should not ignore possible relationships between clients' marital satisfaction and their spouses' work patterns (Karambayya & Reilly, 1992; Leiter & Durup, 1996; Matthews, Conger, & Wickrama, 1996; Orbuch, House, Mero, & Webster, 1996). *Spillover* is a process in which psychological stress in one area of life accumulates and is experienced in another area or domain. The quality of family life is affected when work-related stress, driven by the need to be productive, spills over into the home domain (Leiter & Durup, 1996). High levels of family involvement, however, can mediate high levels of stress that contribute to marital dissatisfaction.

A historical perspective may help explain how socially sanctioned role expectations for men and women have contributed to women's marital dissatisfaction with spouses who are compulsive high performers. Traditional gender roles regarding work have contributed to men becoming workaholics and their spouses feeling neglected or inconsequential. Family structure and development in the United States have largely centered on the role of men as "breadwinners" and, until the census of 1980, as legal "head of household." From the time of the Industrial Revolution, men have been expected to work to provide material sustenance for their families (Bernard, 1981). Early in the 19th century, de Tocqueville (1840/1945) observed that in the United States

> Among a democratic people, where there is no hereditary wealth, every man works to earn a living, or has worked, or is born of parents who have worked. The notion of labor is therefore presented to the mind, on every side, as the necessary, natural, and honest condition of human existence. Not only is labor not dishonorable among such a people, but it is held in honor; the prejudice is not against it, but in its favor. (p. 161)

Women frequently have lacked marketable skills and had household obligations to which to attend. Their contributions to the welfare of society, although substantial, have not been considered equal to those of men. De Tocqueville implied that women's status was a just condition and that their work was not as demanding as that of men: "If, on the one hand, an American woman cannot escape from the quiet circle of domestic employments, she is never forced, on the other, to go beyond it" (p. 223).

In the past, women generally were not welcomed in the labor force, and thus did not acquire knowledge-based or skill-based competencies. Instead, they became dependent on men who would "take care of" them. The goal of many women was to find "a good provider." For many men, being lovingly attentive and emotionally involved with their wives and children was not a priority. Instead, they concentrated on work and thereby provided for their families (Bernard, 1981). To be a good provider meant that men were behaving responsibly, and by so doing, were not only materially rewarded but achieved social standing and family domination. (See chapter 3 in this monograph for further discussion of this issue.)

Men who resented having the responsibilities of breadwinner and their families' and society's expectations imposed on them sometimes punished their wives, who had little financial independence. The women were humiliated by being forced to account for their expenditures and were blamed for the cost of goods they purchased. Highly competitive men, however, often flaunted their earning power by extravagant spending and using their families and homes as showcases for their wealth (Bernard, 1981).

Although women have entered the workforce in greater than usual numbers in recent years, the role of men as providers has persisted. In 1955, Warner and Ablegglen wrote about men who are intensely focused on their careers at the expense of their families. Such men seem to be so stimulated by their work that they are, like people addicted to substances, unable or unwilling to stop their destructive behavior. Paradoxically, society considers men who act as if they value work above all else to be highly successful and acclaims them as role models. Their accomplishments are extolled and their behavior thought to be worthy of emulation. For example, Glenn, a recovering alcoholic, wrote,

> Where was I when my children needed me? I was doing what every father is supposed to do—working hard, *being a provider* [italics added], and being successful. Driven by internal forces that seemed greater than me and strongly supported by a culture that prizes its men for being self-sufficient, hard workers, I became more and more a success at my work and felt more and more like a failure at home . . . . Where did I want to spend my time anyway? At home where I felt like a failure? Or at work where I felt like a success? (Robinson, 1998, p. 44)

Compulsive Work Behavior and Family Discord

Within the context of a family system, each person influences and has influence on other members of the family as they work together to attain a balance in their structure and functioning that works for them. For example, families may maintain balance (homeostasis) by organizing to support compulsive work behavior by the husband/father. Perhaps the wife assumes all of the domestic chores and child rearing, freeing the husband/father from household responsibility. Perhaps an adolescent daughter becomes a drug abuser, a means of deflecting attention from the emotional pain caused by the always-absent and frequently nonresponsive father. The husband/father may be compulsively working in response to circumstances over which he thinks he has no control. His dominant role in the family dictates the family rules, themes, and myths that the family espouses and to which it responds (Curtis, 1999).

Glenn's story illustrates the thinking of those who conceptualize compulsive work behavior, or work addiction, as a family disease. He and his family organized around the workaholic father and maintained balance by encouraging the family myth of the supremacy of the role of "the good provider." Glenn wrote,

> It was only when I grew up, went to work, married, and had children of my own that I could begin to see my own emerging patterns of work addiction. And even then insight didn't come easily. Someone once asked me what is it like to grow up with a workaholic father. That's like asking a fish to be aware of what it's like to live in a pond. It was the water I swam in, the air I breathed. My father traveled, that's all. He was a hard-working and successful provider. What more could one ask for? What better role model could one have in a father?
>
> As a child, I could no more have identified what was wrong with our family than the fish could identify what was wrong with the pond. As a husband and father, I simply and blindly followed for a decade the modeling I had received as a child . . . I found a place where I could swim in my familiar waters. (Robinson, 1998, p. 43)

Excessive work behavior has not always been explained in contextualist terms such as "family disease." Miles and his colleagues (Miles et al., 1975) wrote from an essentialist perspective about physicians who are married to "dependent, histrionic" women who have "an inordinate need for affection and nurturing" (p. 486). The authors wrote that the physicians' response to their "depressed, angry, and desperately unhappy" wives included "immersion in work" (p. 486). They noted that such work behavior was often cited by other writers as etiologic for marriage difficulties, but in the opinion of Miles et al., overworking was a symptomatic means for a physician/husband to be physically separated from his disturbed wife and to receive positive attention from others. Miles et al. explained that as antagonism in the marriage escalates, the husband increases "the amount of time spent in the practice which effectively removes him from the arena of conflict" (p. 483). A more current view is that the high-achieving husband disengages from his family, thereby contributing to both his feeling like an outsider and his role as a marginal family member (Robinson, 1998). The Japanese refer to such a man as a "7–11 husband."

> He tends to have a rather marginal family membership and receives only limited substantive validation for his familial self from the family. When the family forms an internal alliance excluding the marginal father, he is likely to feel displaced and unwanted at home, which in turn reinforces his wish to be back in a familiar working environment. (Ishiyama & Kitayama, 1994, p. 180)

Following a review of medical records of physicians' wives between 1969 and 1973, a team of researchers concluded that working an inordinate number of hours was how the husbands escaped the demands of dependent wives who had become steadily more resentful as their perceived needs went unmet (Miles et al., 1975). The researchers interpreted the content of medical records used in this study to mean that the physicians' wives were women who had a need to be "looked after" by their husbands whose profession it was to "care for others." Common conceptions in 1975 of a woman's ideal marriage are found in the researchers' description of troubled wives in medical marriages.

> Frequently she [the physician's spouse] is bewildered as to why she is experiencing such feelings. Materially comfortable, with secure social status, usually a financially generous husband, and often envied, her unhappiness and anger may seem inappropriate to her. The husband seems no less bewildered. He has "followed the rules"—worked hard, provided amply, and wished the best for his family and is baffled by the turn of events which finds him with a depressed wife and problem children. (Miles et al., 1975, p. 482)

The stereotype of the "good provider" in this description was bolstered by the previous results of Lopata's (1971) study. Lopata found that in the 1960s, 87% of wives considered a husband's primary role to be that of providing for the family. Persistent stereotyping and disparaging of female spouses into the 1990s enabled high-performing husbands to continue their compulsive work behavior. As the wives observe society and the workplace extolling their workaholic husbands, many women refrain from speaking out or seeking help for fear of being characterized as ungrateful. A client, Dorothy, described her feelings:

To everyone else, my husband is perfect. I feel like I'm one of his employees, even at home. He denies there's anything wrong and gets hostile if I confront him about his workaholism. Our friends always want to know why I'm always complaining. I have become the bitchy wife in the eyes of our friends, but they don't understand what it's like being alone. (Robinson, 1998, p. 78)

Profile of Spouses of High Performers

Using case studies and interviews, Robinson (1998) compiled a "portrait" of spouses of workaholics that reflects their isolation and low self-regard and others' vilification of them. This profile reveals that these spouses often

- feel ignored, neglected, and unappreciated;
- believe they are carrying the emotional burdens of the marriage and parenting;
- view themselves as second choice behind work;
- perceive themselves as extensions of the workaholic;
- view themselves as controlled and manipulated;
- use attention-seeking measures for spousal contact;
- view the relationship as serious and overly intense;
- harbor guilt for wanting more in the relationship;
- have low self-esteem because they cannot measure up to their partners; and
- question their own gratitude and sanity.

Susan's Story: A Case Example

Susan's $2^{1}/_{2}$-year marriage ended only after her husband's behavior had ravaged her self-esteem. He had told her he was working only for their future and that she was forcing him to work. He was fond of saying, "You say material things are not important to you, but I know they are." He also asserted that if she could just "let the marriage alone for 5 or 6 years," he would probably have time to pay attention to her "when I have my career in order."

Susan's husband regularly told her that he loved his job more than he loved her and that the job needed him more than she did. He ignored holidays and her birthdays because he said he did not have time to celebrate. He would attempt to postpone, saying, "We can have them later." Meanwhile, families and friends suggested there was something about Susan her husband was avoiding, something that was driving him to spend so much time working. It seemed an unlikely explanation for someone who worked at his computer 72 hours at a stretch without food or sleep. Susan, however, accepted the explanation and repeatedly tried to fix faulty aspects of herself that she was not even able to identify.

Susan's feelings of rage, confusion, and abandonment were such that she often wished her husband would bruise her face or break her arm. She said that if he were to do so, he would confirm her suspicions and she would be able to stop doubting herself. She would be able to say to herself and to everyone else, "See, he really is hurting me. He's doing something terrible to this relationship and it is not my fault." As it was, however, everyone praised him for his work ethic and suggested Susan was nagging, impatient, and ungrateful. "I believed it myself," she painfully acknowledged.

The need for love and acceptance is etiologic in both compulsive high performers and their depressed spouses. For example, Sakinofsky (1980) found that wives of physicians have a high risk of suicide because they are unhappy in their marriages to the hardworking men they perceive as detached, uncaring, stern, and domineering. The wives in Sakinofsky's study reported that their needs for love and acceptance were not met. Pietropinto (1986), however, found that marriage to workaholics may be difficult because they too have an inordinate need for love and acceptance; therefore, they place unreasonable demands on their families.

On the basis of his survey of 400 physicians, Pietropinto (1986) reported that workaholics consider their spouses and children to be extensions of themselves and, therefore, expect them to perform flawlessly in their roles. Such expectations reflect workaholics' fear of failure and are related to their feelings of insecurity. The survey revealed that workaholics seem to have little defense against their fear of being exposed as deficient other than to work compulsively and to expect their family members also to be perfect. Paradoxically, they strive for love and acceptance by attempting to execute a perfect performance and expecting their families to do likewise. Ironically, the findings indicated that children from whom perfection is expected do not feel loving toward their workaholic parents but are resentful because the message the children perceive is that they must be perfect to be loved. The survey also suggested that spousal conflict is further exacerbated because workaholics often lack a sense of humor and capacity for being spontaneous, capabilities people use to counteract stress. They may, however, use sexual relations—sometimes extramarital encounters—to relieve tension or confirm their sexual normality.

Pietropinto (1986) also found that the frequency of sexual relations varies for workaholics and their spouses. Allowing time for intimacy interferes with work schedules. Whatever the circumstances, the experiences are generally unsatisfactory. Additionally, workaholics set unusually high standards for sexual intimacy, which contributes to the anxiety and dissatisfaction that the lifestyle creates for workaholics' spouses.

Gabbard and Menninger (1989) studied the marriages of middle-aged medical couples in which one spouse was a physician (93% of whom were men) and the other was not. They concluded that physicians prefer "work over family life" because of compulsive personality traits. This study was corroborated by Nichols and Rohrbaugh (1998), who found that in marriages in which one partner, more than the other, was more focused on career, there was a greater chance that a demanding-and-withdrawing or pursuing-and-distancing relationship would develop.

Gabbard and Menninger (1989) found that by the time physicians and their wives reached middle age the marital pattern they had established had six features: (a) a gradual erosion of marital intimacy; (b) a reduction or absence of emotional expressiveness; (c) the absence of consistent and meaningful communication and an avoidance of touchy or troubling issues; (d) a diminution, or even cessation, of sexual relations; (e) a gradual divergence of interests to the point when the marital partners have little in common; and (f) mutual withdrawal that results in a subtle estrangement of the couple. When obsession with work is ongoing, spouses do not enjoy the marital satisfaction that comes with less work and fewer parenting demands later in life (Orbuch et al., 1996). Instead, psychological distress in the form of hostility and lack of marital warmth and support results from the conflicting demands of work and family (Matthews et al., 1996).

Physicians' wives who are comfortable with the loss of friendship or love may not react negatively to emotional distance from their husbands. Usually, however, wives become embittered. They respond by (a) pursuing interests and activities independently from their husbands, (b) verbally expressing anger at their husbands because the wives think their husbands have been deliberately withholding love, and (c) developing physical and emotional symptoms to get the attention they need by becoming patients (Gabbard & Menninger, 1989).

Implications for Counselors

Sophocles wrote "that kindred only should behold and hear the griefs of kin." If present-day western society heeded that admonition, the mental health care that society provides for troubled individuals would be radically different. Within the context of empirically researched, theory-based counseling, several approaches and settings are available for female spouses struggling with many of the problems described earlier.

Cognitive Behavioral Therapy

A couple's problems that are related to compulsive work behavior may not always be attributed solely to the high-performing partner. Compulsive workers and/or their female spouses may "endeavor to disavow the existence of [this] disagreeable aspect of life" (Wing & Hammer-Higgins, 1993, p. 14). Although such a response (also called *denial*) often is written about in relation to alcoholism, workaholics' family members also may use it as a coping strategy. Furthermore, denial may serve to maintain congruence between a high performer's behavior and the expectations of his culture. For example, working to achieve tenure at his university, Sam, an assistant professor, is required to teach courses (with all the preparation that work entails), conduct original research, and write manuscripts reporting his findings. He also is required to submit articles for publication in refereed journals and provide service to the profession at the university, local, state, and national levels. Because Sam and his wife expect demands will be made on his time, they rationalize his preoccupation with work as necessary for him to achieve tenure. Moreover, if he exhibits no interest in the family and fails to interact with them or shows other signs of being a workaholic, that behavior may be justified as necessary (Robinson, 1998).

Typically, on entering counseling, clients do not immediately recognize compulsive work behavior as a contributing factor to their mental, emotional, and relationship difficulties. Always keeping cultural influences in mind, the focus of cognitive behavioral counseling with spouses of compulsive high performers is to promote cognitive and emotional development. By better understanding their problems, couples can change their behavior. Experts in cognitive therapy (Beck, Wright, Newman, & Liese, 1993) have written about using this approach with substance abusers. Much of the same information and knowledge can be applied to spouses of workaholics and compulsive high performers. For example, depression, anxiety, and social withdrawal are not uncommon among family members of substance abusers and workaholics (Beck et al., 1993; Carroll & Robinson, in press; Miles et al., 1975; Nichols & Rohrbaugh, 1998). By encouraging clients to tell their stories, counselors can help clients identify the beliefs that sustain mental distress. This permits clients to examine their contradictory and incongruent thinking and behavior.

Three types of beliefs can present obstacles for couples in compulsive high-performing families (Beck et al., 1993). Anticipatory, relief-oriented, and facilitative thinking patterns are common in spouses of chemically dependent people and are found among spouses of workaholics. Anticipatory thoughts are those in which some sort of reward is expected. For example, female spouses who feign illness and expect to receive attention from workaholic husbands may be thus rewarded. A woman seeking romantic love outside her marriage to a high-performing husband may have relief-oriented beliefs. Facilitative beliefs would be those of a spouse who finds it acceptable to shoulder most of the family responsibilities so that her husband can work excessively. Experts suggest using the Socratic method to challenge beliefs with questions such as, "What is your evidence for that belief?" "How do you know that your belief is true?" "Where is that written?" "Where did you learn that?" and "How confident are you in that belief?" (Beck et al., 1993, p. 177).

Counselors can help clients assume responsibility for their difficulties by setting viable goals and taking responsible action. By examining the advantages and disadvantages of acting on beliefs they hold about their partners' work patterns and the subsequent effect on them and their families, clients can distance themselves from the problems and begin working on solutions. Some marriage therapists suggest that when medical couples experience conflict, they need to be authentic and nurturing with each other: "Remember to separate the person from the problem. Work to create an 'us versus the problem' attitude and avoid locking into a 'me versus you' mentality" (Sotile & Sotile, 1996, p. 221). Encouraging clients to learn adaptive problem-solving skills is a feasible route for counselors to take with clients who have difficulties with spousal work behavior.

Family Therapy

Systems theory explains family circumstances within the context of interrelationships between the events that occur and the people involved. Conjoint or couples therapy or family therapy helps clients understand discord in a family from the systems perspective. In such circumstances, adults can see the impact their behavior has on children, and children can be assured that both parents love them (Kaslow & Schwartz, 1987).

Kaslow and Schwartz (1987) contrasted the results of studies published by Goode (1956) and by Kitson and Sussman (1982) of divorced couples who individually ranked their marital complaints. Goode's (1956) study showed no ranking that reflected dissatisfaction with work behavior other than "nonsupport," ranked by the wives as 9th out of 12 in importance, and by the husbands as 11th out of 12. By contrast, Kitson and Sussman's (1982) study showed that former wives ranked "overcommitment to work" as 8th of 29 complaints against their former husbands. The former husbands ranked it 25th. These findings indicate the need for counselors to be aware of the work-pattern problems that are present in increasing numbers of spousal relationships. It is important for counselors to know how to recognize clients who are affected by their partners' work behavior and to learn how to help spouses reach goals for more satisfying lives.

It is significant, however, that some wives of workaholic men consider their husbands' interaction with them as abusive. Family therapists should be mindful, therefore, of Wiehe's (1998) admonition, "no one merits or deserves to be abused," which suggests that when a workaholic man ignores his spouse, socially isolates her, withholds economic support, or assumes his spouse is responsible for all domestic tasks, he may be emotionally or psychologically abusing her. When such men are workaholic, they contribute to eroding their spouses' self-esteem and self-worth. Women come to fear intimacy and exploitation, as the earlier story of Susan illustrated. For all practical purposes, she felt abused. It is sobering to compare Susan's feelings with those that have been attributed to the partners of abusing men (Pfouts, 1978): (a) they blame themselves for being trapped in their marriages in which they cannot change their husbands or find alternative ways to live; (b) they either respond with violence against their husbands and children or enter other relationships in which they express their anger; (c) they leave their marriages or force the men to stop the abusive behavior; and (d) after many years of trying to save their marriages, they disengage and move into nonviolent alternatives.

If spouses of high-performing men feel abused, counselors can offer responses and exhibit behavior that will be instrumental to their recovery. Hamilton and Coates (in Wiehe, 1998, p.123) classified counselor responses that women who felt abused because of their partners' compulsive work behavior said they found helpful and nonhelpful. These women reported that supportive, helpful counselors

1. listened respectfully and took me seriously;
2. believed me;
3. helped me to recognize my strengths;
4. helped me to see how I'd been losing self-confidence;
5. helped me plan for change;
6. helped me understand the effects on the children; and
7. helped me see ways to end the abuse.

These women further reported that non helpful, non supportive counselors

1. gave me unhelpful advice;
2. criticized me for staying with my spouse;
3. did not share information about social agency resources;
4. did not listen carefully;
5. agreed with me when I said the situation wasn't serious;
6. questioned my veracity;
7. suggested I must have wanted the abuse;
8. blamed me for my predicament; and
9. denied the impact of the abuse on my life.

Counselors can help spouses of high-performing men by using a structural approach wherein women are encouraged to reframe their perceptions of low worth, raise their consciousness of their value and abilities, and learn about resources available to them. In small group settings, spouses of high-performing men can acquire the support of others who have had the same or similar experiences. Such groups can help spouses cope with guilt, stress, isolation, and bruised self-esteem. The group can be a refuge for a family that feels alone, hopeless, and fearful they will be denounced for seeking help. Groups can help spouses arrive at constructive actions they can take to change their lives.

Future Research Considerations

With changing social constructions of normal gender roles, more study and effort are needed in three areas. First, clinicians need empirically and theoretically based data on which to base their treatment of spouses of high-performing men, to help these spouses attain independence from the exploitation inherent in such marriages. Clinicians also need to know how and where to refer clients suffering from problems related to being in these marriages. Social policy is currently lacking regarding the needs of such women. Second, male spouses' perceptions of workaholic and high-performing women are unknown because little research has been done on this subject. Parker and Jones (1981) collected data on how female physicians characterized their husbands. These data were, in turn, used to determine the participants' perceptions of the levels of general career support they received from their husbands. The investigation, however, did not address marital satisfaction and husbands' perceptions. Third, more concrete models are needed for counseling couples and families with problems related to high achievement. Sotile and Sotile (1996), who studied the presence of stress in two-physician medical marriages, provided suggestions for managing these high-pressure relationships. Beyond what the Sotiles have offered, however, there is meager information and literally no empirical research on the subject. This is a topic with many unanswered questions that awaits further investigation.

Conclusion

The spousal thoughts, feelings, and behaviors of women related to their husbands' compulsive work conduct can be described as an unceasing systemic array. Lyddon (1989) wrote that such a construction is the basis for Bandura's (1978) notion that "psychological functioning involves a continuous reciprocal interaction between behavioral, cognitive, and environmental influences" (p. 344). Causes of wives' emotional distress often are perceived as originating from their husbands' behavior. Wives frequently relieve their distress in ways that encourage their husbands to continue their behavior and also bolster their own psychological distress. Clinicians may be able to use reliable interventions such as those described in this chapter with spouses to change their pattern of self-defeating negative behavior.

References

Bandura, A. (1978). The self system in reciprocal determinism. *American Psychologist, 33,* 344–358.

Beck, A. T., Wright, F. D., Newman, C. F., & Liese, B. S. (1993). *Cognitive therapy of substance abuse.* New York: Guilford Press.

Bernard, J. (1981). The good provider role: Its rise and fall. *American Psychologist, 36,* 1–12.

Carroll, J. J. (1998). The heigh ho syndrome: An Adlerian perspective on work addiction. In B. E. Robinson, *Chained to the desk: A guidebook for workaholics, their partners and children, and the clinicians who treat them* (pp. 100–102). New York: New York University Press.

Carroll, J. J., & Robinson, B. E. (in press). Depression and parentification among adults as related to parental workaholism and alcoholism. *The Family Journal.*

Curtis, O. (1999). *Chemical dependency: A family affair.* Pacific Grove, CA: Brooks/Cole.

de Tocqueville, A. (1945). *Democracy in America.* (P. Bradley, Ed., Vol. 2). New York: Vintage. (original work published 1840)

Gabbard, G. O., & Menninger, R. W. (1989). The psychology of postponement in the medical marriage. *Journal of the American Medical Association, 261,* 2378–2381.

Goode, W. J. (1956). *After divorce.* Glencoe, IL: Free Press.

Ishiyama, I., & Kitayama, A. (1994). Overwork and career-centered self-validation among the Japanese: Psychosocial issues and counselling implications. *International Journal for the Advancement of Counselling, 17,* 167–182.

Karambayya, R., & Reilly, A. H. (1992). Dual earner couples: Attitudes and actions in restructuring work for family. *Journal of Organizational Behavior, 13,* 585–601.

Kaslow, F. W., & Schwartz, L. L. (1987). *The dynamics of divorce: A life cycle perspective.* New York: Brunner/Mazel.

Kefir, N. (1981). Impasse/priority therapy. In R. J. Corsini (Ed.), *Handbook of innovative psychotherapies* (pp. 401–415). New York: Wiley.

Kitson, G. C., & Sussman, M. B. (1982). Marital complaints, demographic characteristics, and symptoms of mental distress in divorce. *Journal of Marriage and the Family, 44,* 87–101.

Leiter, M. P., & Durup, M. J. (1996). Work, home, and in-between: A longitudinal study of spillover. *Journal of Applied Behavioral Science, 32,* 29–47.

Lopata, H. (1971). *Occupational housewife.* New York: Oxford University Press.

Lyddon, W. J. (1989). Root metaphor theory: A philosophical framework for counseling and psychotherapy. *Journal of Counseling and Development, 67,* 442–448.

Matthews, L. S., Conger, R. D., & Wickrama, K. A. S. (1996). Work–family conflict and marital quality: Mediating processes. *Social Psychology Quarterly, 59,* 62–79.

Miles, J. E., Krell, R., & Lin, T. (1975). The doctor's wife: Mental illness and marital pattern. *International Journal of Psychiatry in Medicine, 6,* 481–487.

Nichols, M. P., & Rohrbaugh, M. J. (1998). Why do women demand and men withdraw? The role of outside career and family involvements. *The Family Journal, 5*, 111–119.

Orbuch, T. L., House, J. S., Mero, R. P., & Webster, P. S. (1996). Marital quality over the life span. *Social Psychology Quarterly, 59*, 162–171.

Parker, G., & Jones, R. (1981). The doctor's husband. *British Journal of Medical Psychology, 54*, 143–147.

Pfouts, J. (1978). Violent families: Coping responses of abused wives. *Child Welfare, 57*, 101–111.

Pietropinto, A. (1986). The workaholic spouse. *Medical Aspects of Human Sexuality, 20*, 89–96.

Robinson, B. E. (1996). Type A children: Empirical findings and counseling implications. *Elementary School Counseling and Guidance Journal, 31*, 34–42.

Robinson, B. E., (Ed.). (1998). *Chained to the desk: A guidebook for workaholics, their partners and children, and clinicians who treat them.* New York: New York University Press.

Robinson, B. E., Carroll, J. J., & Flowers, C. (in press). Marital estrangement, positive affect, and locus of control among spouses of workaholics and spouses of nonworkaholics: A national study. *American Journal of Family Therapy.*

Sakinofsky, I. (1980). Suicide in doctors and wives of doctors. *Canadian Family Physician, 26*, 837–844.

Sotile, W. M., & Sotile, M. O. (1996). *The medical marriage: A couple's survival guide.* New York: Carol Publishing.

Steinglass, P. (1987). *The alcoholic family.* New York: Basic Books.

Warner, W. L., & Ablegglen, J. O. (1955). *Big business leaders in America.* New York: Harper.

Wiehe, V. R. (1998). *Understanding family violence: Treating and preventing partner, child, sibling, and elder abuse.* Thousand Oaks, CA: Sage.

Wing, D. M., & Hammer-Higgins, P. (1993). Determinants of denial: A study of alcoholics. *Journal of Psychosocial Nursing, 31*(2), 13–17.

■ ■ ■

PART

THE INTERSECT BETWEEN HIGH PERFORMANCE IN THE WORKPLACE AND FAMILY PATTERNS AND FAMILY RELATIONSHIPS

3

Workaholics as High-Performance Employees: The Intersection of Workplace and Family Relationship Problems

Gayle Porter, PhD

Workaholics pursue work to the exclusion of other life activities, causing difficulty with interpersonal relations both on the job and in their home life. In contrast to other excessive behaviors, an addiction to work is glorified by society, exacerbating the wedge between the workaholic and those around them who seek a more reciprocal family or friend relationship. This glorification also hinders the opportunity for counseling a workaholic because the problem is camouflaged, which lowers potential to change behaviors once health or relationship difficulties have reached an extreme. This chapter examines workaholism in the business world, where workaholism is often mistaken for high performance, with emphasis on the carryover relationship problems in home and personal life.

Somewhere Over the Rainbow

In a far away place and a different time, the following scene might actually take place. Baxter Hayworth, a midranking executive of a large service firm, has been referred to the company's employee assistance program to explore the potential for achieving better work/ life balance. His latest performance review indicates that he has been putting so much time and energy into career advancement that he may have lost contact with all other life interests. Although he has met or exceeded all assigned objectives, it may have been at the expense of long-term working relationships, as he often placed unrealistic demands on the people around him.

Baxter was somewhat surprised to get this recommendation for counseling. He knew, and the company acknowledged, he had been instrumental in leading his division successfully through some intense times. That evening he talked with his wife about it. She enthusiastically supported the company's suggestion. As she explained her experiences over the past few years caused by his excessive commitment to work, Baxter for the first time realized the pressure she had been under to fill in for him as parent and family member while he focused entirely on his job. Arriving at the appointed time for his first employee assistance program interview, Baxter is receptive to suggestions on how to reinstitute a healthier balance of work, leisure time, and family responsibilities. The changes might not be easy at first, but he knows he has the support of his family, friends, and employer.

Why It Doesn't (Won't?) Happen

The are two major fallacies in the story just provided. The first is the company's concern about Baxter's overworking; the second is the ease with which Baxter is convinced to change his ways. Because the first is a strong contributing factor in the second, the company's response to potential workaholism is paramount in whether the stage will be set for any positive change. Unfortunately, the perceptions and attitudes that create those responses rarely recognize the interconnectedness of life balance with workplace achievement. Rather than seeing balance as a factor that contributes to long-term productivity, traditional management looks to immediate outcomes, which can be influenced by a narrow pursuit of work above all else. This is unlikely to change until the perspective on performance is broadened to include more than hours at the office, this quarter's sales volume, or one-shot improvements in output.

Realistically, any referral to an employee assistance program must be based on performance (Bahls, 1999). Because Baxter has met or exceeded all his objectives, such a referral would likely not take place. Would his boss, perhaps, take him aside and express these concerns off the record? It is unlikely. For the boss to see a problem with Baxter's situation would require an uncommon level of discernment on specific perceptual traps that support workaholic tendencies. Common signals of performance are often surface-level judgments that should be reconsidered for alternative meaning. For example:

1. *Involvement versus face-time.* Being at the workplace (or constantly in contact with the workplace) is interpreted as high involvement with and concern about the job to be done. Workers are very aware of the pressure and sometimes offset this demand by finding ways to conduct more of their personal lives from the work location. For example, time at the office computer may actually be spent managing personal finances or writing to friends (Shellenbarger, 1998b). Yet, managers continue to applaud and reward long hours, because it is more difficult to look for evidence of effective use of time. This unwillingness to look beyond a simplistic assessment of who spends the most hours at the work location can encourage inefficiency. Ongoing rewards for face-time alone can alienate those people who do more in less time.

2. *High standards versus unrealistic expectations.* People can achieve higher performance with two forms of leadership influence. One is notable achievement when led by a person who inspires them to new heights. The other is to hit high performance while they are being coerced toward an even greater unachievable outcome. The first is a sustainable move forward; the second a temporary push that simultaneously destroys morale and long-term potential. In the short-term, the output "numbers" look the same in either case, and companies tend to reward by the numbers. Good numbers lead to quick promotion through the organization. Therefore, a manager who pushes for unrealistic perfectionism may continue to look like the hero, moving rapidly from one assignment to another. Meanwhile, the next manager inherits a longer term problem. The overall organization suffers a gradual deterioration when no one is held accountable for the side effects of his or her management style. As perfectionist managers rise in the company, a greater number of people are subjected to their abusive demands for excessive work.

3. *Crisis resolution versus crisis creation.* Some people seem to be at their best in a crisis situation. Their ability to withstand the intensity makes them heroes when calm is restored. For those who seek intensity and hero status, a shortage of crisis conditions has a stifling effect. A very small delay or a subtle change can make the difference between quiet resolution and the level of turmoil that draws great attention. The individual who enjoys and gains from allowing (or even encouraging) the situation to reach crisis proportion inflicts these conditions on others but still comes out the hero. Today's business organizations face an environment of constant and rapid change. There is much talk about the need to accept this as the new norm—to take it in stride. Still, those who get caught up in crisis and survive are more likely to be recognized and rewarded than the employees who establish a more smooth process for dealing with changing conditions. Individuals who complain about only having time to "put out fires" every day may be stockpiling dry kindling to ensure their important role will always be needed.

4. *Company objectives versus excessive behavior.* Companies look for results, and organizational leaders consider it outside their realm to worry too much about why desired results happen. This stand may be defensible in many ways but, again, is short-sighted. Viewing excessive work as an addictive behavior (detailed more in the next section), reveals that trade-offs are probably occurring on the way to those results. There is lost potential both through the distorted motives for achieving results and through the destruction caused along the way. Company objectives can become secondary to a goal of successfully manipulating people (Schaef & Fassel, 1988). Use of poor time management makes certain everyone stays busy (Robinson, 1989). Failure to include others' input and share information damages interpersonal relationships necessary for ongoing goal achievement (Porter, 1998). Monitoring only the final measure of goal outcomes can ignore important elements of the process in getting there, and the process may be working against the direction of objectives being measured.

Baxter Hayworth may or may not be a workaholic. In fact, his ready acceptance of the need for change suggests he is not addicted to work. His recent past may have been a temporary career push that he can now ease back on. Yet, someone had to initiate his awareness. Imagining that it came from the employer seems nearly as much a fantasy as Dorothy and Toto's journey over the rainbow. In reality, most business organizations would never question his performance. Even when a workaholic's life begins to show evidence of problems, the company will continue to encourage or even demand the outward appearance of high performance. The destruction of family and other relationships may entice the workaholic to invest even more attention in the job, and the company is a willing partner in this unhealthy spiral.

Who Are These Workaholics and Why Are They Difficult to Reach?

Workaholism is work addiction, which implies a number of difficulties in common with other addictions. Addiction isolates the addict from the nonaddicted world (Sells, 1993), and people close to the addict suffer—particularly spouses and children (Robinson, 1998; Seybold & Salomone, 1994; see also chapters 1 and 2 in this monograph).

Defining Workaholism

Not everyone who works long hours is a workaholic. Some people pour tremendous energy into their work, but they are still able to draw enjoyment from other activities as well. Viewing workaholism as an addictive pattern highlights that it is excessive in its exclusion of other activities. A workaholic will neglect other life interests in favor of work. Working more than other people does not identify a workaholic. The determining factor is whether work has begun to interfere with other interests and yet the individual consistently chooses to neglect everything else in favor of work.

A second consideration in defining workaholism is the internal drive for behavior maintenance. The addiction is to work—the behavior or process of work—so the important thing for the addict is to ensure opportunity for that behavior. The workaholic pursuing company objectives is doing so because those objectives provide a framework for continuing work involvement. The rewards for meeting objectives reinforce the workaholic's choice of activities. However, there is nothing in this mix to encourage efficiency. The workaholic may actually choose to work less efficiently for the sake of always having more to do, needing more time at work, or creating spectacular "crunch-time" finishes.

Exploring the Addictive Pattern

People who fit the workaholic profile have some things in common with other addiction sufferers. There is often a background of family problems during childhood (Robinson, 1998) and continuing identity issues during adulthood (Porter, 1996). Individuals are striving to establish worth through their work, but it is never enough to offset the deeply held insecurities and self-doubt. Accomplishments are short-lived; more and more is necessary to recapture the fleeting good feelings. In this way, workaholism includes the same acceleration effect—increased tolerance—as other addictions. It often continues until the workaholic reaches limits of physical endurance, in cycles of increasing external rewards giving way to unabated internal uncertainty.

Rigid thinking is another feature of addiction that is typical of workaholics. Control is one form of rigid thinking. It is important for workaholics to control the supply of work, so they strive to control every decision and process element that might affect how and when the work is done. Considering alternatives might result in greater efficiency and, therefore, poses a threat. Workaholics also apply perfectionist standards—another form of rigid thinking—to self and others. These impossible standards guarantee ongoing work, as does the taking on of additional responsibility. The workaholic as a manager will find it difficult to delegate work to others. Any attempt to do so will likely fail because the standards are impossible to achieve. This, in turn, justifies the workaholics' beliefs that they need to take back responsibility. The workaholic often reasons that no one else cares enough or is willing to work hard enough to do what really needs to be done.

Subordinate and peer-level employees will find it increasingly difficult to interact with the workaholic's demands and inflexibility. This puts a strain on working relationships and isolates the workaholic as others find ways to work around the problem rather than endure unproductive confrontations. The workaholic's extremely high need for control on the job puts a strain on interpersonal relations and gradually erodes trust and cooperation across the organization (Porter, 1998), although individual performance outcomes may still look good.

An addiction has been described as any process or substance that takes control of a person to the extent that he or she will be dishonest with self and others about it (Schaef & Fassel, 1988). Once dishonesty begins, it will spread to any aspect of life being sacrificed to support the addiction. Workaholics are self-centered and dishonest, which, when combined with tendencies of rigid think-ing, leads to an overall ethical deterioration (Fassel, 1990; Schaef & Fassel, 1988). In total, the addictive pattern is ineffective, destruc-tive to relationships in the workplace, and a basis for turmoil among families who are sacrificed for work.

Difficulty Breaking the Pattern

Another sign of addiction is withdrawal when the focal substance or behavior is restricted. Stories abound in which the hard-driving executive finally takes a *real* vacation, only to suffer a fatal heart attack relaxing on the beach. This is an extreme example and one that happens less often than the story is retold. Much more com-mon is the person on the beach with his briefcase or in the coffee shop with her cell phone and laptop computer. These extensions of the workplace are popularly blamed on the demands of today's fast-paced jobs (e.g., Himmelberg, 1998; Kadaba, 1995; Schor, 1992) or exploitative organizations (Wright & Smye, 1996). The workaholic relies on these same arguments but actually depends on the added involvement and will use any available means to not have to let go of it.

Many people may experience uneasiness when they have become accustomed to a certain level of activity and conditions suddenly lower that stimulation. Mamphela Ramphele was a political activ-ist in South Africa during apartheid. As a Black woman dedicated to social change, she maintained this involvement while simulta-neously completing her medical degree, opening clinics to provide health care in poorer townships, and fulfilling the role of a single parent. In her autobiography, she described her feelings in later years when life slowed to a more normal pace.

> Years of activism had left me drained in ways which are diffi-cult to describe to anyone who has not had the experience. It was not simple burn-out; rather it was being programmed for action to such a degree that total relaxation became a rare and strange phenomenon for the body and mind—almost painful. One had to learn anew how to relax—just to stop and smell the flowers. (Ramphele, 1996, p. 161)

That "painful" experience of trying to relax after becoming ac-customed to high activation is withdrawal. Ramphele made the decision to endure that transition, with the realization that it would lead to renewal and growth. The workaholics' addictive pattern drives them to avoid that painful change at nearly any cost. As explained by Rohrlich (1980), work addiction is linked to choice and free will in a person's work habits: "An addiction is measured not by what an individual does, but by what he or she cannot do" (p. 165). When the external demands ease off, the workaholic will find or create new ones. The uneasiness of withdrawal symptoms is a distinct reminder that action is needed to keep the supply of work coming.

The typical corporate working environment has been described as demanding, hostile (Maslach & Leiter, 1997), even abusive (Wright & Smye, 1996). In spite of evidence that cost-cutting strategies do not lead to competitive advantage (Micklethwait & Wooldridge, 1996), businesses continue to reorganize with emphasis on fewer people doing the same total amount of work. All of this provides support for workaholic denial, the other block to breaking the pattern of work addiction.

In open discussions about workaholism, it is usual for several people to speak up about being unfairly accused of being a workaholic. After having lost two or three very close friends, they still claim the problem exists in their friends' lack of understanding. Their conclusion: "I need friends who have similar levels of career involvement, so they'll know it's the job and not me." There is an old line about alcoholics claiming "I don't have a drinking problem, my wife has a problem with my drinking." A workaholic also will blame problems in the marriage on the spouse's lack of sympathy. The difference between the workaholic's blame shifting and that of the alcoholic is the amount of support available for this claim of being unfairly accused. After all, the heavy workplace demands on employees at all levels is well documented, and there is a long history of organizational rewards for the very behaviors a spouse might cite as a problem. While the workaholic is receiving complaints from a handful of friends and family members, daily experience in the workplace supports the choice to work even more. Workaholic denial receives a great deal of organizational support.

Societal Supports That Compound the Organization's Misconceptions

Although we might hope executives would acquire enough insight to facilitate change, we cannot entirely blame the current corporate leadership for standards that have evolved over long periods of time and with a great deal of general social support. Business organizations are also a reflection of the accepted social standards. To accomplish any change, one must examine the operating philosophy of the businesses within the context of related social values. Across time, there have been changes in both family structure and workforce composition, but workaholism has received social support throughout those evolutions.

For most of the time since industrialization, men were the head of traditional family households, expected to be a good breadwinner and make sacrifices toward the financial stability of the family. The wife cared for the children and kept things running smoothly at home. This division of duties had certain clarity and efficiency but helped create a stereotype of the workaholic as a man. Without suggesting that all traditional male heads of households are workaholics, this is the scenario in which the pattern was first recognized. In the course of fulfilling the breadwinner's role, the husband/father's shift to the imbalance of workaholism could develop gradually and not appear out of the norm until reaching an extreme.

Eventually the father hardly knows his children because they are in bed when he leaves for work in the morning and in bed when he returns home at night. Rather than being at birthday parties and important school events, the father's relationship becomes one of promises followed by apologies. Work always interferes. Yet, he is a good "provider" who simply has had to sacrifice a little more than originally expected to uphold his societal role. Certainly, his wife then would be expected to understand this as his duty, fill in as needed, and not complain. Social expectations provided this backdrop for any husband and father with workaholic tendencies. In a home in which this model is still the basic family structure, the workaholic man continues to have strong social support as well as company encouragement for his addiction.

Of course, workaholism is not restricted to the male population. In traditional homes, women did not have the convenience of organizational demands to justify immersion in work, but a willingness to take on responsibility for charities, school organizations, or small business ventures could supply equivalent combined demands. Because the woman's combination included elements of the household and activities related to the children's lives, there would not be the same appearance of sacrificing family for work. If the children themselves sensed little connection between interest in them and their mother's takeover of the PTA, it could easily go unnoticed by anyone else. The various family characters were still within the socially prescribed role set.

As more and more women moved to careers outside the home, new opportunities were created for female workaholics. Reportedly, the feeling of being torn between demands of job and home are worse for women than men (Sefton, 1999)—probably a carryover of the role definitions just described. Still, a workaholic woman who feels compelled to take on more than a reasonable workload now has available both the business demands and the traditional homemaker's responsibilities. Although she might claim to desire relief at home, the pattern often replicates that of the workaholic boss who cannot delegate. Any attempt to turn over tasks to the husband or a third party culminates in frustration for all. The workaholic's perfectionist standards and need to control ensure that the work will not be satisfactory, and she must take back that responsibility if it is ever to be done correctly. The expectation that she can do it all is also unreasonable, but it guarantees an unceasing workload. She may get occasional accolades for her "superwoman" accomplishments, but these are short-lived highs just like the external rewards in the workplace. Whatever she is trying to prove to herself will be an accelerating pursuit with no long-term satisfaction from this path.

In terms of time on the job, women now have greater social support for workaholism than ever before. If the relationship with her husband starts to suffer, she can draw from a number of sources to remind him of how difficult it is for a woman to achieve equal credibility, break through the glass ceiling, hold her own in male-dominated fields, or compete on the job when she is getting so little help at home (Caputo & Dolinsky, 1994; LaPlante, 1999; Segal et al., 1992; Tharenou, Latimer, & Conroy, 1994). However, the influx of more women into the workforce is not a one-sided support for only women's workaholic behavior. Men can also claim they now must work harder than ever to offset the company's efforts to move more women into higher positions (Gates, 1993). The responses differ only in terms of gender-specific detail. Each is still the workaholic's attempt to say the relationship problem is due to the spouse's lack of appreciation for what the workaholic is up against—the claim of external pressure rather than addictive behavior.

Every external pressure mentioned here does exist to some extent. Sacrifices are made to support families; competition for promotion is stiff, particularly as organizations flatten their structure and consolidate jobs; and new populations entering the workforce change the rules about preferred appearance and actions. None of the arguments mentioned are put into this discussion to suggest that they lack credibility entirely. Rather it is to show that the link to reality supplies a generalized social support for workaholic behavior—behavior that, in truth, would continue if none of these conditions existed. Even when situations reach more extreme proportions, there is not the social outrage that would help define where reality stops and fabrication begins.

The following are some current examples of imbalance in work and personal life:

- In reviewing the film *The 24-Hour Woman,* Maslin (1999) described the character Grace, who has her nanny videotape counterfeit birthday party scenes. She missed her child's party by working late but wants to have evidence for posterity that suggests she made it on time.
- A real-life "wonder woman" who runs Chicago's snow removal crews is described as being so devoted to her position that it precludes any concern about sleep, food, or anything else. She is not married and concedes that she has structured the job in a way that it would be difficult for a married person to manage (Spielman, 1999).
- A pregnant director of corporate affairs for a power company was closing a big deal when her water broke, tried to continue working, but finally had to go to the hospital for delivery. Two days after giving birth, she was back on the job to put finishing touches on the deal (Sullivan, 1999).

These stories about women get attention because they represent decisions about level of work involvement that previously were only available to men. These women are making choices about marriage and children that many men have made. Among those who might see a potential problem in these situations, public reaction often is either that "it comes with the territory if you want that level of career" or "this is why it's better for men to hold these positions." If the problem of work/life balance were taken more seriously, there would be more commentary about the new spread of a pattern that has *always* represented potential problems. Seeing women do what men have done in the past neither creates a new problem nor solves an old one. It may only serve to bring attention to something that deserved attention all along.

Among the male population, there are a few brave souls who have tried to break the pattern long associated with male breadwinners. Some fathers have chosen to take advantage of family leave policies or take a break from their career to cover child-care and home responsibilities. Few companies support these choices. There are very real obstacles, including the perception that the man is a slacker or not serious about the job. Those who simply want to leave on time, perhaps stay home occasionally to care for a sick child, or otherwise share in home responsibilities often feel the need to conceal those decisions (Poe, 1999). For example, some have been creative in use of sick leave and vacation days, and they have learned that leaving the computer and desk lamp on gives the impression of still being in the office while handling a family situation (Jackson, 1999b).

The view that families and other relationships should give way for greater time on the job is familiar to U.S. culture in general, as well as being actively promoted by specific organizations. Trying to convince a workaholic to change this addictive behavior means taking on more than the views of one individual. It is no wonder that spouses, friends, and even children often feel they must choose either to exit (physically or psychologically) or to join forces with the workaholic in distorted relationship patterns (Fassel, 1990; Robinson, 1998).

When Will You See the Workaholic in Counseling?

Addiction continues until the motivation to stop is strong enough to break through denial and justify the discomfort of both immediate withdrawal symptoms and struggle of long-term behavior changes. In most jobs, physical overwork has been replaced by psychological overload (Michie & Cockcroft, 1996), but the outcomes of excessive work can manifest in physical, psychological, or social problems.

Deterioration of Personal Health

Companies do recognize some ultimate downside to the habit of high work involvement and long hours, usually in the form of health deterioration. A cynic might say that this recognition is fueled by self-interest. An employee hospitalized for heart problems, ulcers, or other stress-related illness is missing time from work—although the workaholic will set up office in the hospital room as quickly as possible. Employee health insurance costs are a concern. In recent years, Japanese firms have lost legal judgments for *karoshi*—death by overwork—requiring them to pay settlements to the widows (Kato, 1995), a new and not insignificant expense to the company. The management task, then, becomes one of getting as much out of people as possible and stopping them just before their condition shifts to costly health problems.

A less cynical view would allow for the possibility that the employer does hold some genuine concern for worker's health, in addition to protecting the company's investment. Starting from either assumption, a company might attempt to take action to lessen the possibility of work-related health problems, but it is difficult to determine what is appropriate, and when. Each individual's threshold is different. Wellness programs can help employees recognize their own needs, make lifestyle changes, and take action to alleviate stress, but individual initiative is the key. A workaholic uses denial, avoids any action initiating feelings of withdrawal, and primarily recognizes only the need to work. This is not an individual who is going to take advantage of the opportunity to create a more balanced workday.

When physical health problems do occur, a blunt doctor's warning to "stop or die" may lead the workaholic to seek help. There is likely to be resentment that the body has failed to keep up with the desired lifestyle rather than any initial admission that it was pushed beyond reasonable expectations. Those who willingly listen to suggestions may also revert to taking their chances with health when withdrawal discomfort sets in. After all, withdrawal hurts now, a few minor concessions can be implemented, and it is somewhat speculative that another heart attack is imminent. By definition, the workaholic has chosen work over all other potential sources of pleasure and satisfaction. The suggestion for less work puts that only source of pleasure at risk. The physical health problems that lead workaholics to seek help may improve noticeably in the time immediately following medical intervention. In terms of initiating counseling, it gets them in the door, but dedication to a long-term solution may fade rather quickly.

Burnout

During and since the 1980s, the term *burnout* has become a recognized term in business vocabulary (Maslach, 1982; Pines & Aronson, 1988; Schaufeli, Maslach, & Marek, 1993). When people suffer mental and emotional exhaustion, adopt a distant cynical attitude toward work and their coworkers, and feel they are inadequate in their jobs, they are in a state of burnout (Maslach & Leiter, 1997). Workaholics do experience burnout, although they are driven to increase work involvement at the same time they feel inadequate, exhausted, and cynical. They may even have greater susceptibility to burnout because of their perfectionist standards and tendency to take on responsibility and control of work. But workaholics are less likely to consider a change in job or work habits to resolve feelings of burnout.

On the surface, a workaholic's accelerating need for more and more work (increased tolerance) may appear to be the organization's dream come true—the employee who just cannot get enough, no matter what the cost. This illusion assumes that the individual is efficient and productive in his or her increasing responsibilities and time devotion. When one looks past the surface-level activities to the addiction pattern, it is apparent the organization is admiring what it thinks is a high threshold for work but which is, in fact, an inefficient and destructive influence. The impossible standards, inability to delegate or give up any control to others, potential crisis creation, and erratic nontrusting interpersonal relations on the job all are extremely detrimental to others' mental and emotional state. While it is true that a workaholic may end up in counseling, it is also very likely that those who work in contact with the workaholic would be seeking help for this reason.

Family Problems

The complaints counselors get from the spouse are still the most likely introduction to the workaholic. The spouse may seek joint counseling, with the hope that another person can provide some backup to the feelings of neglect or burden in support of the workaholic's all-consuming job. The workaholic, in turn, may agree to participate only with the expectation that it will help clarify it is the spouse who is being unreasonable. As with other addictions, causality is likely to have been a household debate (see Miller & Gold, 1990). Family counselors must often deal with what is termed *circular causality* (Robinson, 1998), as with questions such as the following: Does unpleasantness at home drive the workaholic to greater immersion in work, or does the work addiction cause family problems? With the extent of social and organizational support favoring the workaholic's views, strong arguments are needed to solicit further cooperation if initial discussion frames the work involvement as excessive.

Children can be excellent monitors of whether there is a true imbalance. However, they may not always speak up or may be easily influenced to restrain the very feelings that would identify the problem. One man tells of a turning point in his life when seeing a picture his son had drawn of the family for a school assignment (Dobrzynski, 1995). He was not in the picture. When he asked where Daddy was, his son replied without any apparent emotion that Daddy was at work. This depiction of his absence, treated as the normal condition, was a strong enough message to prompt changes in that father's work/home priorities. If someone had asked his son about problems, would he have mentioned his father's absence? He may not have had any comparison basis on which to identify it as a problem.

Another father did receive complaints from his children about his choice to work so much rather than be present at ballgames and family functions. He drove them through a very poor neighborhood and explained that this was how they would have to live if he only worked 9 to 5 every day. That put an end to their complaints. In his view, he had provided an explanation in terms the children could understand. If they were later asked about the amount of attention they received from their father, would they have brought it up again? Maybe not, if they felt they would be expressing a selfish desire for his time balanced against the well-being of the entire family. Another adult might have brought up a condition that is midground between the two extremes of the comparison, but these children apparently accepted the rigid reasoning as valid.

Some parents find that having children can increase their productivity at work because parenthood supplies the motivation to be more efficient and enable time at home with the kids ("Parenthood May Improve Productivity," 1999). The workaholic's choice is more work. Reports of recent studies continue to link parenting and home environment with children's ability to grow into confident, happy adults (Boodman, 1998; Thomas, 1999). For children from addictive households, counseling may not occur until they experience problems in adulthood. By this time, workaholic parenting can only be dealt with as a past influence (Robinson, 1998).

In addition to family members, good friends may attempt to convince the workaholic that the breakdown in their friendship is closely linked to work being given more importance than anything else. These people are the least likely to be able to influence a workaholic to seek help. Most ambitious business people have heard that "it's lonely at the top." Losing friends in pursuit of promotion and career success is, therefore, to be expected. While a consistent pattern of lost friendships can be revealing information for identifying a *real* workaholic, it is at best a contributing factor in any decision to make a change, not the triggering event.

Problems on the Job

Earlier comments have indicated there is little chance the employer will instigate any examination of the workaholic's behavior.

Those higher ranking in the organization will look at the activity level and short-term outcomes that the workaholic so effectively generates. It is much easier to accept the surface appearance of high performance than to look for issues that might cause longer term difficulty. However, there are changes taking place in the workplace that make life more difficult for the workaholic.

As organizations flatten their structure, the convenience of authoritarian rule is diminished. Team-based structures, shifting project assignments, and collaborative partnerships are becoming more common. The rigid control and perfectionism that a workaholic could inflict on others as a manager or supervisor now become more visible in difficulty working as part of the team. In a management position, the workaholic's performance ratings may now include more difficult criteria, such as encouraging participation or generating advantages through employee diversity. The currently popular 360° performance reviews (input from organizational levels above, equivalent, and below the employee) lessen the potential of looking good to the boss at the expense of others.

Workaholics want control to ensure their work supply, and one source of control is holding (and withholding) information. Current trends toward organizations' knowledge management are based on dissemination of information, so that all employees have easy access to what they need to do the job, when they need it. Workaholics may seem to get involved in early stages of knowledge management initiatives, when the project startup justifies extra time and effort. Ultimately, though, they will resist full sharing of information in their personal domain. In addition to the threat of losing control, they may perceive that others will not use the information properly (perfectionism) and keep clinging to the responsibility. Depending on the organization and others' awareness, the workaholic either may continue to look like the hero for saving the group from flawed information sharing or will finally be seen as a blockage in the process.

These trends also may gradually help identify workaholic tendencies among workers previously excluded from many discussions of the problem. It is easier to imagine potential workaholism among those in jobs or at organizational levels known to have more discretionary control of their schedules. The executive who takes work home at night is viewed as voluntarily extending his workday. The production line worker or payroll clerk who is instructed to add overtime hours appears to be the recipient of others' decisions. A deeper look might reveal that each person could have gained enough efficiency to avoid extended hours. At any level, the workaholic who is manipulating situations and people to create a need to work more is disrupting more than his or her own range of responsibilities. As new workplace trends illuminate the more complete picture, it may help to better identify workaholics at all ranks.

A person caught in these transitions will not walk into a therapist's office saying that the latest organizational changes have revealed his or her workaholism and forced realization that it is time to change. If changes in the workplace do initiate any search for new answers, it will more likely be due to a sense of extreme frustration with new working conditions. In the workaholic's view, "those people" refuse to acknowledge that the workaholic is the only one who can see the right way to do things and is willing to put in the time and sacrifices necessary to make it happen. Simply put, some of the current changes seen in organizations make it more difficult for the workaholic to continue the game under familiar rules. Any search for new strategies to support the addictive pattern may allow a window of opportunity to bring the real problem to light.

The most drastic job change for a workaholic would be loss of the job itself. A workaholic has much personal identity and day-to-day survival wrapped up in the job. If that singular source of satisfaction is suddenly removed, the distress of withdrawal and insecurity might manifest in a number of ways that would lead the individual into some sort of counseling. Without the anchor of required work each day, the workaholic may lash out at anyone nearby, and this is usually going to be family members or a few close friends. Although they will be understanding about the loss of the job, they will probably not understand the depth of loss that has occurred. The workaholic will increasingly be focused on how to regain the process of his or her addiction. Anyone who gets in the way, no matter how sympathetic or well meaning, will readily be sacrificed as needed. Loss of a job is likely to cause more turmoil among family members of a workaholic than for other workers who may, in fact, have much greater financial jeopardy or fewer new employment options.

Is This a Growing or Declining Problem?

The general population seems to be getting busier and busier. To accommodate the need or desire to do more in each 24-hour day, the individual's solution, increasingly, is to do with less sleep (Fulmer, 1999; Shellenbarger, 1999a). This trend—large numbers of people choosing sleep deprivation in order to do more—in itself is disturbing. Is high performance now generally accepted to mean quantity of accomplishments without much quality-of-life consideration? Has doing everything become such a basic need as to justify inattentive drivers, groggy or accident-prone workers, grouchy parents/partners, and reliance on caffeine to make it through each day?

The need to keep doing more and more has also been referred to as a "busyness trap," invading most of the population (Moses, 1998). Even the extreme of work addiction has been credited to entire organizations (Schaef & Fassel, 1988). Are we headed in an irreversible direction, or can we still distinguish workaholic behavior from the pace of the general population? Reviewing some key work-related issues that are often linked with workaholism can help draw attention to the extremes of the addiction.

Those Labor-Saving Devices

Not long ago, the workaholic had to stuff a briefcase with work to make it through the evening, weekend, or vacation. Now, thanks to advances in technology, the office umbilical cord reaches anywhere at any time. Pagers, wireless phones, and computers that fit in any briefcase make it easy to keep the entire job at one's fingertips. Videoconferencing allows joint discussion on issues that travel costs otherwise would have prohibited. This is a positive addition to the workplace, when leading to faster resolution or higher quality decisions. But it can also help generate new work by bringing superfluous questions and concerns into an otherwise simple task.

Telecommuting can be a time saver, but it also blurs the line between work and home. Some workers can enjoy having the option to cover a home situation in the middle of the afternoon and make up that lost work time at the end of the day or on the weekend—flexibility is key. The workaholic will simply add evening time and weekends to the work schedule, with the usual neglect of other interests.

An employee who really wants to spend the weekend at home with family will seriously attempt to be efficient enough to make that happen. The workaholic prefers to let conditions develop, so that weekend work is necessary. When work is constrained to one location, the inefficiency of the workaholic is very often rewarded because the hours spent at work are assumed to indicate dedication and hard work. When work input is electronic, it is easier to stay constantly involved, but the identity issues of the workaholic may require finding ways to maintain visibility and the illusion that involvement is necessary. Some may find small rewards in displaying their importance to bystanders—being so critically important that cell phone conversations *must* take place in a restaurant or on the golf course. To gain organizational rewards, however, it will also be necessary to ensure company visibility of the hours and constant attention to work. As constant contact becomes the corporate norm, this will be easier and easier to accomplish.

New technology is a workaholic's dream because work can now so easily be a constant companion. Technology has also been cited as accelerating corporate abuse (Wright & Smye, 1996) and increasing the incidence of burnout (Maslach & Leiter, 1997). Abusive or excessive demands that have increased because of available technology are more appropriately blamed on the organization making the demands than the technology itself. Also, these demands are likely to continue as long as employees allow it to happen. Some individuals fear for their jobs and believe they cannot object for that reason. Some people have personal reasons for allowing those impositions for a limited time and will eventually move to a less abusive environment. Some—the workaholics—just plain like it.

White Collars, Knowledge Workers, and Entrepreneurs

Combining societal trends and availability of technology, the question arises whether there are certain professions or types of employees in which the workaholic is more likely to thrive. For example, if technology so easily supports workaholism, are workers heavily involved with technology more likely to fit the workaholic profile? Not according to a survey by ITManpower, a firm specializing in recruitment of information technology (IT) professionals (Butler, 1999). In a sample of mostly young (ages 18–33) men (72 of 100), 84% reported working less than 50 hours per week. Nearly 40% said they spent most of their spare time with family. Some individuals admitted to spending home hours on personal projects that might resemble their work activity, but the results suggest these technical workers are not overwhelmingly workaholics.

In 1992, Juliet Schor initiated a controversy with her book *The Overworked American*. She claimed a steady increase in the amount of time people spend on the job. *Fortune* magazine expressed similar concern (Fisher, 1992), speculating that the heavier workload resulting from layoffs and mergers would become the standard of the future rather than fading as a temporary bad patch when recovery takes hold. Specifically, the *Fortune* article focused on middle managers who claimed to be investing well over 40 hours per week (some in excess of 60 hours per week) and unable to get the work done. In contrast to these reports, others have responded that reported work hours are exaggerated and this publicity was overattentiveness to baby boomers who are at the prime career-building stage of their lives (e.g., Kane, 1995). Common throughout the debate is the tendency to characterize current overworkers as white-collar professionals working as much for career advancement as job security.

Whether these aspiring professionals are workaholics depends on the extent to which they are sacrificing other life interests for work involvement and whether it is internally motivated rather than a reaction to external pressure. Possibly workaholics are attracted to these positions as an environment supportive of their existing preference. Or, those who survive the longest may do so because they are workaholics. Consider the situation of one CEO whose company now dominates the U.S. market with a stock price quadruple that of before his leadership, and profits up 55% (J. Kaufman, 1999). He relishes the job, despite the fact it has caused stress in his family. His wife does not understand why, as CEO, he cannot find a way to work less. He describes the job as one that has changed dramatically from the past when the leader could focus primarily on strategic decisions.

His predecessor kept strong managers in place, people in which he had high confidence, and dealt more with strategic direction. This CEO decided to flatten the organization, eliminating the senior executive positions. In his view, the person in the top position now must have more direct involvement. Is his sacrifice best for the organization? Companies do experience some savings when management layers are eliminated. However, a look at corporate CEO pay levels in the past few years suggests that a few more senior people could be kept in place for the same total amount of money, without seriously damaging the lifestyle of any one individual. It may be reasonable to suspect many CEOs and other high-ranking executives do fit the workaholic profile—trading family time for more work, greater control, and the identity established through an extraordinary pay check.

Entrepreneurs often retain similar control of all the business details. The excitement in the process of building up a company is so alluring that they frequently move on to a new venture as soon as activity and risk start to level out in the current one. Kets de Vries (1996) summarized frequent traits of entrepreneurs from existing research to include a need for control, sense of distrust, desire for applause, difficulties with self-esteem, and a tendency toward denial. Baechler (1996) described it as living for being needed.

You have to be at all the meetings because people might make a bad decision without your presence to show them the error of their ways. What if there's a crisis? Nobody's as good as you are in a crisis, right? . . . . . Somewhere in the depths of your mind there's a buzzer saying that your family needs you too, but when a phone call comes in at 5:15, you just can't hang up. (p. 29)

Baechler (1996) referred to this as being a hog-all-the-fun manager and has since changed her own approach to work and learned to protect her family from her problem with workaholism.

Another spate of articles has appeared on the theme of pressure to work more hours (e.g., Bond, Galinsky, & Swanberg, 1998; Himmelberg, 1998). The general problem seems to range across most industries and all types of organizations. True external pressure seems inextricably interwoven with individuals' need to achieve, making it difficult to pinpoint those who pursue this type of routine from an addictive drive. Not all white-collar professionals, executives, and entrepreneurs are workaholics. However, the business environment is one that offers ample opportunity to live out those preferences, and there is evidence many workaholics have found a home in both large and small companies (Bond et al., 1998).

Internationality of Workaholism

A variation on the theme of increasing work demands is a tendency to compare U.S. workers with those in other countries— another sign of increasing globalization of commerce. Business people who balk at the idea of a shorter workweek often cite the rise of international competition as reason for more work rather than less. Schor (1992) reported on sending out 300 letters to business leaders, and the mailing failed to yield a single favorable response to her suggestions advocating shorter work hours. Both the willingness to work extended hours and the expected outcomes for overwork seem to be common around the globe.

One comparison shows that the United States ranks high on the percentage of workers who admit taking time off work as a result of stress (Kadaba, 1995)—27%, second only to 28% of Hong Kong workers. Kabada also wrote about others' envy of Europeans who stop work for enjoyable lunch hours and get away for longer vacations. "Until the mid-'70s, the United States was among the countries leading the industrialized world in shorter work hours and weeks. . . . In recent years, Americans have a far greater desire for work than Europeans" (Kadaba, 1995, p. F6).

The Japanese have been referred to as a workaholic society, because they work longer hours than people in most other countries (Kato, 1995). Although statistics are not officially kept on *karoshi*, there are reports that the Ministry of Labor compensated 196 cases of work-related death between 1987 and 1994. These *karoshi* victims are believed to have worked in excess of 3,000 hours a year—roughly twice the norm for people in France, Germany, and Sweden (Kato, 1995). Recent government settlements also include payments to families who can substantiate that suicide was caused by overwork. This is another recognition of the intense Japanese work ethic (Kageyama, 1999). As conditions change and younger workers influence organizational life, the Japanese may begin to learn the advantages of less work ("Learn to Enjoy Life," 1999), but change will be slow.

Workaholism is not unique to the United States by any means, but national culture does seem to be a strong influence on attitudes that encourage, or at least tolerate, workaholic behavior. Family relationships or friendships between people from different cultural backgrounds may be an added factor in dealing with a workaholic. On the one hand, the cultural tendency may provide an opening to talk about the problem in a way that is less personally threatening. On the other hand, the workaholic might cling to strong identification with a supportive culture as one more evidence of being misunderstood by those who do not share that indoctrination.

Generational Push

The baby-boomer generation has not exactly set the stage for ending workaholism. As role models, they have shown that it is important to work long hours (or at least claim to work long hours); as the higher ranking managers in many companies today, they set the demands for the workers who follow. A great deal has been written about Generation X, the subsequent employees who do not seem to follow the same rules. One view is that the attitudes of "Xers" and "Boomers" are so vastly different that they have created a special management challenge for companies (Tulgan, 1995). Contrary to the stereotypes that have evolved, recent surveys have found that both loyalty and desired incentives to stay with a job are not as different across the generations as once believed (Bond et al., 1998).

In many instances, the Gen-Xers seem more comfortable drawing the line at too much work (Jackson, 1999a). If this is the case, they will gradually push organizations for better work-life programs and help remove any stigma attached to use of existing programs (Poe, 1999). This generation of workers is more likely than ever before to be members of a couple in which both parties work full time (Bond et al., 1998). This pervasive dual-career norm might eliminate some of the family tension linked to social roles and expectations (provider vs. support member). What is unclear is whether that will focus more or less attention on workaholic behaviors. Somewhat surprisingly, Generation X respondents to the workforce survey indicated that "They work substantially longer hours on average and find their jobs more demanding than young workers 20 years ago did" (Bond et al., 1998, p. 14). As they age and progress in careers from this starting point, will they replicate or reverse the trend for overwork and traits of workaholism?

Many Gen-Xers are already moving into the management role. Who will follow them into the workforce? Today's teens, the baby boomlet, are now reaching adulthood. There are distinct indications that they will follow in the footsteps of their overworked parents. In pursuit of a stellar resume, they already overload on coursework and extracurricular activities, always pushing to perfectionist standards. Many hold jobs as well, to add some work experience to their credentials. They believe their parents expect this behavior and consider it nothing out of the ordinary (Shellenbarger, 1998a).

At one high school, freshmen take a careers class that contains a heavy dose of training in the work/family balancing act (Shellenbarger, 1999b). By highlighting the trade-offs between career and family at such an early stage, a course like this might create enough consciousness that these students can intercept problems while they are more manageable. The process could avert a few young people from unconsciously following a pattern of excess, based on what seems to be the accepted norm in their household. An awkward side effect to this might be new consideration of the existing family patterns, questioning—or criticism—of parents' decisions, and resurfacing of any previously buried feelings of neglect. Those who need the awareness most might also have to survive the family turmoil of facing issues that have been quietly buried in day-to-day routine.

Workaholism generates from within the individual. While external factors may lend support, workaholism is not caused by technology, the type of job, or the person's age, generation, or nation of origin. These factors are considered here because they have all been linked to tendencies for overwork. Each one, therefore, is a topic likely to complicate the identification of an individual whose addiction is working.

Conclusion

Companies continue to make strong demands on employees' time and energy. At the same time, there is growing attention to the impact of excessive work in the form of burnout or lower creativity. Many organizations profess a commitment to work/life balance, although they admittedly struggle with how to shift into living out that commitment. More aggressive companies are beginning to mandate shorter working hours and goal-setting sessions that include leisure objectives (L. Kaufman, 1999). Initiatives of this type will not cure the workaholic, but they may help reveal those individuals whose work excess is self-inflicted.

It is reasonable to speculate that these changes in corporate operating philosophy would not occur unless social attitudes about the role of work are also changing somewhat. However gradual it may be, the removal of organizational and societal support for workaholic behavior will help focus relationship problems on the underlying difficulty of the addictive pattern.

The direction of the trend looks promising, but it is deserving of only cautious optimism. In a recent survey of more than 700 people, every respondent said someone they care about works too hard. Reasons for the excess included a desire for money (40%), a demanding supervisor (22%), and workaholism (55%) ("Workplace Briefs," 1999). In spite of positive change in some organizations, the prevalence of excessive work has reached monumental proportions.

For each person who pursues work as an addiction, multiple relationships are affected. The problem is perpetuated through home environments that instruct young people in the addictive pattern while tearing apart the marriage partnership. The intersection of workplace and family problems will continue to be destructive to personal relationships until workaholism is more effectively recognized and treated as an addictive behavior.

References

Baechler, M. (1996, May). I'm Mary, and I'm a workaholic. *Inc.*, *18*, 29–30.

Bahls, J. E. (1999, March). Handle with care. *HR Magazine*, *44*, 60–66.

Bond, J. T., Galinsky, E., & Swanberg, J. E. (1998). *The 1997 national study of the changing workforce*. New York: Families and Work Institute.

Boodman, S. G. (1998, June 1). Study links childhood experience to later illness. *Philadelphia Inquirer*, pp. D1, D3.

Butler, G. (1999, February 20). New breed of IT professionals explodes myth. *Australian Financial Review*, p. 19.

Caputo, R. K., & Dolinsky, A. (1994). Women's choice to pursue self-employment: The role of financial and human capital of household members. *Journal of Small Business Management 35*(3), 8–17.

Dobrzynski, J. H. (1995, June 18). Should I have left an hour earlier? *The New York Times*, Section 3, pp. 1, 12.

Fassel, D. (1990). *Working ourselves to death*. San Francisco: Harper.

Fisher, A. B. (1992, November 30). Welcome to the age of overwork. *Fortune, 126*, 64–71.

Fulmer, M. (1999, January 11). Careers/Zen at work: The Zen of clockwork. *Los Angeles Times*, pp. C2, C21.

Gates, D. (1993, March 29). White male paranoia: Are they the newest victims—or just bad sports? *Newsweek*, 47–53.

Himmelberg, M. (1998). Workers wonder: What became of the 8-hour work day? *The Philadelphia Inquirer*, pp. C1, C8.

Jackson, M. (1999a, February 21). Adjusting to the "X" factor: As new generation of workers emerges, corporations reconsider training, benefits. *The Boston Globe*, p. J4.

Jackson, M. (1999b, February 6). Working dads strive for balance. *Philadelphia Inquirer*, p. D1.

Kadaba, L. S. (1995, February 21). The stress of work. *The Philadelphia Inquirer*, pp. F1, F6.

Kageyama, Y. (1999, March 13). Japan ordered to pay after overworked man kills self. *Los Angeles Times*, p. A5.

Kane, M. (1995, April 23). Overworked? Maybe, maybe not. *Star Ledger*, p. C1.

Kato, T. (1995, February). Workaholism: It's not in the blood. *Look Japan*, pp. 1–4.

Kaufman, J. (1999, May 3). For latter-day CEO "all in a day's work" often means just that. *The Wall Street Journal*, pp. A1, A8.

Kaufman, L. (1999, May 4). Some companies derail the "burnout" track. *The New York Times*, p. 1.

Kets de Vries, M. F. R. (1996). The anatomy of the entrepreneur: Clinical observations. *Human Relations, 49*, 853–882.

LaPlante, M. (1999). Illegal interview questions fuel hiring bias. *Women in Higher Education, 8*(3), 6.

Learn to enjoy life. (1999, February 7). *South China Morning Post*, p. 2.

Maslach, C. (1982). *Burnout: The cost of caring*. Englewood Cliffs, NJ: Prentice Hall.

Maslach, C., & Leiter, M. P. (1997). *The truth about burnout: How organizations cause personal stress and what to do about it*. San Francisco: Jossey-Bass.

Maslin, J. (1999, January 29). Women's work: 9 to 5 in daydreams only. *The New York Times*, p. 10.

Michie, S., & Cockcroft, A. (1996). Overwork can kill. *British Medical Journal, 313*, 921–922.

Micklethwait, J., & Wooldridge, A. (1996). *The witch doctors: Making sense of the management gurus*. New York: Random House.

Miller, N. S., & Gold, M. S. (1990). The disease and adaptive models of addiction: A reevaluation. *Journal of Drug Issues, 20*, 19–35.

Moses, B. (1998, November). The busyness trap. *Training, 35*, 38–42.

Parenthood may improve productivity. (1999, May). *HR Magazine, 44*, 24.

Pines, A., & Aronson, E. (1988). *Career burnout: Causes and cures*. New York: Macmillan.

Poe, A. C. (1999, July). The daddy track. *HR Magazine, 44*, 82–89.

Porter, G. (1996). Organizational impact of workaholism: Suggestions for researching the negative outcomes of excessive work. *Journal of Occupational Health Psychology, 1*, 70–84.

Porter, G. (1998). Can you trust a workaholic? How work addiction erodes trust throughout the organization. *Journal of Contemporary Business Issues, 6*(2), 48–57.

Ramphele, M. (1996). *Across boundaries: The journey of a South African woman leader*. New York: Feminist Press.

Robinson, B. E. (1989). *Work addiction: Hidden legacies of adult children*. Deerfield Beach, FL: Health Communications.

Robinson, B. E. (1998). *Chained to the desk: A guidebook for workaholics, their partners and children, and the clinicians who treat them*. New York: New York University Press.

Rohrlich, J. B. (1980). *Work and love: The crucial balance*. New York: Summit Books.

Schaef, A. W., & Fassel, D. (1988). *The addictive organization*. San Francisco: Harper & Row.

Schaufeli, W., Maslach, C., & Marek, T. (Eds.). (1993). *Professional burnout: Recent developments in theory and research*. Washington, DC: Taylor & Francis.

Schor, J. B. (1992). *The overworked American: The unexpected decline of leisure*. New York: Basic Books.

Sefton, D. (1999, January 28). Two together half as happy: Stress is taking its toll on many working couples. *The Kansas City Star*, p. E1.

Segal, A. T., Landler, M., Shine, E., Zinn, L., Flynn, J., & Marcial, G. G. (1992, June 8). Corporate women—progress? Sure. But the playing field is still far from level. *Business Week*, 74–83.

Sells, B. L. (1993, December). Workaholism. *ABA Journal*, 70–71.

Seybold, K., & Salomone, P. (1994). Understanding workaholism: A review of causes and counseling approaches. *Journal of Counseling and Development, 73*, 4–9.

Shellenbarger, S. (1998a, June 3). Teens are inheriting parents' tendencies toward work overload. *The Wall Street Journal*, p. B1.

Shellenbarger, S. (1998b, September 16). Workers offer views about productivity and long workweeks. *The Wall Street Journal*, p. B1.

Shellenbarger, S. (1999a, February 17). Rising before dawn, are you getting ahead or just getting tired? *The Wall Street Journal*, p. B1.

Shellenbarger, S. (1999b, February 24). Students get lessons in how to manage a well-balanced life. *The Wall Street Journal*, p. B1.

Spielman, F. (1999, January 24). City's snow warrior. *Chicago Sun-Times*, p. 6.

Sullivan, J. (1999, January 23). Rejecting hard labor. *The Age*, p. 8.

Tharenou, P., Latimer, S., & Conroy, D. (1994). How do you make it to the top? An examination of influences on women's and men's managerial advancement. *Academy of Management Journal, 37*, 800–931.

Thomas, D. (1999, January 30). Why boys need a father's guiding hand: A workaholic with no time for his son may be throwing away that child's future happiness. *The Daily Telegraph*, p. 21.

Tulgan, B. (1995). *Managing Generation X*. Santa Monica, CA: Merritt.

Workplace briefs. (1999, February 17). *The Detroit News*, p. B4.

Wright, L., & Smye, M. (1996). *Corporate abuse: How "lean and mean" robs people and profits*. New York: Macmillan.

■ ■ ■

4

Attorneys: High Performance and Family Relationships

Clarence Hibbs, PhD

Those who choose the practice of law find themselves in a profession that requires the practitioner to consistently achieve a very high level of performance to succeed. Because the quality of attorneys' work may be crucial to their clients' lives, the rewards may be considerable, both in terms of satisfaction and in compensation. Their families also may enjoy high regard in the community, with high performance expected of them as well. However, along with the rewards and satisfactions, the practice of law also brings with it inherent hazards and risks for the life of the family. The constant pressure for high performance, the sustained effort often required, and the frequently precious little time for recovery from long hours at the office take their toll on both the attorney and the family. All too often, the results are tragic. Witness the following example.

Melissa could not have been more astounded when Jim, her husband of 7 years, announced that he was leaving the marriage. She had no idea that he was unhappy and had given up on the relationship. Jim had been very supportive of Melissa's desire to be an attorney, and he had worked hard to support her through law school. In the early years of her career, he had made few complaints about the long hours she spent at the office. He did more than his share of child care for which she was very grateful indeed. It is true that they had to cancel many social engagements because of her work and that she had often been too exhausted to go out when they had planned an evening together. It was also true that their sex life had suffered for much the same reasons. It was not a lack of interest on her part, but by the time everything was done in the evenings, she fell asleep almost before her head touched the pillow. Their disagreements about child raising, finances, and other household matters had seemed to her as just a part of being married, but not that serious. Jim's contention that she treated him like one of her court cases seemed overblown. He should not be so oversensitive about normal marital conflict, she thought. However, his view was that family life had become peripheral to her professional life, which she valued over everything else. The crisis that ensued gave Melissa and Jim an opportunity to examine the erosion of their relationship, including the way her work had contributed to the situation.

Although Melissa and Jim's case may be a little unusual for several reasons, the scenario they were experiencing is disturbingly familiar. High stress, long hours, demanding clients, and an adversarial and competitive climate are elements that dramatically affect the lives of attorneys and, consequently, their families and close relationships. As the work becomes increasingly demanding, the attorney may become more distant and unavailable at home, which in turn contributes to the deterioration of the marriage. Although accurate statistics are difficult to access, anecdotal evidence seems to indicate that, over the past two decades, the divorce rate for attorneys has remained abnormally high (Drogin, 1991; Hibbs & Himes, 1985), even as the divorce rate for the general population has leveled off (National Marriage Project, 1999).

It will become evident that many aspects of attorney families are similar to other high-profile families such as celebrities (Mitchell & Cronson, 1987), medical families (Gabbard, Menninger, & Coyne, 1987; Sotile & Sotile, 1996; Yandoli, 1989), families of executives (Keele, 1984), social work academics (Spence & Robbins, 1992), and other "fast track" families (Brooks, 1989). In some aspects, however, families of attorneys face challenges that contribute to family difficulties that are more particular to the profession of law. Therefore, this chapter is primarily concerned with the lives of attorneys and their families, and particularly the effects of the legal profession on family life. Along with many positive aspects of the career of law, there are many factors that put lawyers and their families at risk for difficulties in their relationships. Many of these difficulties, such as those experienced by Melissa and Jim, are avoidable if attention is given to the potentially destructive elements associated with the high-performance demands of the practice of law.

For purposes of this discussion, a broadly systemic viewpoint is assumed. This means that the reciprocal, mutual interaction of all facets of the social system is influential in determining the course of the conduct of life (Atwood, 1992). A systemic view directs attention to the widest context possible because no problem can be understood without examining the context in which the difficulty occurs (Watzlawick, Beavin, & Jackson, 1967). When families such as that of Melissa and Jim come for counseling in their difficulties, every factor of their lives, past and present, is of interest. It is not possible to understand a family unless attention is paid to the interaction of culture, society, and, in this case, the particular culture of work to intervene with high-performance families such as "lawyer families" (Robinson, 1998a). Because it would not be possible to investigate here all the contextual factors of these families, we have chosen to focus on those that come most directly from the environment of the legal profession.

Choosing the Legal Profession

There are four motivations for choosing law that are most often mentioned by researchers and law professors who have observed students over a period of time. Undoubtedly these motivations have origins in family background and experience and affect the way the lawyer's family will conduct itself, especially in light of the expectations and demands that are placed on the family. The first is the motive of power. Lawyers are perceived as powerful people. Those who have an interest in influencing society or who desire to control their own destinies may choose the law partly as a path to power (Arron, 1999). Some young people may have very idealistic reasons for wanting to exercise power and may see their ambition as a way of making a positive contribution to society. In any case, seeking power influences family performance. The second motivation is prestige. The desire to be recognized, valued, and esteemed by others is closely associated with the motivation of power because prestige is also powerful. The drive to be noticed may arise from a sense of insecurity, and gaining recognition from others is a way of establishing one's identities (Arron, 1989; Drell, 1994). The visibility that comes with power and recognition will influence the performance of the family in both public and private aspects of its life. Money is a third motivation. The perception that lawyers have high incomes is often given as a reason for wanting to be a lawyer. These three motivations are in many ways variations on the same basic theme. However, a fourth motivation often cited is the desire to do public good. When a person sees the law as a way to exercise his or her talent to help others and promote the welfare of society, then some of the other motivations may not be as compelling. Family expectations and performance may adjust to be congruent with the altruistic motivations of the lawyer. Still others, often those educated in the social sciences, enter law school because they do not know what else to do. They are often multitalented but undirected, and they see the law as a challenging intellectual profession (Arron, 1989; A. V. Baker, personal communication, July 30, 1999).

The experience of law school is a crucial element in the socialization of lawyers (Drell, 1994; Hibbs & Himes, 1985). One adopts behaviors, beliefs, and attitudes that are similar to those of colleagues and begins to act in ways that are consistent with those beliefs. The primary skills of the law profession are the exercise of reason and logic, coupled with the verbal skills to articulate persuasive arguments supporting one's position (Arron, 1989; Drell, 1994). Perfecting intellectual and logical abilities and honing reasoning and verbal skills are necessary to be a successful attorney. The ability to remain objective and uninvolved emotionally is one of the unique features of legal training and practice. It is essential in carrying out the lawyer's obligation to the client. While countless hours of careful and diligent effort are necessary to acquire these skills, the experience is sometimes described in negative terms. One lawyer said that in law school he focused on "being the super-rational, super intellectual super-logician. I submitted to a lobotomy of my emotional corpus" (Arron, 1989, p. 48). Another attorney described the experience as an indoctrination. He said, "what law school applicants do not understand . . . is that law school is not intended for the generalist. It is, instead, an indoctrination into a new way of thinking that significantly alters one's view and approach to the world" (Arron, 1989, p. 58). Both of these instances make the important point that legal education seeks to reshape the person's value system and behavior patterns to focus primarily on what is logical and rational. Although this socialization process molds the law career, it is often at odds with the role of a nurturing and involved spouse or parent.

The element of competition and the development of skills in argument and advocacy arising primarily out of concentration on the intellectual and logical are all part of what Elkins (1985, p. 28) called learning to "think like a lawyer." In the classroom, the Socratic method is the primary classroom methodology used to accomplish the goal of thinking like a lawyer. The professor questions students on their understanding of the subject matter by calling on a class member and repeatedly probing for further refinements of the issue at hand. The students' anxiety of waiting to be called on, especially if unprepared, is intense. The experience underscores the need to think quickly on one's feet and be prepared with an adequate response for any occasion.

Legal scholars and law school professors question whether their own methods are effective in producing legal professionals who are suited to the present climate or if, in fact, they may be contributing to students' dysfunction (A. V. Baker, personal communication, July 30, 1999; Iijima, 1998). If legal education neglects crucial factors necessary for the well-being of legal practitioners, it is likely that it also produces people who will have difficulties in their relationships and families.

Characteristics of the Legal Profession and Attorneys and Their Effects on Family

Married Law Students

Law school, especially the first year, is intensively competitive. The well-known lawyer and novelist Scott Turow's first book, titled *One L/* (1977), was a description of his first year at Harvard Law School. He described the unrelenting pressure of competition and the unbearable tension that students felt while waiting for the posting of grades after the first term. Students then obsessed over their relative positions in the rankings based on the grades and whether they would make law review, a particularly important measure of whether they were "making it" in relation to their colleagues. Turow, who was married during his law school days, gave a vivid description of the effect of law school on his marriage. When the law students are married, the effect of law school socialization is quickly felt in their marriages. One professor warned wives of first-year law students that their spouses would be more aggressive, more hostile, more precise, more impatient, more cynical, and more distrusting (Schwartz, 1980). One woman commented that after her first year of law school, she was the only person who was still married out of her class. She divorced during her second year. Similar reports are common.

Impact on the Family

There are many positive and beneficial aspects to the profession of law, both to the lawyer and to his or her family. Many areas of law provide excitement and intellectual challenge that make each work day something to look forward to (Blodgett, 1986; Hirsch, 1985). Job satisfaction is an important element in having a satisfying family life and brings an optimistic atmosphere home. Intellectual stimulation, a feeling of personal power, and the excitement of doing a good job greatly contribute to job satisfaction (Blodgett, 1986; Hirsch, 1985). Family support for one's career has been associated with positive marital adjustment for lawyers (Spendlove et al., 1990). Such family support supplies impetus for going back into the workplace with renewed energy and adds to job satisfaction.

The desire for recognition is an important motivator (Arron, 1999). Choosing a high-profile career is one way of receiving recognition and visibility. Being recognized by important people and having them depend on you is a potent motivator. One lawyer quipped that as soon as he moved to his new home and it was discovered that he was a lawyer, he was quickly asked to be on the board of the local Little League. As visibility and prestige grow, larger opportunities typically open to the lawyer, increasing his or her influence, which can be used to benefit others and increase life's satisfaction.

The life of high-performance families is practically a blueprint for what Sotile and Sotile (1998) called the "Big Life," defined as relentless hard work, a perfectionistic approach, always in a hurry, an ability to think about more than one thing at a time, being competitive, and having the stamina to respond to multiple demands. These are also characteristics of medical families (Gabbard et al., 1987; Sotile & Sotile, 1996) and are similar to Robinson's (1998b) description of workaholics. Although some thrive on this fast-paced life, eventually the stress points may begin to show. Nearly all lawyers report substantial dissatisfaction with at least one aspect of their employment, especially as it interferes with their personal lives (Blodgett, 1986; Dahl, 1996; Drogin, 1991; Hirsch, 1985). Whether or not these elements may be seen individually as positive or negative, they all have significant implications for the family. The following discussion describes elements most often mentioned when lawyers complain about the downside of their jobs. The intensity of the complaints ranges from mild annoyance to unacceptability. What is important for this discussion is the impact on attorneys and their families.

One of the negatives most often mentioned is the long hours necessary to carry out job responsibilities. Especially in private practice, and particularly when a new attorney begins practice, the pressure to turn in billable hours is intense (Dahl, 1996). Reports of 80-hour weeks are common (Arron, 1989). One male lawyer described a typical week of 8:00 a.m. to 7:00 or 8:00 p.m. The fact that he has an hour's commute makes a 14-hour workday the norm. Evening engagements often take him late into the night before returning home. This leaves him little time or energy to engage with his family. As a result, his wife complains that he is emotionally unavailable, and his children confide that they do not know him well at all. One young couple considering marriage and struggling with their relationship reported that the female lawyer's legal cases often lasted several weeks, and the hours they could spend together were limited to weekends. They found this insufficient time to establish their plans for the future since her work schedule occasionally included weekends as well. Some lawyers have stated that they become intolerant of clients wasting their time because that time is time away from their family (Arron, 1989).

In private practice, the ability to produce billable hours may be the difference between being retained or fired, regardless of the quality of the work done or the reputation among one's colleagues (A. V. Baker, personal communication, July, 30, 1999; Dahl, 1996). The bottom line for the firm often determines who stays and who goes. This pressure is the reason some attorneys choose to practice in smaller communities and others to work in small firms—and have more control over their lives (C. J. Tyler, personal communication, August 10, 1999; L. Gose, personal communication, August 11, 1999).

Long hours at work may function as a distance regulation in the family. The pattern that develops in this instance decreases the psychological intensity of the family interaction, as well as physical and emotional contact (Alexander & Parsons, 1982). There are fewer opportunities for conflict, but also fewer opportunities for intimacy. The effect on the family of the unavailability of the attorney often is that the family members feel that they are unimportant and take last place in the attorney's priorities, or in the words of one lawyer's wife, "the marriage is on hold."

The life of the lawyer and his or her family is also affected by the unpredictability of the demands of work. Firm plans can never be made. A last-minute call or an unexpected complication can require that the lawyer stay at work, or go back to work, or perhaps miss an important family event. It may be necessary to leave town on short notice without knowing when he or she will return. Years of family interruption and disappointment are bound to damage relationships (Arron, 1999). Even those who attempt to scale back the time spent on the job find objections, such as Stint (1988), who complained that the competitiveness of the practice of law is such that it does not allow for the luxury of such personal choices. It is obvious that the consequences of the absence of the attorney from so much of the family's life is enormous. One lawyer who was questioned about the conduct of his son retorted, "It couldn't have been because of me, I was never there."

In addition to the monumental time requirements, the culture in which the work takes place is significant. It has already been noted that traditional law training tends to shape lawyers to depend primarily on the logical and rational (Arron, 1989; Drell, 1994). If in the home, only that which makes sense and can be justified is permitted, anything not meeting the rational standard may be discounted or derided. Lawyers and their family members may come to believe that unsubstantiated opinion, based on preference or feelings, may be too dangerous to express. The ability to remain objective and emotionally nonreactive may be learned so well that it is hard to reengage at home, and as a result, family members do not feel well connected. Dependence on logic tends to keep one out of touch with one's own emotions and insensitive to the feelings of others (Arron, 1999; Robinson, 1998a).

Legal work requires meticulous attention to detail. Because any mistakes will quickly be identified by others, perhaps an opponent, constant focus on flawless work is necessary to avoid costly and embarrassing errors or oversights. The pressure to make every detail correct can encourage a pattern of perfectionism (Arron, 1999). At home, if every detail of life comes under scrutiny and mistakes or imperfections are forbidden, a demoralizing atmosphere will likely develop. People cannot possibly live up to such expectations and may respond by giving up trying or rebelling. Children may give up on being perfect and grow up acting irresponsibly because they could never meet the standard expected of them; and in such cases, the way the rebellion is expressed would be chosen to embarrass the parents (Pittman, 1985).

Much legal work is adversarial in nature and as a result encourages suspicion, hostility, and aggression (Elwork & Benjamin, 1995) that likely will be continued outside the office. Some people enjoy arguing some of the time, but few want to debate every issue that comes up in conversation. Being constantly cross-examined may make family members feel abused. People quickly learn to avoid those who batter them with words and argument.

The atmosphere of competition is often pervasive within law practices. It is part of what makes the profession interesting. One can compete by getting new clients, producing billable hours, making the best arguments, or getting high awards by the court. Lawyers often come from families in which competition is encouraged. Obviously, competition is the name of the game in business, and it makes money for everyone. But when taken to the extreme, competition produces a dog-eat-dog context in which walls are erected between people (Drell, 1994). For some, not only is it not enough to win, but also the other person has to lose, and winning becomes equated with personal efficacy (van Zyverden, 1996). One never admits to being wrong. The fear of losing clients by not being perceived as tough enough in specialties such as litigation may set the tone for other success-oriented lawyers. Kohn (1992) described competition as a disease that spreads from office to home, affecting the living room and bedroom as well. The lawyer may carry competition home and compete with family members and encourage competition rather than cooperation. Not being able to admit being wrong and always winning an argument are not helpful in the family setting. One lawyer caught himself always winning games with his children and realized why they became discouraged and avoided playing with him; his naturally competitive patterns were inappropriate at home.

Because legal work can be absorbing and intense, it is difficult to disengage from it even when away from the office (Hirsch, 1985). Family members may complain that even when the lawyer is at home, he or she is not really there. The attorney may be still thinking about the cases and emotionally unavailable to the family (Robinson, 1998a). This is what Lansky (1985) called *preoccupatio*: a person is emotionally absent but physically present and is experienced by family members as remote and rejecting (Vande Kemp, 1997). Family members, especially the spouse, will feel that there is something wrong with them and may attempt even more to compensate. Thus, addiction to work further affects the family's functioning (Chase, 1999; Jurkovic, 1997; Robinson, 1999). It is not surprising that the American Academy of Matrimonial Lawyers found preoccupation to be one of the top four causes of divorce (Robinson, 1998a).

The high stress of the constant pressure of legal work can have cumulative effects on the health and well-being of legal professionals, and the price includes not only burnout but likelihood of heart attacks and a lowered immune system (Dahl, 1996; Drogin, 1991; Elwork & Benjamin, 1995; Hirsch, 1985). Workaholics such as attorneys suffer from more health complaints and also psychologically debilitating symptoms of depression, anxiety, and anger. The health of family members may also be affected (Robinson, 1996;

Spence & Robbins, 1992). Stress, however, can become addictive. Constant pressure, and the excitement that accompanies it in professions such as law, may make one bored in times when the stress is lowered (Arron, 1999). Even on vacation, many lawyers take their computers, frequently check their E-mail, or are constantly on the phone, so they never are really away from work (S. Bost, personal communication, August 2, 1999; Robinson, 1998a). This is not lost on the family. It may take a week of vacation before stress begins to moderate.

The abuse of alcohol and drugs is a frequent hazard in high-performing professions like law. One study suggests that as many as 15% of lawyers may be alcoholics (Drogin, 1991). To maintain the pace during intense periods of work, lawyers may use drugs to medicate and cope. The use of alcohol is common to enable one to slow down and relax, as well as to cause a numbing effect (Arron, 1989; A. Johnson, personal communication, July 30, 1999; Margolick, 1992; Robinson, 1998b). Often preparation for cases may require nearly round-the-clock work. Cocaine is sometimes utilized to keep up the energy level while going without sleep for long periods (Arron, 1999). One author has witnessed an outpouring of testimonial articles, many of which are anonymous or second hand, recounting how careers and personal lives have been affected by alcohol (Drogin, 1991).

Women in Law

The increase of women entering the law profession is the phenomenon that has changed it most dramatically in the past two or three decades. The number of women receiving law degrees is approaching 50% (White, 1998; Wightman, 1996), and the proportion of women in law firms is currently at 30.3%, up from 26.6% in 1998 (Goldhaber, 1998). Will the increase of women in law change the way the profession is practiced? Arron (1999) indicated that she does not believe that women are changing the way law is practiced, and in fact believes that competition and the lack of the collegiality are becoming even worse. A. V. Baker (personal communication, July 30, 1999) and A. Johnson (personal communication, July 30, 1999) agreed that there is little or no change. In fact, they believe that there is a decline in civility among lawyers and with clients. Therefore, according to this opinion, the professional courtesy extended in the past seems to be just that—in the past (Arron, 1989). The health cost for women can be high. Female attorneys are twice as likely to be single, three times as likely to be childless than the general population (Smith, 1984). They may have more difficulty becoming pregnant and carrying a child to full term than the general population because of stress (Gatland, 1997). Women still contend with traditional attitudes toward women's achievements (Smith, 1984) but may also be looked down on if they make the choice to prioritize home and family over the firm. Even in the late 1990s, choosing to spend more time at home was interpreted as not being able to "make it" at the firm, and this applied to both women and men (A. Johnson, personal communication, July 30, 1999).

Workaholism

A clinical description of workaholics includes work taking precedence over everything and everyone, difficulty forming and maintaining intimate relationships and close friendships, always hurrying and staying busy, the need to control, perfectionism, difficulty relaxing and having fun, "brownouts" and memory losses because of exhaustion and preoccupation, being impatient and irritable, and feelings of self-inadequacy and self-neglect (Robinson, 1998b).

A relevant question at this point might be, Is the practice of law an example among many professions in which work addiction is a characteristic feature, or is law a profession that shares many similarities with work addiction, but because of its unique focus is distinct from other professions? Whichever answer one might choose, studies of work addiction reveal striking similarities. In one study that included attorneys, physicians, and psychologists/therapists, more attorneys fell into the workaholic classification compared with the other professions (Doerfler & Kammer, 1986).

Family Patterns

The effects of the characteristics just discussed obviously affect family relationships, but caution is advised in assuming that these are the only determinants of family life. This being said, working long hours with little time for anything else, having the spouse not being able to count on the lawyer for anything to do with family and household responsibilities, and then bringing home a pattern of competitive, adversarial, and perfectionistic behavior would have a devastating effect on the family, leading to unsatisfactory family relationships and contributing to family conflict (Robinson & Post, 1997). It is unlikely that any lawyer would embody all these characteristics, and no family would display all of the patterns discussed.

However, given the tendency for lawyers to fit this pattern to some degree, some comments are possible about the kinds of families that may emerge in professions such as law, in which work is a dominating part of the context. Workaholics have a characteristic difficulty in maintaining social and intimate relationships, and the worse the addiction, the greater the "difficulty in family communication, problem solving, expressing feelings, valuing others, and functioning as a unit" (Robinson, 1999, p. 68).

It is worth noting that, although an attorney may be largely absent at home, it does not mean he or she does not consider the family to be important. For some attorneys, family relationships are extremely important, despite their absence most of the time. The relationship with the spouse may be the one enduring relationship he or she has. Having distanced and destroyed relationships at work by the combative and competitive work, the attorney may feel that the family may be the only place with any emotional comfort (Arron, 1999).

From a structural perspective (Minuchin, 1974), some possible patterns emerge. A typical structure of the family would be the disengaged, emotionally distant lawyer parent. The nonlawyer spouse has learned to be very independent and overfunctioning at home, and to carry the major responsibility for maintenance and discipline of household and children. The parental coalition could be expected to be weak but might or might not be conflictual. It is likely to have closeness–distance struggles as the spouse periodically pushes for more closeness (Sotile & Sotile, 1998). It would be expected that children would be more closely connected with the nonlawyer spouse, and thus may be parentified (Jurkovic, 1997) or "spousified" (Chase, 1999). The work of the lawyer may be considered so important that the family organizes around accommodating to the demands imposed by the lawyer's work. Work is important and what happens at home is trivial, therefore work takes first place, and family occasions and obligations take whatever is left. The family may learn to function with the lawyer as a peripheral part of the interaction and adjust adequately. Similar patterns have been found in celebrity families (Mitchell & Cronson, 1987) and executive families (Keele, 1984). Hierarchical shifts occur that alternate between periods of time when the professional is at home and away. These shifts are confusing to everyone, because the family accommodates to the presence or absence of the workaholic parent (Mitchell & Cronson, 1987; Robinson, 1998a). Behavior patterns develop over time that organize the family around the demands of the profession, which both enable the professional to continue the work addiction and at the same time reveal circular patterns of closeness–distance oscillations. It may also result in irresponsible behavior on the part of children (Mitchell & Cronson, 1987; Pittman, 1985; Robinson, 1996, 1998a).

Over the past 15 years, however, an alternative pattern seems to be emerging, with many lawyers marrying other high-performing professionals (Arron, 1999). In families of this kind, the executive subsystem will more likely be symmetrical and more egalitarian. Both spouses are likely to be involved in decision making; both careers will be valued and household duties shared. The emphasis is on the equality of both spouses with responsibilities shared and negotiated. The boundaries between parents and children can be clearer because both parents are likely to be involved in supervision and care of the children and execution of household duties. It is likely that interactions in this pattern will be more competitive than the more complementary relationship (Sotile & Sotile, 1998). Decision making and problem solving have both the potential for cooperative collaborative processes and the potential for lengthy, drawn-out negotiation if these skills are not used well. In any case, dual-career families really have three jobs to perform with multiple obligations and with fewer hours to accomplish them (Piotrkowski & Hughes, 1993).

For instance, the dual-career couple, one of whom may be a lawyer, find ways of forming habits and rules that make their life work. Sometimes, however, circumstances change and necessitate renegotiation of the rules and patterns of the family. For instance, when the decision is made to have children, everything changes. Decisions about whether one parent will return to work, arrangements for child care, and the operation of the household are only the beginning of issues for which change is evident. An unexpected result of these changes is the way the person staying home thinks of himself or herself. Home care may have less status than work, even for the person staying home. If the marriage partners have pursued their careers for several years before having children, the adjustment may be dramatic (A. Johnson, personal communication, July 30, 1999).

Interventions

There is little to indicate that high-performing families are any better equipped than the general population with the skills needed to navigate through the many difficult waters of family life. Given the additional stresses of families that are connected with professions requiring high performance, the risks may even be higher. When couples or families such as Melissa and Jim come for assistance with their relationship, it is vital that contextual issues such as the influence of work be addressed. The unique culture of the law profession needs to be understood to make effective interventions. Clinicians working with families of lawyers, as with other high-performance families, will recognize that interventions may be made at more than one level, but changes in the approach to work will surely be involved.

The first and perhaps most difficult issue to be faced is whether one or both of the spouses are willing to make some value and lifestyle changes to improve their relationship. Changes of priorities, which may mean significant alterations of work patterns, may be necessary to save the family (Sotile & Sotile, 1998).

Individual Interventions

Changes can be made in the habits of the lawyer to make him or her more available and attentive to the family. Small changes can result in large effects. Clinicians may offer suggestions that may seem obvious but that often come as welcome and workable changes for the person receiving them.

The first suggestion is to compartmentalize work and home (Drell, 1994). The attorney has already learned to stay focused on whatever case is before him or her, even though numerous cases may be active. The same skill is needed in separating work from home if there is a tendency to allow work to intrude into the home. Leaving the lawyer skills in the office and adopting more relational skills such as being focused and attentive to family members and attending to feelings and reactions of spouse and children are obvious suggestions. Some spouses enjoy discussing issues that arise at the office, especially those with professional training. However, the emotional tensions that have been necessary to function as a lawyer become destructive if they persistently invade the home environment. The commute home can be productive as a buffer between home and office. Listening to music or the news on the radio is very effective.

The second suggestion is to develop interests other than work pursuits (Drell, 1994). Spending time on something totally different from what absorbs the mind at work gives a wider perspective on life. The problem for the workaholic is that such activity may be perceived as a waste of time (Robinson, 1998a). Another tendency is to work at a hobby with the same intensity as lawyering. Some persuasion may be necessary to convince a busy professional that time spent in non-work-related activities is in the long run productive for him or her.

Hiring help recovers time for family and spouse. "Hire all you can," one lawyer said. His point was not that he hated doing home chores, but being with the kids was more important than mowing the lawn or waxing the car, even though he enjoyed these activities. Saving time for the family is money well spent, and a good income makes it possible. More than one lawyer who decided to leave practice lamented that the kids grew up so fast and that what lawyers do is frivolous compared with raising children (Arron, 1989).

Family Interventions

Clinical interventions for working with high-performance families may not be very different than working with other populations of clients. Skill-building programs are effective in helping families build the patterns of effective parenting and communication skills such as problem solving and decision making. "Fighting for Your Marriage," "Family Wellness," "Pairs," and "Family Works" are examples of well-established programs in which clinicians can be trained to effectively equip families with skills for daily life. What is different is the perspective of a profession that places high demands on both the attorney and his or her family through the extremely long hours, high expectations, and work environment that often results in family difficulties.

Resilience

Rather than surveying therapeutic approaches that concentrate on the deficits of families and that attend to what is wrong, a positive approach by looking for the strengths of high-performance families is advocated. Walsh (1998a) called for a resilience-based approach to therapy rather than one that concentrates on resolving pathology. The concept of resilience calls on clinicians to concentrate on the ability of individuals and families to persevere and rebound from adversity and emerge from it strengthened and more resourceful (Walsh, 1998b; Wolin, 1999; Wolin & Wolin, 1993). Furthermore, resilience refers to the positive ways families go about managing crises by using qualities of their families under stress, especially those that promote coping, endurance, and survival (McCubbin & McCubbin, 1988), and having endured crises, the families emerge stronger and better able to cope (McCubbin, Thompson, & McCubbin,

1996). Because resilience should be considered a process over time and not a brief event or a bag of tricks, it reveals the ability of families to adopt their strengths to fit the situation (Hawley & DeHaan, 1996).

No family is so resilient that it is free of difficulties or disappointments (Walsh, 1998b; Wolin, 1999), therefore assessment of a family's unique strengths is essential to using them as the method of intervention. In the case of families in which high performance is expected, an approach that looks for positive, optimistic solutions is likely to be well received.

Walsh (1998b) and Wolin (1999) suggested components of resilient families that are useful in activating the resources they have to find solutions to their problems. The family's belief system is the first powerful component in producing resilience. This has to do with the convictions, attitudes, biases, and assumptions about the world and about the past, present, and future (Walsh, 1998b). Specifically with regard to marriage, a commitment to family as an institution worth protecting is fostered as part of the belief system (Wolin, 1999). Families with a system of transcendent values that provide meaning and purpose beyond themselves have been shown to be effective in coping with adversity and to have a sense of well-being and wholeness that sustains them in times of crisis and enhances the belief that challenges can be overcome (Beavers & Hapson, 1990; Walsh, 1998b). A positive outlook is essential to coping in the face of adversity and maintains an interpretation that problems are solvable and the family can overcome difficulties as they arise (Walsh, 1998b). Clinical work that helps develop a positive stance to problems frames them in terms of strengths rather than deficits. Research data support the notion that there are strong positive effects of an optimistic orientation to coping with crises and stress (Walsh, 1998a).

The second key to resilience is the ability to develop family organizational patterns that are able to adapt to the challenges families face. This includes the balance of stability and flexibility as well as a balance of connectedness and separateness (Hawley & DeHaan, 1996; Walsh, 1998b). On the one hand, families require the stability of predictable, consistent rules and patterns of interaction so members can know what is expected of one another, and members can be relied on to follow through with commitments that have been made. On the other hand, families need to be able to change, especially in times of crisis. There is the need to be able to alter rules, routines, and conditions (Walsh, 1998b). Families in which a high level of performance is required need to develop both the consistency that produces the stability and the flexibility to change when it is needed. Often conditions change quickly and new demands may be made of the family, thereby making great demands on the strength of the organizational patterns that govern the family.

The balance between connectedness and separateness requires the ability to remain connected, to be able to give mutual support, to collaborate and remain committed, and at the same time to respect individual needs and to appreciate the differences of individuals in the family. In developing the balance of connectedness and separateness, the family needs strong leadership that includes nurturing, protecting, and guiding children. There also needs to be the ability for reconnection and reconciliation, the ability to forgive and move on (Walsh, 1998b), also known as quality *initiative.* This includes an honor for the struggle that comes out of a team approach to problem solving (Wolin, 1999).

A strong support system is crucial to withstanding crises. Resilient families are able to turn to outside the family for help in managing problems. This means both maintaining good relationships with the extended family and being able to contact community resources (Hawley & DeHaan, 1996; McCubbin et al., 1996; Walsh 1998b). This may prove to be a substantial challenge to high-performance families like those of attorneys, because asking for help may be seen as a sign of weakness or failure. Validating the need for developing a strong support system may be needed. Overcoming resistance to getting help may be a major issue.

A third key to resilience is clear, consistent communication (Walsh, 1998b). Family members can communicate without worrying about mixed messages and can seek information from each other in a crisis. It is especially important that one can communicate emotions and feel validated and supported to manage crises (Hawley & DeHaan, 1996; McCubbin et al., 1996; Walsh, 1998b). This means developing good problem-solving skills in which problems can be identified and openly discussed in a collaborative way. It also means that conflicts can be resolved and the family can focus on achievable goals (McCubbin et al., 1996, Walsh 1998b). Wolin (1999) emphasized the necessity of each person being able to say what his or her contribution to the problem is, and each person will make a contribution to the solution to the problem. One lawyer's wife appreciated the way her husband put his problem-solving skills to work to solve family problems and saw it as a great strength for their family. However, if collaboration in solving problems is difficult and there is an autocratic pattern of solutions only coming from one person, difficulty will result.

Conclusion

Families of attorneys are an example of families in which the nature of the work that one or more of the parents do has particular effects on the nature of the family interaction. Although some of these characteristics are not unique to the law profession, the combination of factors does seem to produce patterns that may be difficult for their families. Lawyers do extremely demanding work that requires long hours and is characterized by high-performance demands in an atmosphere of competition, with meticulously exacting standards, in which there is often adversarial interaction. They are trained to trust their logical and rational facilities to do the best for their clients. Conversely, lawyers tend to discount feelings and reject unsubstantiated conclusions. These conditions promote the tendency to act in much the same way at home. The same high-performing professionals are also able to use their intelligence and skill to change the atmosphere at home into a safe, supportive, and intimate one. For this reason, an approach that uses the resilience of the family is recommended. Working with attorney families to capitalize on transcendent values and on communication skills that produce consistent and flexible rules, with a positive outlook and a strong support system, is believed to be an effective method of intervention.

References

Alexander, J., & Parsons, B. V. (1982). *Functional family therapy.* Monterey, CA: Brooks/Cole.

Arron, D. L. (1989). *Running from the law: Why good lawyers are getting out of the legal profession.* Seattle, WA: Niche Press.

Arron, D. L. (1999, October). Connection gaps. *American Bar Association Journal 85,* 60–63, 96.

Atwood, J. D. (1992). The historical aspects of marriage and family therapy. In J. D. Atwood (Ed.), *Family therapy: A systemic behavioral approach* (pp. 5–28). Chicago: Nelson-Hall.

Beavers, W. R., & Hapson, R. B. (1990). *Successful families.* New York: Norton

Blodgett, N. (1986, September). Time and money: A look at today's lawyer. *American Bar Association Journal, 72,* 47–53.

Brooks, A. A. (1989). *Children of fast-track parents: Raising self-sufficient and confident children in an achievement-oriented world.* New York: Viking Penguin.

Chase, N. (1999). Parentification: An overview of theory, research, and social issues. In N. Chase (Ed.), *Burdened children: Theory, research, and treatment of parentification* (pp. 3–33). Thousand Oaks, CA. Sage.

Dahl, D. (1996, April 14). The trouble with lawyers. *Boston Globe Magazine*, pp. 26–29.

Doerfler, M. C., & Kammer, P. P. (1986). Workaholism, sex, and sex-role stereotyping among female professionals. *Sex Roles, 14*, 551–560.

Drell, A. (1994, October). Chilling out. *American Bar Association Journal, 80*, 70–73.

Drogin, E. (1991). Alcoholism in the legal profession: Psychological and legal perspective and interventions. *Law and Psychology Review, 15*, 117–162.

Elkins, J. R. (1985). Rites de passage: Law students "telling their lives." *Journal of Legal Education, 35*, 27–55.

Elwork, A., & Benjamin, G. A. H. (1995). Lawyers in distress. *Journal of Psychiatry and Law, 32*, 205–229.

Gabbard, G. O., Menninger, R. W., & Coyne, L. (1987). Sources of conflict in medical marriage. *American Journal of Psychiatry, 144*, 567–572.

Gatland, L. (1997, December). Dangerous deduction. *American Bar Association Journal, 83*, 28–30.

Goldhaber, M. D. (1998, December 21). Women's numbers rise at the bigger law firms. *National Law Journal*, pp. A1, A11.

Hawley, D. R., & DeHaan, L. (1996). Toward a definition of family resilience: Integrating life-span and family perspectives. *Family Process, 35*, 283–299.

Hibbs, C., & Himes, L. K. (1985, October). *Enriching graduate student marriages: Coping with the stress.* Paper presented at the 43rd Annual Conference of the American Association for Marriage and Family Therapy, New York.

Hirsch, R. L. (1985, Winter). Are you on target? *Barrister, 12*, 17–20, 49–50.

Iijima, A. L. (1998). Lessons learned: Legal education and law student dysfunction. *Journal of Legal Education, 48*, 524–538.

Jurkovic, G. J. (1997). *Lost childhoods: The plight of the parentified child.* New York: Brunner/Mazel.

Keele, R. R. (1984). Executive families: From pitfalls to payoffs. In N. M. Hoopes, F. L. Fisher, & S. H. Barlow (Eds.), *Structured family facilitation programs: Enrichment, education, and treatment* (pp. 209–229). Rockville, MD: Aspen System.

Kohn, A. (1992). *No contest: The case against competition.* Boston: Houghton Mifflin.

Lansky, M. (1985). Preoccupation and pathologic distance regulation. *International Journal of Psychoanalytic Psychotherapy, 11*, 409–425.

Margolick, D. (1992, April 10). At the bar: Beyond confrontational law, the feel-good approach. *The New York Times*, p. B-10.

McCubbin, H. I., & McCubbin, M. A. (1988). Topologies of resilient families: Emerging roles of social class and ethnicity. *Family Relations, 37*, 247–254.

McCubbin, H. I., Thompson, A. I., & McCubbin, M. A. (1996). *Family assessment: Resiliency, coping, and adaptation*. Madison: University of Wisconsin Press.

Minuchin, S. (1974). *Families and family therapy*. Cambridge, MA: Harvard University Press.

Mitchell, G., & Cronson, H. (1987). The celebrity family. *American Journal of Family Therapy 13*, 235–241.

National Marriage Project. (1999). *The state of our unions, 1999*. New Brunswick, NJ: Author.

Piotrkowski, C. S., & Hughes, D. (1993). Dual-earner families in context: Managing family and work systems. In F. Walsh (Ed.), *Normal family processes* (2nd ed., pp. 185–207). New York: Guilford Press.

Pittman, F. (1985). Children of the rich. *Family Process, 24*, 461–472.

Robinson, B. E. (1996). Relationship between work addiction and family functioning: Clinical implications for marriage and family therapists. *Journal of Family Psychotherapy, 7*(3), 13–29.

Robinson, B. E. (1998a). *Chained to the desk: A guidebook for workaholics, their partners and children, and the clinicians who treat them*. New York: New York University Press.

Robinson, B. E. (1998b). The workaholic family: A clinical perspective. *American Journal of Family Therapy, 26*, 65–75.

Robinson, B. E. (1999). Workaholic children: One method of fulfilling the parentification role. In N. Chase (Ed.), *Burdened children: Theory, research, and treatment of parentification* (pp. 56–74). Thousand Oaks, CA: Sage.

Robinson, B., & Post, P. (1997). Risk of addiction to work and family functioning. *Psychological Reports, 81*, 91–95.

Schwartz, A. J. (1980). Law, lawyers, and law school: Perspectives from the first-year class. *Journal of Legal Education 30*, 437–469.

Smith, R. S. (1984). A profile of lawyer lifestyles. *American Bar Association Journal 70*, 50–54.

Sotile, W. M., & Sotile, M. O. (1996). *The medical marriage: A couple's survival guide*. New York: Birch Lane Press.

Sotile, W. M., & Sotile, M. O. (1998). *Supercouple syndrome: How overworked couples can beat stress together*. New York: Wiley.

Spence, J. T., & Robbins, A. S. (1992). Workaholics: Definition, measurement, and preliminary results. *Journal of Personality Assessment, 58*, 160–178.

Spendlove, D. C., Reed, B. D., Whitman, N., Slattery, M. L., French, T. K., & Horwood, K. (1990). Marital adjustment among housestaff and new attorneys. *Academic Medicine, 65*, 599–603.

Stint, T. E. (1988). An 80% solution is not realistic. *California Lawyer 8*(3), 88.

Turow, S. (1977). *One L/*. New York: Putnam.

van Zyverden, W. (June, 1996). Lawyer dissatisfaction. *Vermont Bar Journal and Law Digest*, 33–34.

Vande Kemp, H. (1997, April). *Commitment, courtesy, and the courage to be.* Paper presented at the Sixth Annual Wheaton College Theology Conference, Wheaton, IL.

Walsh, F. (1998a). Beliefs, spirituality, and transcendence: Keys to family resilience. In M. McGoldrick (Ed.), *Re-visioning family therapy: Race, culture, and gender in clinical practice* (pp. 62–77). New York: Guilford Press.

Walsh, F. (1998b). *Strengthening family resilience.* New York: Guilford Press.

Watzlawick, P., Beavin, J., & Jackson, D. (1967). *Pragmatics of human communication.* New York: Norton.

White, R. A. (1998). *Association of American Law Schools: Statistical report on law school faculty and candidates for law faculty positions, 1997–98* [On-line]. Available: www.aals.org/statistics/rpt9798w.html#women.

Wightman, L. F. (1996). *Women in legal education: A comparison of the law school performance and law school experiences of women and men.* Newton, PA: Law School Admission Council.

Wolin, S. (1999, July). *The seven qualities of resilient marriage.* Paper presented at the Third Annual Conference of the Coalition for Marriage, Family, and Couples Education, Washington, DC.

Wolin, S., & Wolin, S. (1993). *The resilient self: How survivors of troubled families rise above adversity.* New York: Valerate.

Yandoli, A. H. (1989). Stress and medical marriages. *Stress Medicine, 5,* 213–219.

■ ■ ■

PART III

HIGH PERFORMANCE
AND PARENTIFICATION
OUTCOMES IN FAMILIES

5

High Performance, Parentification, and Personality Development From an Object Relations Perspective

Marolyn Wells, PhD
Robert Miller, EdD

In healthy families, high performance can reflect the realization of healthy ambition (Kohut, 1971), initiative, industry, and generativity in adulthood (Erikson, 1963), built on a bedrock of secure attachment (Bartholomew & Horowitz, 1991) and basic trust (Erikson, 1963). In families that induce *parentification*—a relational dynamic in which children fulfill inordinate and prolonged responsibilities, either of a practical or emotional nature, in service to the needs and expectations of their parents—high performance often reflects an overfunctioning role assigned by one or both parents to a receptive, bright, talented, and precocious child. The parental role played by the child is unconsciously crafted to meet the previously unmet needs of the parent or parents. When this overfunctioning childhood role rigidifies, it can persist into adulthood as a driven, often perfectionistic, overdoing style of relating focused on performance goals (Carroll & Robinson, in press). In general, unhealthy parentification reflects some combination of the following underlying aims: a substitute of admiration for love (overt narcissism), efforts to earn love (masochism, covert narcissism), or a means of regulating self-worth through a special association with an idealized other (covert narcissism). In this chapter, we discuss the proposed relationships among high performance, parentification, and personality development.

Previous theory and supporting research (Jones & Wells, 1996; Wells & Jones, 1999) have already demonstrated a correlation between parentification and narcissistic as well as self-defeating (masochistic) personality characteristics in college students. Other research has linked parentification with shame-proneness (Carroll & Robinson, in press; Wells & Jones, 2000) and defensive splitting (Wells & Jones, 1998). These findings have supported the conceptualization of pathological childhood parentification as representing the inducement of a shame-based false self-construction based on chronic parent–child role reversal, which is designed to assure relational proximity to the parent. Inasmuch as parentification is associated with a shame-based self-concept (Wells & Jones, 2000), high performance may represent strivings to compensate for or avoid intolerable feelings of shame associated with real self-expression.

Understanding the relationship between parentification and personality development can thus help clinicians better understand what drives at least some types of chronic overfunctioning, high performance, urgency addiction, and workaholism in parentified adult clients. This understanding may then provide insight into how to help parentified clients protect themselves against or mediate burnout, clinical depression, alcohol, or drug abuse. This understanding may also help clinicians predict what insights and corrective relationship experiences would be most therapeutic for a particular client (e.g., Glickauf-Hughes & Wells, 1997; Robinson, 1998, 1999).

The first section of this chapter describes childhood parentification in terms of attachment, separation, security, and self-esteem issues. Then we relate these developments to typical personality adaptations and the resulting proclivities for different kinds of overfunctioning. The final section explores therapeutic approaches that might be effective in intervening with each clinical presentation.

Parentification and Attachment, Separation, Security, and Self-Esteem Issues

The dialectical tension between attachment and separation that occurs across the human life span has been termed the human paradox. In healthy development, humans "seek constantly for the object with and through whom one regresses and restores oneself, while also seeking incessantly independence from the object, apart from whom one can and must progress and fulfill oneself" (Ekstein & Caruth, 1972, p. 201). The healthy family system reassures the child that the child's efforts to negotiate the human paradox will not induce undue anxiety, needfulness, abandonment, or shame. Healthy parents who recognize and respond to the attachment and separation issues facing their child will affirm the child's efforts to explore outwardly from the primary attachment figures, yet also remain available when the child needs to reattach or return for refueling.

Although individuals encounter the attachment and separation dialectic across the life span, at particular developmental stages the process becomes more pronounced. This is most true during critical developmental periods such as rapprochement, launching from one's family of origin, the birth of a child, and periods of grief and mourning. Individuals with a solid sense of self, based in healthy object relations, have the internal resources to successfully negotiate these life stages. Where the self-system is damaged, a failure to thrive and develop may result, accompanied by an impasse or rigidity.

Pathological parentification is an example of a dysfunctional parent–child dynamic that disrupts the healthy resolution of separation and individuation. The parentification process results in a fused or collusive parent–child relationship that undermines the child's efforts to make age-appropriate reconciliation of the attachment–separation dialectic. Parentification refers to the formation of a parent–child collusion signified by chronic role inversion (Bowlby, 1969, 1973) or role reversal (Zeanah & Klitaker, 1991). The collusion crystallizes the child's character formation toward taking care of the parent at the expense of the child's true self (Winnicott, 1965) and induces an insecure attachment style (Alexander, 1992; Benoit & Parker, 1994; Main & Goldwyn, 1984; Main & Hesse, 1990).

Projective Identification as Instrument of Collusion

The link between parentification and high performance is solidified when the parent needs the child to excel or overfunction to reduce the parent's anxieties. Typically the parent's anxieties originated in his or her own childhood experiences. The following case example describes how one client, Carol, became a container for her father's unmet and unresolved needs. The father used projective identification to instill in his daughter his unmet needs and, in turn, to control and contain his own anxiety over personal losses. The link between parentification and high performance was established because this father needed his child to excel or overfunction in a particular way to reduce his anxieties.

Carol first entered therapy as a college student. She was an intelligent young woman whose natural inclinations were more artistic in comparison with the scientific orientation preferred by her father. Carol was doing well in her premed courses but found herself fighting feelings of chronic dissatisfaction, emptiness, and depression. She defended against these feelings by hard work and fantasizing about how wonderful life was going to be once she became a medical doctor. A recent breakup with her fourth boyfriend because he was not ambitious enough challenged Carol's defenses and left her feeling more reflective and concerned about her future.

In examining her feelings and history during treatment, Carol realized she was really "forcing" herself to become a medical doctor to realize her father's unfulfilled dreams of becoming a physician. Her father had immigrated to the United States as a young man and had felt compelled to give up his dream to provide for his family. He recruited Carol, his intelligent and sensitive eldest daughter, to satisfy his own ambition in the unconscious hope of restoring his self-esteem and undoing his disappointment. He did this by promoting an atmosphere of guilt and pressure to comply in order for Carol to deserve his love. For example, he repeatedly told his wife, in earshot of Carol, "If it wasn't for marrying you and raising this family, I could have been a great surgeon by now." He also repeatedly told Carol, "You are so like me, so very smart and responsible, you can do anything you want to." In addition, he told anyone who would listen in his family that if he had but one wish, "it would be to have his family honor restored by someone in the family becoming a true healer." In addition, he did things like buy a stethoscope for Carol when she was 3 years of age. He loved telling the story of how he remembered her asking for one for her birthday after she had seen a rerun of *Dr. Kildare* on television.

Carol's intelligence and determination permitted her to succeed at premed, but she found no intrinsic reward in her pursuits to be a physician. Her own musical talent and childhood dream of being a piano teacher were being sacrificed to meet her father's needs and realize her role as the family heroine. When she began therapy, she largely agreed with her father that being a physician was the only "real profession" and that any other career was not good enough. Her loyalty to the family definition of success is indicative of the power inherent in the parent–child collusion. The father's projective identification successfully met his desires through the achievements of his daughter.

Parents who carry unresolved narcissistic wounds from their own childhood can recapitulate those issues with their own children. The key element of the recapitulation is an unconscious collusion fostered by the parent who, through the primary mechanism of projective identification, induces the child into acting out a parentified role designed to meet the unmet childhood needs of the parent. Because the child is the more dependent and vulnerable member of the parent–child dyad, he or she is particularly susceptible to unconscious communications from the parent to think, feel, and behave in a prescribed manner.

The parent's unconscious use of projective identifications induces the child to assume emotional or instrumental social support functions in the family that are designed to meet the parent's needs rather than the child's evolving needs. In particular, the child is induced to serve as a caretaker in the relationship in such a way as to reduce the parent's own long-standing anxiety around personally unsatisfactory experiences involving attachment and separation. For the parent, projective identification has the dual purpose of ridding the parent of internal conflict (projecting unmet needs that generate intolerable feelings) while simultaneously gaining from the object of the projection (the child) a response soothing and sympathetic to the projector's self (fulfillment of unmet needs). For the child, the acceptance of the induced role guarantees his or her proximity to the needed parent.

Projective Identification and Damage to the True Self

Sue came to therapy with a successful and high-functioning social work practice, three children, and major volunteering commitments at church where she sang in the choir and taught Sunday school. She complained about her problem saying no to anyone or anything that seemed to need her. She presented as an exhausted young woman, and yet she kept pushing to take on more. She acted as a confidante to her friends and was best friend to her father and husband. She realized she was overrelying on her eldest daughter to listen to her complaints and said she had come to therapy to help her daughter not be so serious and perfectionistic. She was partly aware that it was easier for her to seek professional help for her daughter's sake rather than directly for her own sake.

Sue reported that at a young age she had assumed a prescribed role as her mother's and then her father's partner. Following the death of her mother from heart disease, Sue, at the age of 10, ran the house, paid the bills, took care of her baby sister, and made daily household decisions. Even when her mother was living, Sue was reinforced for assuming the role of "mother's little helper." It was a simple and natural step to raise her younger sibling and care for the household once her mother became ill. In a letter to his brother, her father wrote that he had worried that his daughter would require more support than he could give her, but it turned out that she became his support as he weathered the loss of his wife.

Over the years no one ever asked Sue how she felt about her mother's death. Her father, neighbors, and other relatives all seemed relieved and proud that Sue continued to overfunction and remain visibly unneedful. Her father reinforced Sue's overfunctioning by allowing himself to indulge his severe depression, thus making himself unavailable to meet his daughter's needs. He instilled in his daughter a lifelong fear that, out of his own grief, he was capable of taking his own life and leaving her orphaned. She was compelled to "keep it together" and "keep everything running smoothly." This prescribed script translated into "biting her tongue" whenever she felt upset or irritated.

Sue's father periodically "bragged on" Sue to his friends. He called her "his little balabusta," a Yiddish term referring to someone who knows all the things you need to make a home. She reported that he even "let her boss him around about getting the bills out or getting ready for an appointment." Sue remembered often waking her father up to go to work in the morning when he overslept. As a result, Sue felt special, important, and indispensable during a time when she easily could have felt deprived, depressed, and ignored. It would not be until much later, in her late 20s, that she would recognize how deprived she had felt in her childhood.

In therapy, it became apparent that Sue never received the nurturance she had needed as a child, even before her mother's illness. She described her mother as "a perfect mother who knew everything about taking care of us physically and giving good advice" but who was "emotionally preoccupied and very reserved." Family members knew her mother had been abused as a child, but she never talked about the abuse she had suffered in her family of origin. Sue's mother's attachment, intimacy, and separation problems were evident, however, in her discomfort with physical affection and personal disclosures of any negative feelings as well as her need for her eldest child to remain high functioning and unneedful.

The result of the multigenerational dysfunctional family dynamic in Sue's development was inhibition of personal needs and desires. She missed out on sufficient experiences of holding, attunement, and validation of self necessary for healthy development. She developed the unspoken assumption that self-worth was associated with doing for others at the sacrifice of knowing, much less doing for, her true self.

The core message transmitted from the parent to the child in the parentification dynamic is that the child can go through the motions of separation, but accomplishments must be in service to the parent. The process engenders a pseudo separation–individuation so that the child may look and act grown up, responsible, and independent but, in fact, maintains an enmeshed relationship with the parent. The struggle to resolve the human paradox is supplanted by a more ominous paradox wherein "achievement, while encouraged, must be based upon the child's failure to separate" (Rinsley, 1989, p. 29) from the parent. The self of the child becomes distorted and is defined by how well the needs of the parent are satisfied. In this manner, the "false self" emerges and gains predominance in the developmental course of the child's life.

The pseudoadult role draws implicit, if not explicit, admiration or approval. The parentified child is able to feel needed, useful, important, and "grown up" as a result of his or her special relationship to the parent. However, in the role of caretaker for the parent, the child loses out on being the recipient of the nurturing necessary for development. In particular, the child does not receive the empathy, attunement, interest, guidance, and consistent responsiveness from the parent that is representative of healthy parent–child relationships and that underlies the development and evolution of true self.

The Multigenerational Context of Parentification

Parentification has been described as a family ledger of accounts due that accrues across generations (Boszormenyi-Nagy & Krasner, 1986). Adult family members, like Carol's father and Sue's mother, whose own needs were not met in childhood, compensate by focusing on one of their children. The parent induces the child to assume and fulfill the parental functions not received by the parent in his or her own childhood. The child selected for this induction often manifests a disposition (e.g., sensitivity and responsiveness) and natural gifts (e.g., talents, athleticism, and intelligence) that make him or her particularly vulnerable to such inductions. The child's genetic predisposition may foster the assumption of pseudoadult functions where another child might not be predisposed or able to do so.

The adult who was parentified as a child is theoretically expected to seek emotional supplies in a manner paralleling his or her parent's behavior. In this way, the multigenerational die is cast. The multi-generational process of parentification resulted in Sue shaming herself for being weak whenever she expressed a negative feeling. She was inarticulate in expressing herself as she had little practice in intimate self-revelation. She was wholly uncomfortable crying in front of anyone or receiving help from anyone. She was overidentified with being the helper and the functional one in the family. Her family and friends relied on her as a confidante without expecting reciprocity. When she had children, she found herself looking to her own sensitive and hypervigilant daughter for solace and help around the house in a way that was reminiscent of her own childhood. To her dismay, she was recapitulating a family dynamic. As a result, and to her credit, she sought therapy.

Variations of Personality Development and Overfunctioning

Parentification presumably represents a relational template that is internalized by the child and crystallized into his or her personality. The parentified child's relational template develops from the parenting style in the family of origin and results in the child developing a shame-based character style (Wells & Jones, 2000). Dweck and colleagues (Dweck, 1986; Dweck & Leggett, 1988; Heyman & Dweck, 1992) described two parenting styles that foster different relational templates in children. These parenting styles are the *performance goal focused style* and the *learning for understanding focused style*. It is the performance goal focused style that characteristically underlies the parentified relational template.

In examining the differential parenting of academically talented children, Ablard and Parker (1997) found that while most parents focused on learning for understanding with their children, a minority of parents focused on higher performance outcomes and external recognition for performance. Those parents who focused on performance goals had children who were significantly more likely to exhibit dysfunctional perfectionism, doubts about actions, and a high concern about mistakes, parental expectations, and parental criticism. These parents often tell their children that they can do anything they want, including extraordinary accomplishments, if they only put their minds to it.

Parents using the performance goal style focus on high performance because it signifies competence and high intelligence. Ablard and Parker (1997) agreed with Hills (1987) that some of these parents may wish for their children to demonstrate exceptional levels of performance because of their own desire for personal recognition or high social status resulting from having intelligence. Such high parental expectations combined with a child's desire to please can foster the belief that parental love and social acceptance are contingent on one's high achievement (Hewitt & Flett, 1991; Hills, 1987; Pacht, 1984). This belief supports the link between parentification and high performance in those gifted and talented children who were raised by parents with unrealistic goal expectations of their child.

The parentification literature has delineated two parentified roles in children that are consistent with the performance goal focused style. One role forms to fulfill instrumental parenting tasks and the other forms to fulfill expressive parenting tasks (Jurkovic, Jessee, & Goglia, 1991). These roles are consistent with the narcissistic vulnerability of gifted individuals who have been used by their parents to gratify parental needs (Glickhauf-Hughes, Wells, & Genirberg, 1987). In this section, we first discuss the relationship between parentification and shame-proneness. Following that are descriptions of the link between rigidified parentified roles and the pathological, compromised, and maladaptive personality development manifested in narcissistic and masochistic personality traits. Although we describe three parentified styles (i.e., inflated narcissistic style, deflated narcissistic style, and masochistic style) that adult clients can manifest, most parentified adults whom we have seen in our practices present with some mixture of these three styles or adaptations.

Shame-Proneness, Parentification, and Defensive High-Performance Drive

It is proposed that the parentified relational template stemming from the aforementioned parental styles and childhood relational roles results in a shame-based syndrome in the child (Cleary, 1992; Wells & Jones, 2000). High performance or overfunctioning can represent a defense against the activation of painful feelings of shame about the true self (Winnicott, 1965), as well as attempts to survive or preserve the self and maintain proximity to the needed other. In addition, it is further proposed that unhealthy parentification may vary somewhat in its manifestations depending on the mixture of narcissistic and masochistic personality traits induced by the parents to meet their own unmet childhood needs (Jones & Wells, 1996; Wells & Jones, 1998, 1999). The messages communicated from the parent to the child result in the child developing a false and shame-based core sense of self. Table 5.1 outlines three different styles of parentified messages, which are unconsciously communicated from parent to child through projective identification, with the complementary self-concept, which develops in the parentified child.

When a child is prematurely and chronically exposed to unrealistic performance expectations or expectations that are a mismatch to the child's real self or level of development, shame is likely to become associated with the child's developing self-concept. Shame has been associated with feeling bad about one's self, with feeling small, inadequate, not enough, degraded, or humiliated. Shame results from feeling oneself cut off from attunement and loving because one is essentially defective or unlovable. Shame is the experience of one's person being insufficient and unwanted.

Goldberg (1988) conceptualized shame-proneness as a result of premature exposure to unrealistic expectations, which casts self-doubts about one's personal adequacy and evokes the belief that one is "incapable of achieving the conditions necessary for physical and psychological preservation of the self" (p. 119). Boszormenyi-Nagy and Spark (1973) linked this type of premature exposure to parentification, and Cleary (1992) hypothesized that parentification is a shame-based syndrome. Wells and Jones (2000) recently found preliminary empirical evidence for this relationship.

Under conditions of premature exposure, preservation of the self is invested in the development of a false self designed to realize projected parental demands. The true self (Winnicott, 1965) is discredited or denied as a way to deal with the shame associated with authentic impulses, needs, and wishes that compete with or are a mismatch with the parent's needs for the child. In the case of parentification, the child sacrifices the true self to develop a false self intended to parent the parent through role reversal and identification with the parent's projected ego ideal. Wells and Jones (2000) noted that "the child often becomes emotionally invested in the parentified role (and in the identity provided by the parent's ego ideal), as it provides the only identity the child can discover within him/herself and have supported in the family" (p. 20).

TABLE 5.1
High Performance, Parentification, and Personality Development:
Formation of Narcissistic and Masochistic Character Styles

	Parent–Child Relationship	Message Communicated From Parent to Child Through Projective Identification	Core Self of the Child
Overt Narcissism	Form of narcissism in which the parent provides admiration and love if the child becomes a reflection of the parent's unfilled needs and wishes.	The parent uses projective identification to communicate to the child: "I love you and admire you because you have become what I admire and want to be."	The child develops a false self defined by the pursuit of achievement in order to gain the parent's admiration. The false self deprives the child of access to personal needs and feelings. Example: the overachieving child who must "shine" in order to please parent.
Covert Narcissism	Form of narcissism in which the parent coerces the child to admire the parent in order for the child to receive love and admiration.	The parent uses projective identification to communicate to the child: "I love you because you admire me."	The child develops a false self defined by admiration of the parent resulting in the child becoming an extension of the self of the parent. Example: the underachieving child who cannot "outshine" the parent; the overachieving child who can never satisfy the parent who needs to be the most admired.
Masochism	Parent–child relationship based in the child being caretaker of parent in order to receive love, affection, and validation of self-worth.	The parent uses projective identification to communicate to the child: "Take care of me and I'll love you."	The child develops a false self defined by assuming parental and caretaker roles in order to achieve self-worth. Example: the underachieving or overachieving child who under- or overachieves in service to the parent (e.g., as a means to take care of the parent)

Parents whose own ego ideal involves recognition for great accomplishments will have high performance goals for their targeted parentified children. These children will then be likely to use high performance ambitions as a way to secure the emotional support of the parent and defend against feelings of shame toward the inadequate self. This situation is likely to lead to burnout and involve narcissistic vulnerability to disappointments, empathic failures, or lack of acclaim.

Narcissistically Parentified Individuals

A number of authors (e.g., Reeves, 1999; Robinson, 1999) have noted the connection between the parentification of a designated child and narcissistically depleted parents who were, in all likelihood, themselves parentified by narcissistically injured parents. Reeves (1999) noted that the child, "too psychologically unformed to protect herself, is made to believe that she must provide the parent with the narcissistic supplies denied the parent during her own formative years. . . . Instinctively the child knows that noncompliance guarantees psychic abandonment" (pp. 176–177).

In a complementary vein, Jones and Wells (1996) proposed that childhood parentification could result in the development of narcissistic defenses and character traits designed to afford the child a sense of self-worth and relational proximity by internalizing and then realizing the parents' ego ideal. Narcissistic parentification thus reflects an induced adaptation to narcissistically injured parents who suffer from serious self-esteem problems and depression and then emotionally demand that their child attune to their emotional needs. Wells and Jones (1999) noted that narcissistically parentified children "give up true self-actualization to become the parent's ego ideal and, thus, in fundamental ways, live out someone else's life in order to stay connected with the parent who is overwhelmed with his or her loss or self-esteem deficiencies" (p. 118).

These children develop unusual sensitivity to the narcissistic needs of early caretakers and subvert their own authentic feelings and needs in order to conform to an adaptive "false" self. In addition to realizing the parent's ego ideal, this false self may conform to the narcissistically injured parent's ideal parent. If this ego ideal or ideal parent projection necessitates grandiose or bigger-than-life recognition of exceptional performance, then the links among parentification, narcissistic strivings for specialness, and high performance are crystallized.

Inflated Narcissistic Parentification

Carol, who was realizing her father's dream of becoming a physician, is a concrete example of the more grandiose form of narcissistic parentification. She sought the prestige, admiration, and acclaim associated with realizing her father's dream and being the family heroine. More importantly, however, she unconsciously wanted to undo her father's lifelong sense of failure and retain her connection to her father by internalizing his ego ideal of being a great surgeon who would be sought after to save people. She believed that in order to be lovable and loved by the vitally needed others in her life, she would have to live up to their expectations. Carol's father once told her that "surgeons are like gods. They hold life and death in their hands. You will be always needed and never without great value to yourself and great honor to your family." Carol described her mother as someone who always supported and agreed with her father and whose life revolved around her father, his occupations and moods, and her family. Her mother agreed with her father that Carol had special abilities and thus special obligations to the family, given her status as the eldest child.

Carol reported that she eventually believed she had to be recognized as the best medical student and then the best surgeon in the country to fulfill this family legacy. She fantasized about developing break-through surgical procedures and receiving the Nobel Prize with the world's admiration. In therapy, she came to understand these fantasies as the alienated and aggrandized symbols of her natural childhood wish to be good enough to be loved and cherished by her parents. "I wanted them to love me no matter what . . . even when I was stinky and failing, not just when I came out smelling like roses and got Phi Beta Kappa."

The intact grandiose or exhibitionistic narcissistically parentified child, like Carol, deals with emotional or self-esteem injury by a highly effective, sustained attack or indifference aimed at the nongratifying or nonadmiring, nonempathic others (Issel, 1995, p. 283). As adults, these parentified individuals typically devalue those who do not meet their expectations and then move on to others who hold more prospect of providing needed libidinal supplies. Carol, for example, reported a pattern of having intense infatuations with men with whom she broke up when she discovered some fatal flaw. Carol rationalized to herself that she needed someone who would support her, especially her ambitions, and not hold her back.

Narcissistically parentified adults who are more exhibitionistic high performers typically have developed a progressive (Willi, 1982), inflated (Bach, 1999), or grandiose (Masterson, 1993) relational style. This style differs from the regressive (Willi, 1982), deflated (Bach, 1999), or closet (Masterson, 1993) style of narcissistic relating. Grandiose forms of narcissistic parentification are usually reflected in an individual's longing to be acclaimed as special and to receive constant admiration and perfect empathy. To achieve the admiration of the valued parent, the parentified individual with an inflated narcissistic style attempts to personify the parent's ideal self or ego ideal by exhibiting the brilliant, beautiful, or extremely accomplished parental projection (Glickauf-Hughes & Wells, 1997). This parentified child strives for admiration or conditional love because unconditional love is presumably unavailable.

Deflated or Closet Narcissistic Parentification

Pam, a bright, very attractive, and always perfectly well-groomed young woman, reported that she attended law school with the intention of selecting and marrying the most talented and successful, up-and-coming young man who would function like her attorney father whom her entire family idealized and catered to. Pam focused on performing well in the area of interest to her fantasy object in order to be a good catch and be noticed. She responded to even minor external stressors and internal events with fragmenting self-doubt, feelings of inferiority, and inadequacy. Her use of defensive fusion with significant others was designed to help her avoid these disquieting feelings about her self. She thus allowed the significant other to set the structure or direction for both of them, empathizing with the other's point of view, taking up the other's interests, and even favoring the same cigarettes to create the illusion of fusion as a defense against her own abandonment anxieties. Pam's most extraordinary talent manifested in her extreme sensitivity to the other's narcissistic needs. When she dated someone who seemed to fit her fantasy, she would attune herself to his unspoken narcissistic needs and then carefully tend to those needs, mostly through admiration, good listening, and emotional support (Miller, 1981).

In therapy, to defend against her abandonment anxieties and self-esteem regulation problems, Pam strove to merge with the therapist as a powerful and special other. She attempted to accomplish this merger through projective identifications in which she would pressure the therapist into feeling that he possessed special clinical ability to work with her unique issues. The therapist and client thus developed a mutual admiration collusion. Pam also pressured the therapist to directly gratify her wishes to feel soothed, safe, accepted, and understood. She was finely attuned to each of the therapist's interventions and actively reinforced those that felt soothing and reinforcing to her, while devaluing those that did not serve that purpose for her. For example, she told the therapist that his anecdotes were quite insightful and seemed to reflect a special sensitivity and perceptiveness. Pam also tended to overfocus on being a perfect client who brought appropriate dreams and other material to sessions. At the same time, Pam tended to avoid those core anxieties that would reflect her profound desire to feel truly known and her great difficulty accepting her real self. She tended to either ignore the therapist or tell him he was being too intellectual and abstract whenever the therapist ventured an intervention aimed at increasing Pam's self-awareness, and thus her anxieties, into her struggles with shame-related issues.

The narcissistically parentified child with a deflated (Bach, 1999) or closet (Masterson, 1993) style of relating is more likely to regulate his or her self-esteem by fusing with the valued or idealized parent or significant other ("I am special because I am associated with you, and you are wonderful"). Closet or deflated narcissists have the same underlying self-deficits and narcissistic vulnerabilities as grandiose narcissists. However, rather than focusing on obtaining perfect empathy and admiration directly from others, they attempt to regulate self-esteem by gratifying the narcissistic needs of an idealized other and then fusing or merging psychically with that other's strength and ambition. They are thus more likely to fuse with idealized others by being their confidante or emotional admirer, sweeping others off their feet, and by being whatever the other needs. High performance may offer them the means or the vehicle to charm the other into a relationship.

Their perfectionistic performance orientation may also be fueled by their need to stave off feelings of intense shame, guilt, and inferiority. In addition, because the deflated narcissist is often uncomfortable with the immediate experience of himself or herself as a center of thought, feelings, and action (Bach, 1999), the performance or work role may also help provide a structure for self-expression and self-confidence.

Masochistically Parentified Individuals

As Bill, one of our male clients, noted, "I know my worth by how useful I feel to others. So I do both my sisters' taxes and financial investments, I provide for my wife and three kids, I volunteer at my kid's school, I'm their Boy Scout leader and Little League coach, and I listen to my secretary's home problems to keep her happy. The only problem in all this is that I cannot seem to get past my depression, which worries my wife." Like the Type A kids in Visintainer and Matthews (1987), Bill had learned to suppress his fatigue and become a compulsive overachiever, with an underlying sense of urgency and perfectionism. He could not rest, bringing work with him on all his vacations and feeling restless, guilty, or irritable whenever he was not being productive.

His boss gave him wonderful performance evaluations but noted he could not promote Bill to a supervisory position because Bill did not seem to be able to delegate to others when the boss thought he really needed to. Bill seemed to think he had to do everything himself and not burden others. Bill experienced great difficulty saying no to others, even when setting limits was not only reasonable but needed in order for Bill to meet other obligations in his life. He had an especially difficult time setting limits with his immediate supervisor, who often asked him to stay late on a project, telling Bill he "needed someone he could trust to pull things together." Whenever there was a conflict, Bill invariably thought it was his fault and thus assumed more than his share of responsibility in making any reparation. Even when another employee made it clear that Bill's interventions were more disruptive than helpful, Bill would still feel compelled to give advice or lend assistance to regulate his self-esteem.

Masochistically parentified clients are extremely vulnerable to feeling overextended, burnt-out, and exhausted but are unable to "back off" or set good limits for themselves. They err on the side of feeling badly about themselves for not being able to do more. These individuals usually talk about feeling "not enough" and feeling excessively guilt-ridden as well as being secretly proud of how much they can accomplish. These clients may enter therapy when they are experiencing extreme distress related to feeling overburdened or even mistreated by significant others (e.g., boss, lover, or partner). Typically in their families of origin they adapted to inconsistent parental attunement and hostility by focusing on the physical or concrete needs of others, thereby assuring security in relationships by making themselves as indispensable as possible.

West and Keller (1991) noted that childhood parentification could result in self-defeating characteristics that afforded the child the "best opportunity for achieving proximity to the parent" (p. 426) who may otherwise be inconsistently available, emotionally detached, or self-absorbed. High performance for the masochistically parentified individual often involves compulsive physical and emotional caretaking, which reflects the child's assumption that he or she must earn parental love through self-sacrifice. In families of origin, these children are usually noted by their behavior as mother's little helper or junior social workers.

Valleau, Bergner, and Horton (1995) found empirical evidence correlating parentification with a culturally determined caretaker syndrome vis-à-vis the parents. The syndrome is defined as pathogenic when (a) the child is overburdened with the role; (b) the child is charged with responsibilities beyond his or her years or competencies; (c) the parents assume complementary childlike roles in response to the child; (d) the child's best interests are neglected in the role determination; and (e) the child is not explicitly recognized or appreciated in his or her parental roles and may even be punished at times for enacting them (Bergner, 1982; Boszormenyi-Nagy & Spark, 1973; Haley, 1976; Mika, Bergner, & Baum, 1987; Minuchin, 1974).

As adults, masochistically parentified individuals enact this syndrome through a pervasive pattern of taking care of others (e.g., fixer, rescuer, adviser, advocate, or therapist), even when others do not want them to or when this pattern is obviously self-destructive (e.g., making the person ill, burnt-out, chronically fatigued, or resentful). When one's sense of worth is linked with earning love and worth through service, one may feel compelled to serve even when serving is counterproductive or paradoxically pushes people away.

Recommendations for Treatment

A significant amount of evidence supports the clinical observation that individuals base current relationships on past relational experiences (Glickauf-Hughes & Wells, 1997; McWilliams, 1994; Scharff & Scharff, 1998). Urist (1980) wrote, "In the experiencing of the 'real' relationships between self and others in the external world, the individual processes and registers present experience in the context of the ways in which past experience has been organized" (p. 821). Early life relationships form the psychic maps that help a person navigate relationship dynamics. It is these maps, which originate in childhood, that eventually provide the guidance for one's interpersonal behavior in adulthood. Conversely, the adult's relationship style provides clues to the individual's childhood experience and how he or she adapted to and learned to organize interpersonal experience.

The object relations/self-psychology approach to psychotherapy uses an appreciation of formative childhood experiences and object relations to inform the therapy process. In particular, the relationship between therapist and client is central to treatment. The therapeutic relationship is the lab in which the underlying relational dynamics manifest and can be explored. Central to this approach are the concepts of transference, countertransference (objective and subjective), and projective identification.

Therapeutic Work With the
Narcissistically Parentified Client

The narcissism inherent in parentification, as described earlier, affects the evolution of the individual's identity and experience of separateness and connection with others. The dangers of unhealthy grandiosity and the need to merge with the idealized object represent opposing dimensions of the human paradox identified by Ekstein and Caruth (1972). Morrison (1989) wrote, "This paradox constitutes the narcissistic quandary and can be resolved only by a state of 'good enough' autonomy and identity to merit fantasied fusion with the idealized parent/other" (p. 63). In the parentification dynamic, the child adapts to this narcissistic quandary by "taking control" and assuming the role of the parent, giving the illusion of autonomy while remaining attached through fulfilling the needs of the parent.

It is central to the therapeutic process with the parentified individual that the therapist be aware of the client's dual striving for attachment and autonomy. Furthermore, the therapist must recognize that the parentification role is, or was, adaptive for the client despite its seemingly pathological results. For example, as the case examples describe, the parentified child recognizes at some level that to remain attached and secure, he or she must fulfill the needs of the parent. To do otherwise would invite abandonment, either real or imagined. Kohut understood well the use of defense mechanisms as a means of adaptation and communication. He wrote (1966, as cited in Morrison, 1989), "My personal preference is to speak of the 'defensiveness' of patients—and to think of their defensive attitudes as adaptive and psychologically valuable—and not of their resistances" (p. 130).

Rinsley (1982), in discussing the treatment of the borderline personality, made a point equally appropriate to understanding and treating the parentified individual. He wrote, "An effective therapeutic approach recognizes the survival importance of this sensitivity, including the ever-present nucleus of the patient's perceptions, which are in fact accurate" (p. 131). This sensitivity refers to the client's exquisite sense of "tuning into" the needs of the other individual. Rinsley continued by pointing out how this essential appreciation on the part of the therapist underlies effective treatment, stating, "such an approach witnesses a growing alliance between the therapist's ego and the reality-oriented part of the patient's ego as basic for the effective interpretation of the patient's hypersensitivity to . . . object relations and representations" (p. 131).

As long as the overperforming, narcissistically parentified client's defenses are working, the client's underlying shame, pain, and strain may remain unconscious. The client's lack of entitlement to real-self feelings and impulses may only be seen in glimpses, and the major work will occur during moments of empathic failure or when the therapist otherwise disappoints the client, and the client's longings for perfect mirroring or idealized reliance on the other's strength will manifest. For the narcissistically parentified adult client who is overperforming, one of the turning points of treatment is when the client realizes that all the attention she or he has captured with so much effort and self-denial was not love or concern for his or her real self but represents admiration for his or her high achievements. Grief and pain follow the client's exploration of these issues, but a new empathy with his or her fate is born out of the mourning (Miller, 1981, p. 15).

The therapist who engages in empathic immersion will by definition become the recipient of projective identifications from the client. The question becomes, "How do I as a therapist see the projective identification as it is occurring?" Projective identification is probable when the therapist believes that (a) he or she has developed a narrow perspective of self in relationship to the client, and (b) the client appears to share this narrow view (Ogden, 1982). One can visualize numerous situations in working with parentified individuals that qualify: (a) the therapist feels "taken care of" by the client; (b) the therapist feels idealized by the client; (c) the therapist idealizes the client; (d) the therapist pities the client; and (e) the therapist withers under the gaze of the client.

The therapist can facilitate the narcissistically parentified client's growing awareness and understanding of his or her unconscious longings and compensations by focusing on the client's developing transference and core projective identifications. Often the therapist first becomes aware of these mechanisms through his or her own objective countertransference reactions. Table 5.2 introduces the typical transference, projective identifications, and countertrans-

TABLE 5.2

Relationship Dynamics in the Treatment of Parentified Adults: Inflated Narcissism

	Transference	Projective Identification	Objective Countertransference	Subjective Countertransference	Therapeutic Response
Inflated Narcissism	Client sees therapist as a valued and admiring audience or a devalued and un-needed object. The client's unconscious aim is: "I am perfect and you must admire me or you are worthless."	Client pressures therapist to affirm client's specialness by showing off, charm or self-promotion, and devaluations of anything ungratifying. The client's underlying assumption is: "If you see me as wonderful, I must be wonderful."	Therapist typically feels charmed and impressed by the client or feels vaguely constricted, emotionally blackmailed, set up, or pressured to be the client's audience as a result of the client's inducement behaviors.	Examples: Therapists with unresolved narcissistic issues may feel envious or devaluing with client. Therapists with unresolved masochistic issues may feel challenged to win over the client or seek the client's approval.	Therapist contains reactions to projective identification and examines self to differentiate between objective and subjective countertransference. Interpretations mirror client's longing for empathy and appreciation by valued other. Interpretations center on client's substitution of admiration for love, impression management, real vs. false self, and devaluation of the object.

ference reactions when working with an inflated narcissistically parentified client. The grandiose narcissistic projective identification usually induces admiration or makes an impression through showing off and charming engagements. Objective countertransference represents the reactions anyone would have as a result of the client's inducements, whereas subjective countertransference reactions reflect the therapist's personalized emotional and cognitive reactions shaped by the therapist's own unique history and psychological makeup. Whereas objective countertransference reactions may give the therapist insight into intolerable aspects of self or quality of relationship with which the client struggles, subjective countertransference says more about the therapist and needs to be differentiated from issues introduced by the client.

The projective identification process is by definition unconscious; therefore, if the therapist recognizes the projective identification at all, this awareness will often only be in retrospect. Sometimes it is more obvious for supervisors or colleagues to observe the projective identification. Critical to the therapy with the parentified adult is the therapist's self-acknowledgment that he or she has been "taken into" reenacting the client's process (Ogden, 1982).

For example, during treatment with Carol the therapist recognized feeling taken into a grandiose projective identification in which the therapist often felt placed in the role of Carol's admiring audience while Carol held forth on important topics of concern or regaled the therapist with interesting family stories. The therapist was able to empathize with Carol's longing for accurate mirroring when Carol experienced an empathic failure with the therapist. Eventually, Carol realized how invested she was in eliciting admiration through achievement and how resistant and afraid she was to allow herself any vulnerability. She equated her own vulnerability with weakness rather than with loveableness. During treatment, Carol came to realize that the mirroring she had received in her family was conditional on her realizing the role prescribed for her; that is, the role of a strong, powerful, successful, perfect medical doctor.

Carol gradually realized she had not really allowed others to know her as she did not know herself, both because of her other-oriented focus and because of her strong investment in impression management and false self-development. The therapist and Carol then began the slow process of coming to know and appreciate Carol's real self—her values, interests, ambitions, strengths, and growing edges.

Over time Carol was able to mourn the developmental neglect of her real self and risk exposing her real feelings and thoughts to the therapist. The mourning process is central to the therapy with these clients and typically follows the awareness or insight into their role in the family of origin. In this phase of the therapy, the therapist needs to remain alert to how the client can attempt to minimize the pain of loss through denial in order to protect the parent.

As Carol allowed herself to experience the healing aspects of being truly known in an interpersonal atmosphere of acceptance and empathy, she saw the benefits of reasonable risks of vulnerability. The therapist worked with Carol on developing a working alliance with Carol's real self and developing a relational atmosphere characterized by mutual empathy to demonstrate the opportunities and rewards of true intimacy. In the words of Alice Miller (1981), "But the experience of one's own truth, and the post ambivalent knowledge of it, make it possible to return to one's own world of feelings at an adult level—without paradise, but with the ability to mourn. And this ability does, indeed, give us back our vitality" (pp. 29–30).

The foundation of effective treatment is the formation of a solid working alliance with the client. It is through the working alliance that the deeper wounds of parentification can be therapeutically addressed. The shame that accompanies narcissism is frequently masked by depression, but too often only the depression is treated (Morrison, 1989). In the case example of Carol, if the therapist had approached her presenting concern by conceptualizing it as depression about not becoming a doctor, the therapy would never have addressed the underlying shame related to upholding the family myth. Indeed, a therapeutic failure to immerse empathetically might have resulted in a recapitulation of the dysfunctional family process with the therapist unwittingly supporting Carol's false self and encouraging her pursuit of a medical career to avoid her depression through the presumed activation of initiative and industry. Carol's unconscious belief that she had to become a doctor to undo her father's shame and avoid emotional abandonment by her family would never have been addressed. In addition, her own shame related to a real self rejected and neglected by her family would never have been explored.

Thus, it is critical for therapists to recognize how shame motivates clients to conceal (Morrison, 1989). The concealment occurs not just in relation to the therapist (or others) but also with respect to the self. Effective therapy unveils what is concealed at the proper pace so that the client can examine and understand it.

Table 5.3 presents the core transference, projective identification, and countertransferences typically encountered in treating parentified clients with deflated narcissistic defenses, aims, and

TABLE 5.3
Relationship Dynamics in the Treatment of Parentified Adults: Deflated Narcissism

	Transference	Projective Identification	Objective Countertransference	Subjective Countertransference	Therapeutic Response
Deflated Narcisssism	Client idealizes therapist as special, omnipotent, perfect, and/or omniscient. Client's sense of self-worth is attached to an idealization of therapist. The client's unconscious aim is: "You are wonderful and I am a part of you."	Client induces therapist to assume role of powerful and perfect other by idealizing therapist and fusing with the idealization. The client's underlying assumption is: "If wonderful you values me then I must be special too."	Therapist typically feels flattered, powerful, and special as a result of the client's inducement behaviors. Conversely, therapist may feel discomforts related to being misrepresented as perfect.	Examples: Therapists with unresolved narcissistic issues may feel superior and entitled to client's adoration or may feel contempt toward the client's idealization stemming from therapist's entitled role in family of origin. Therapists with unresolved masochistic issues may feel unworthy or guilty about being idealized stemming from a personal history of being devalued in the eyes of significant others.	Therapist contains feelings induced by client as well as subjective countertransference responses. Therapist engages in self-examination to differentiate subjective from objective countertransference. Interpretations mirror the client's need to idealize the therapist and help the client recognize the real self vs. idealization of the object in support of a false self.

characteristics. The client's idealizing projective identification induces objective countertransference reactions in the therapist that include feeling flattered and being made important, big, special, omniscient, or omnipotent.

The therapist working with Pam not only found himself feeling uncomfortably idealized at times but eventually found himself feeling resistant to challenging or confronting her in ways he normally would with other clients. In consultation with another colleague, the therapist realized he had been feeling flattered and taken care of by Pam, who had read every article and book he had written and who pointedly told him he was obviously more skilled than other therapists with whom she had worked. She would tell him stories of how she told her friends, many of whom were other therapists in town, how insightful and helpful he was. She referred him a number of clients out of her admiration of his skills. She also told the therapist in a clearly devaluing manner how other therapists were unhelpful, by "calling me sensitive" and "not understanding me." In both obvious and subtle ways, Pam interacted with the therapist in such a way as to induce a feeling in the therapist of being idealized and admired as long as the therapist provided perfect mirroring and did not say or do anything that would challenge Pam's narcissistic collusion with the therapist. The therapist felt vaguely trapped or overconstricted and afraid to offend Pam in some way lest she prematurely terminate and "ruin his reputation" with other therapists in town. The therapist would come to understand that Pam was inducing uncomfortable self-states in the therapist that Pam had struggled with as a child and needed help to understand and work through.

Ogden (1982) identified several technical problems related to containing projective identification. He noted that it is essential to process the projective identification without acting on the feelings engendered by the projective identification in the therapy. The projective identification must be understood as a form of communication whose message must be understood by the therapist. The therapist must accept the projective identification rather than react to it. Therefore, interpretations are best saved to the proper time when the therapist senses the client is receptive.

The content of a projective identification may take several forms when working with the parentified client. Morrison (1989) described several shame-related phenomena that, although not specifically identified as related to parentification, are consistent with how a parentified client can present. A common means of defending against shame and expunging it from the self is through anger and rage. If this affect is directed toward the therapist, the resultant affect and repercussion on the therapist's sense of self can be (a) anger in return, (b) defensiveness under attack, or (c) helplessness. The therapist who appreciates the nature of projective identification understands that the effect on his or her sense of self in this situation likely stems from the client's sense of self.

This understanding engenders the therapist to contain the situation (e.g., by appreciating the communication) rather than react to it (e.g., by taking it personally). Similar manifestations of projective identification can occur through the parentified client projecting contempt, smothering behaviors, attempting to humiliate the therapist, envying the therapist, and feeling guilt because the client has in some way "wronged" the therapist (e.g., missed an appointment).

Therapists working with narcissistically parentified clients are advised to explore and observe the transference–countertransference patterns that develop through projective identifications (Kohut, 1971). By entering the therapeutic relationship with the parentified client, the therapist also enters into the client's attachment–separation struggle and shame-based adaptations. It is the therapist's ability to immerse himself or herself into the client's psychic world of parentified self-objects that will allow the therapist opportunities to empathize through induced emotional experience with what has been intolerable, unmanageable, or unresolved for the client.

Through examination of the therapist's countertransference reactions, Pam's inducement behaviors, and her conflictual relational patterns in her family of origin and current life, the therapist hypothesized that Pam was communicating important emotional information to the therapist through projective identifications that recapitulated the emotional binds Pam had experienced in her family. Pam had been used by her mother to meet her mother's needs for a confidante and an empathic listener. In a bad marriage with an active alcoholic, her mother had felt isolated, overwhelmed, and deprived. To remain aligned with her mother and support her, Pam felt "obliged" to mirror her mother and resist confronting her. She was thus left with an intense longing for a strong, calm, and understanding other on whom she could rely.

The therapist's work with Pam thus followed three steps. First, he noted and contained his emotions elicited by Pam's behavior toward him. He recognized that attempting to interpret or intervene in the moment would be damaging to the therapeutic relationship. Second, when the projective identification was not activated, the therapist invited Pam to explore the role she felt induced to assume with her mother in her family. The therapist helped Pam to empathize with both herself as a child and her mother in an intergenerational context. In particular, the therapist helped Pam to see how both she and her mother were understandably left with a longing to rely on a strong, idealized other who could take care of them. Third, when the therapist did not feel defensive but sustained an attitude of neutrality and interest, he invited Pam to explore the recapitulation of family roles within the therapy relationship. The therapist thus explored the projective identification as a means of communication that needed to be decoded, understood, and responded to in the here-and-now relationship through self-reflection in action, opening the topic up for discussion, determining the conscious and unconscious needs and aims of the transaction, and providing a larger contextual perspective. Pam was thus assisted in gaining insights into how the parentification dynamic was being recapitulated in the here-and-now with the therapist.

Later in the treatment, when Pam appeared to be inducing the idealizing projective identification, the therapist worked with her on articulating the interactive story that was being induced between them. This narrative would usually include (a) some event (internal or external) that induced insecurity in Pam; (b) Pam responding to that feeling of insecurity by longing for a strong and competent other who could understand her needs and take care of her; (c) Pam then using the approach she experienced her mother using with her as a child to induce the therapist to gratify that longing and soothe her; and (d) the therapist, implicitly feeling invited to assume the role of Pam as a child, then experiencing both the desire to take care of Pam and an uncomfortable feeling of constriction that paralleled Pam's feelings as a child. Promoting a discussion of the client's longings, roles, and use of projective identification serves many purposes, not the least of which is empathizing with the client's core discomforts, needs, and binds. Developing the alternative of empathically talking through feelings and insecurities in a safe and supportive relationship rather than unconsciously acting them out serves as a corrective relational experience for the client.

For both Pam and Carol, healthy functioning included learning more about themselves separate from what others wanted for them and reclaiming their "entitlement" to being true to themselves. For Carol, this meant a redirection of her energy from realizing her father's dream to realizing her own, rather than pulling back and reducing high performance. Carol eventually chose to pursue a degree in social work, applying her musical talents to her work with troubled children.

For Pam, this meant discovering what her ambitions were separate from others' ambitions and learning to enjoy learning for its intrinsic rewards rather than performing to avoid shame. Pam could then risk choosing a nonglamourous but personally meaningful career as a kindergarten teacher. In Pam's treatment, disappointments in the therapist as an idealized object provided opportunities to empathize with Pam's longing for someone big to help her or soothe her, as well as to be genuinely interested in her as a person, not just in her ability to meet the other person's ego needs. Pam had a period of mourning the absence of an interested and available parent who tracked her evolving needs as a child and responded appropriately to further the development of her unique personhood. The therapist empathically worked with Pam to help her focus on her real self, to explore and learn about who she was and heal the self-esteem wounds she suffered through neglect and shaming of her real self early in life.

Therapeutic Work With Masochistically Parentified Clients

Whereas the transference with the narcissistically parentified adult client is likely to assume either a mirroring or idealizing form, transference with the masochistically parentified adult client is likely to assume a caretaking form. These clients may bring food or coffee for the therapist. They may watch for how tired or preoccupied the therapist is and do things to emotionally take care of the therapist. They will typically experience discomfort in a receiving role. In group therapy they often become "junior therapists," finding it easier to listen to others than to talk about their own problems.

Their high performance is often witnessed as a perfectionistic overdoing at school or work. They may seem to be in a self-imposed, painful struggle with their work. They appear burdened and yet cannot be stopped from overdoing. In some cases, the client may report feeling mistreated or underappreciated by an overdemanding boss. This client may appear to think that he or she knows what is best for everyone. In some cases, the overdoing takes on a manic flavor. For example, even though one client's workload was strenuous around the holidays, she spent all her precious personal time making special handmade cards for each and every person in her office.

Table 5.4 presents the transference–countertransference and projective identification patterns typically experienced in working with the masochistically parentified client. Countertransferentially,

TABLE 5.4
Relationship Dynamics in the Treatment of Parentified Adults: Masochism

	Transference	Projective Identification	Objective Countertransference	Subjective Countertransference	Therapeutic Response
Masochism	Client views therapist as a narcissistic rescuer. Client goes to great lengths to care for therapist out of concern that therapist will abandon client if she or he fails to satisfy the other's needs. The client's unconscious aim is: "I satisfy your needs, so you owe me relational security and will not abandon me."	The client pressures the therapist to be taken care of, or even rescued, by the client. Furthermore, the client pressures the therapist to feel grateful for the assistance provided by the client. The client's underlying assumption is: "I will feel secure in relationship if I earn love."	Therapist is typically aware of feeling appreciated, thankful, taken care of, and may feel pulled to experience the client as a "favorite client." Conversely, the therapist may be aware of feeling controlled, manipulated, smothered, and/or misrepresented by the client. Therapist may experience the client as resistant to receiving from the therapist.	Examples: Therapists with unresolved masochist c issues may feel competitive with client for rescuer position or for who is more burdened. Therapists with unresolved narcissistic issues may feel gratified by client's attention or devalue client's need for approval and fear of abandonment, and become rejecting or distancing toward the client.	Therapist contains objective and subjective countertransference induced by the client. Therapist mirrors client's need for rescue. Interpretations directed at helping the client see patterns of other-oriented care taking at expense of self. Therapist helps client recognize importance of learning how to receive from others and care for self.

therapists can find themselves grateful to a masochistically parentified client who never expresses anger when the therapist is late or makes a mistake in scheduling an appointment; a client who notices when the therapist is tired and empathizes with what a difficult job the therapist has; a client who watches the time for the therapist and always ends promptly at the designated hour; a client who notices that the therapist is running late and looks a little stressed and responds by bringing up an interesting dream and talking about issues that are less intense and demanding for the therapist. A tired and emotionally drained therapist may find himself or herself disinclined to explicitly articulate his or her observation of the client's subtle caretaking efforts and simply enjoy the break, thus recapitulating the client's parental collusion and defensive efforts at emotional fusion with the significant other. Addressing the meaning of the client's tendencies to excessively caretake and self-sacrifice are thus essential to treatment.

One of the turning points in treatment may come when the masochistically parentified adult client understands how he or she was induced to hold and take care of the parent's anxieties by literally caretaking the parent. Another critical phase of treatment may occur when the client begins to understand all of the different ways that his or her compulsive caretaking serves to maintain insecure attachments to significant others, defends against interpersonal and intrapsychic anxieties, and keeps the effects of past trauma out of awareness.

For example, Sue discovered in therapy how her compulsive caretaking made her feel indispensable, provided her with the security of a structured role in relating to others, and kept the trauma of her mother's death and her intense, unresolved feelings of loss and mourning out of her consciousness. The therapeutic challenge for Sue then became tolerating the ambiguity and anxieties of practicing real self-expression in treatment to get to know herself outside of the caretaker role and learn how to trust the development of mutuality in relating.

Another turning point in the treatment of the masochistically parentified adult client is thus related to the client's realization that it is just as important to be a good receiver as it is to be a good giver, and the most rewarding and intimate relationships are built on mutuality and reciprocity rather than unilateral giving. Bill, for example, was very uncomfortable being in the role of receiver. This discomfort made the therapeutic experience of self-exploration very difficult for him to tolerate. Bill felt most comfortable in the role of either the fixer or the listener. He tried at various times to be his own therapist, beating the therapist to the punch whenever he sensed something about himself could evoke criticism.

Bill's therapist thus helped Bill to gain a larger perspective, in part by encouraging him to observe how hard it was for him to receive the therapist's undivided attention and interest as well as how difficult it was for Bill to focus on himself. Bill tended to try to deflect the spotlight from himself by asking the therapist for advice when what he really needed was understanding for some part of his experience that was generating insecurity or anxiety. The therapist worked with Bill by tracking the process as much as the content with the aim of helping Bill become more comfortable as a receiver in the give-and-take of mutual relating.

Masochistically parentified clients also need to mourn the lack of unconditional parental love and gain more empathy for themselves. They are especially in need of learning how to set good limits and, more importantly, feel the right to do so; that is, to believe that their limits are essentially good enough. Working with these clients to understand where their bottom lines are is an essential part of treatment. For Bill, healthy functioning would include coming to know, appreciate, and respect his limits, as well as living a more balanced life, and thus developing the range of his innate interests so that his self-esteem was not excessively tied to his work performance.

For Sue, healthy functioning would include learning how to listen to, acknowledge, and take care of her true self. She began to differentiate her true self from the overfunctioning, other-oriented false self-construct she had developed to assure relational proximity and self-worth in her family of origin. Healthy functioning for Sue eventually included more balance and less high performance. To accomplish this, she first had to mourn the loss of a carefree childhood and learn how to play as well as self-nurture.

Conclusion

In this chapter we have examined the ways in which high performance can reflect various overfunctioning roles induced by unhealthy parentification in one's family of origin. In particular, we have examined three shame-based parentified templates that result in high-performance strivings aimed at regulating self-esteem and maintaining relational proximity to significant others. Understanding narcissistic and masochistic parentification dynamics will help therapists tailor more effective treatment plans when working with parentified clients. Critical treatment goals and intervention strategies have been presented that target each form of parentification examined in this chapter.

References

Ablard, K. E., & Parker, W. D. (1997). Parents' achievement goals and perfectionism in their academically talented children. *Journal of Youth and Adolescence, 26,* 651–667.

Alexander, P. C. (1992). Application of attachment theory to the study of sexual abuse. *Journal of Consulting and Clinical Psychology, 60,* 185–195.

Bach, S. (1999). *The language of perversion and the language of love.* Northvale, NJ: Jason Aronson.

Bartholomew, K., & Horowitz, I. M. (1991). Attachment styles among young adults: A test of a four-category model. *Journal of Personality and Social Psychology, 61,* 226–244.

Benoit, D., & Parker, K. C. H. (1994). Stability and transmission of attachment across three generations. *Child Development, 65,* 1444–1454.

Bergner, R. M. (1982). Hysterical action, impersonation, and caretaking roles: A descriptive and practical study. *Advances in Descriptive Psychology, 2,* 233–248.

Boszormenyi-Nagy, I., & Krasner, B. R. (1986). *Between give and take: A clinical guide to contextual therapy.* New York: Brunner/Mazel.

Boszormenyi-Nagy, I., & Spark, G. M. (1973). *Invisible loyalties: Reciprocity in intergenerational family therapy.* New York: Harper & Row.

Bowlby, J. (1969). *Attachment and loss: Vol. 1. Attachment.* New York: Basic Books.

Bowlby, J. (1973). *Attachment and loss: Vol. 2. Separation.* New York: Basic Books.

Carroll, J. J., & Robinson, B. E. (in press). Depression and parentification among adults as related to parental workaholism and alcoholism. *The Family Journal.*

Cleary, M. J. (1992). Shame and shame-based syndromes: Implications for health educators. *Health Values, 16*(6), 47–54.

Dweck, C. S. (1986). Motivational processes affecting learning. *American Psychologist, 41,* 1040–1048.

Dweck, C. S., & Leggett, E. L. (1988). A social–cognitive approach to motivation and personality. *Psychological Review, 95,* 256–273.

Ekstein, R., & Caruth, E. (1972). Keeping secrets. In P. L. Giovacchini (Ed.), *Tactics and techniques in psychoanalytic therapy* (pp. 200–215). London: Hogarth Press.

Erikson, E. (1963). *Childhood and society* (2nd ed.). New York: Norton.

Glickauf-Hughes, C., & Wells, M. (1997). *Object relations psychotherapy: An individualized and interactive approach to diagnosis and treatment.* Northvale, NJ: Jason Aronson.

Glickauf-Hughes, C., Wells, M., & Genirberg, R. (1987). Psychotherapy of gifted students with narcissistic dynamics. *Journal of College Student Psychotherapy, 1*(3), 99–115.

Goldberg, C. (1988). Replacing moral masochism with a shame paradigm in psychoanalysis. *Dynamic Psychotherapy, 6,* 114–123.

Haley, J. (1976). *Problem-solving therapy.* San Francisco: Jossey-Bass.

Hewitt, P. L., & Flett, G. L. (1991). Perfectionism in the self and social contexts: Conceptualization, assessment, and association with psychopathology. *Journal of Personality and Social Psychology, 60,* 456–470.

Heyman, G. D., & Dweck, C. S. (1992). Achievement goals and intrinsic motivation: Their relation and their role in adaptive motivation. *Motivational Emotion, 16,* 231–247.

Hills, T. W. (1987). Children in the fast lane: Implications for early childhood policy and practice. *Early Childhood Research Quarterly, 2,* 265–273.

Issel, S. Z. (1995). Disavowed narcissism: Fusion and externalizing defenses in the closet narcissistic disorder of the self. In J. Masterson & R. Klein (Eds.), *Disorders of the self: New therapeutic horizons—the Masterson approach* (pp. 281–297). New York: Brunner Mazel.

Jones, R., & Wells, M. (1996). An empirical study of parentification and personality. *American Journal of Family Therapy, 24,* 145–152.

Jurkovic, G. J., Jessee, E. H., & Goglia, L. R. (1991). Treatment of parental children and their families: Conceptual and technical issues. *American Journal of Family Therapy, 19,* 302–314.

Kohut, H. (1971). *Analysis of the self.* New York: International Universities Press.

Main, M., & Goldwyn, R. (1984). Predicting rejecting of her infant from mother's representation of her own experience: Implications for the abused–abusing intergeneration cycle. *Child Abuse and Neglect, 8,* 203–217.

Main, M., & Hesse, E. (1990). Parents' unresolved traumatic experiences are related to infant disorganized attachment status: Is frightened and/or frightening parental behavior the linking mechanism? In M. Greenberg, D. Ciccetti, & M. Cummings (Eds.), *Attachment in the preschool years* (pp. 161–182). Chicago: University of Chicago Press.

Masterson, J. (1993). *The emerging self.* New York: Brunner/ Mazel.

McWilliams, N. (1994). *Psychoanalytic diagnosis.* New York: Guilford Press.

Mika, P., Bergner, R. M., & Baum, M. C. (1987). The development of a scale for the assessment of parentification. *Family Therapy, 14,* 229–235.

Miller, A. (1981). *Prisoner of childhood: The drama of the gifted child and the search for the true self.* New York: Basic Books.

Minuchin, P. (1974). *Families and family therapy.* Cambridge, MA: Harvard University Press.

Morrison, A. P. (1989). *Shame: The underside of narcissism.* Hillsdale, NJ: Analytic Press.

Ogden, T. H. (1982). *Projective identification and psychotherapeutic technique.* Northvale, NJ: Jason Aronson.

Pacht, A. R. (1984). Reflections on perfection. *American Psychologist, 39*, 386–390.

Reeves, P. M. (1999). The archetype of the parentified child: A psychosomatic presence. In N. Chase (Ed.), *Burdened children: Theory, research, and treatment of parentification* (pp. 171–184). Thousand Oaks, CA: Sage.

Rinsley, D. B. (1982). *Borderline and other self disorders: A developmental and object-relations perspective.* Northvale, NJ: Jason Aronson.

Rinsley, D. B. (1989). *Developmental pathogenesis and treatment of borderline and narcissistic personalities.* Northvale, NJ: Jason Aronson.

Robinson, B. E. (1998). The workaholic family: A clinical perspective. *American Journal of Family Therapy, 26*, 63–73.

Robinson, B. E. (1999). Workaholic children: One method of fulfilling the parentification role. In N. Chase (Ed.), *Burdened children: Theory, research, and treatment of parentification* (pp. 56–74). Thousand Oaks, CA: Sage.

Scharff, J. S., & Scharff, D. E. (1998). *Object relations individual therapy.* Northvale, NJ: Jason Aronson.

Urist, J. (1980). Object relations. In R. W. Woody (Ed.), *Encyclopedia of clinical assessment* (2nd ed., pp. 821–833). San Francisco: Jossey-Bass.

Valleau, M. P., Bergner, R. M., & Horton, C. B. (1995). Parentification and caretaker syndrome: An empirical investigation. *Family Therapy, 22*, 157–163.

Visintainer, P., & Matthews, K. A. (1987). Stability of overt Type A children: Results from a 2- and 5-year longitudinal study. *Child Development, 58*, 1586–1591.

Wells, M., & Jones, R. (1998). The relationship between parentification, splitting, and dissociation: Preliminary findings. *American Journal of Family Therapy, 26*, 331–339.

Wells, M., & Jones, R. (1999). Object relations therapy of narcissistic and masochistic parentification styles. In N. Chase (Ed.), *Burdened children: Theory, research, and treatment of parentification* (pp. 117–131). Thousand Oaks, CA: Sage.

Wells, M., & Jones, R. (2000). Parentification and shame-proneness. *American Journal of Family Therapy, 28*, 19–28.

West, M. L., & Keller, A. (1991). Parentification of the child: A case study of Bowlby's compulsive caregiving attachment pattern. *American Journal of Psychotherapy, 155*, 425–431.

Willi, J. (1982). *Couples in collusion.* Northvale, NJ: Jason Aronson.

Winnicott, D. W. (1965). *The maturational process and the facilitating environment.* New York: International Universities Press.

Zeanah, C. H., & Klitaker, M. (1991). Role reversal and the self-effacing solution: Observations from infant–parent psychotherapy. *Psychiatry, 54*, 346–357.

■ ■ ■

6

Parentification in the Lives of High-Profile Individuals and Their Families: A Hidden Source of Strength and Distress

Gregory J. Jurkovic, PhD
Richard Morrell, JD
Sean Casey, MEd

And while they were walking along, Isaac spoke unto his father, "Behold, the fire and the wood, but where then is the lamb for a burnt offering before the Lord?" And Abraham answered Isaac, saying, "The Lord hath chosen thee, my son, for a perfect burnt offering, instead of the lamb." And Isaac said unto his father, "I will do all that the Lord hath spoken to thee with joy and cheerfulness of heart." (Ginzberg, 1956, p. 131)

Impelled by powerful psychosocial forces, many children like Isaac dutifully respond to their family's direct or indirect call for loyalty, succor, and self-sacrifice. They engage in a variety of instru-

We wish to acknowledge James Dabbs, PhD, Gabriel Kuperminc, PhD, and the editors of this volume for their help in identifying examples of parentification in high-profile individuals. The second and third authors contributed equally to this chapter. The order in which they are listed was determined by a coin toss.

mental and emotional caregiving activities to satisfy the needs of parents, siblings, and the family as a whole. Similar dynamics may operate between generational equals. Partners often parent one another. Referred to as *parentification* by Boszormenyi-Nagy (1987) and his colleagues (Boszormenyi-Nagy & Krasner, 1986; Boszormenyi-Nagy & Spark, 1973), this relational process has become the focus of increasing clinical, theoretical, and empirical attention (see Chase, 1999; Jurkovic, 1997, 1998; Jurkovic, Morrell, & Thirkield, 1999). Despite its Eurocentric roots, parentification has proven to be a useful construct for understanding and helping a widely diverse group of individuals and their families.

Parentification appears endemic to family life. It is not tantamount to pathology and, indeed, frequently characterizes adaptive family relationships, particularly during stressful periods (Boszormenyi-Nagy & Spark, 1973). The construct appears to be gaining increasing visibility. For example, Maria Echaveste, President Clinton's deputy chief of staff and the oldest child of migrant farmworkers who immigrated to the United States from Mexico, had to "grow up fast," according to one of her sisters, Carmella. A social worker, Carmella referred to Maria as a "parentified" child (Dart, 1999). It is likely that Ms. Echaveste's familial role was part of a culturally prescriptive process. In some cultural contexts, instrumental parentification of children is normative (Jurkovic et al., 2000; Jurkovic, Morrell, & Thirkield, 1999). Growing evidence further suggests that individuals, including young children, are motivated to help and heal those with whom they share a significant relationship (see Jurkovic, 1997). These "innate psychotherapeutic strivings," as Searles (1971) referred to them, are an essential source of family cohesion and individual growth.

According to Boszormenyi-Nagy and Krasner (1986), whether parentification becomes destructive depends on the balance of give-and-take in the family. An imbalance develops when the beneficent activities of children or partners are not acknowledged, legitimized, and reciprocated in the family and the larger sociocultural context in which they live. Destructively parentified children often grow up in families plagued by substance dependence, workaholism, parental mood disorders, divorce, marital conflict, poverty, and other stressful conditions. They are at risk of suffering from various short- and long-term problems, for example, depression, anxiety, low self-esteem, and overfunctioning in relationships (see Chase, 1999; Jurkovic, 1997, 1998).

At the same time, even imbalanced forms of childhood parentification may facilitate the development of desirable personality traits, such as interpersonal sensitivity and resourcefulness, that serve the child well in future roles (Jurkovic, 1997). It is interesting to note that a number of investigators (Jurkovic, 1997; Lackie, 1983; Miller, 1981; Sessions, 1986) have pointed to evidence of parentification, often of a destructive nature, in the family backgrounds of social workers, psychoanalysts, clinical psychologists, and marriage and family therapists. One of the professionals interviewed by Jurkovic (1997) reported, "My career as a therapist began when I was four. . . . I just needed the structure of a formal education to do what I've always been doing" (p. 173). Speaking about those who enter the psychoanalytic profession, Miller (1981) asked rhetorically, "Who else, without this previous history [of parentification], would muster sufficient interest to spend the whole day trying to discover what is happening in the other person's unconscious?" (p. 91).

Miller, a psychoanalyst herself, shares the pathos of her own parentification in the preface of her book, *Prisoners of Childhood: The Drama of the Gifted Child and the Search for the True Self* (1981). She, and others (Jurkovic, 1997) have observed that the same conditions conducive to the successful pursuit of a career in the therapy field contribute to the therapist's greatest professional and personal difficulties (e.g., narcissistic disturbances, boundary problems, compulsive giving, and burnout). These professionals are truly "wounded healers" (Jung, 1966).

Along the same lines, in addition to discovering that parentified children are at risk of developing various internalizing problems, Hetherington (1999) subsequently found evidence of strength (namely, social responsibility) in their early adult years. Accordingly, she coined the phrase "competent at a cost" to characterize the parentified child's development. From a systemic perspective, however, the meaning of Hetherington's apt descriptor applies not only to the parentified youngster but also to other family members. For example, because of the parentified role assumed by one or more of their brothers or sisters, the remaining members of the sibling subsystem are often free to pursue childhood interests and age-appropriate tasks. The cost for their freedom is the parentification of their siblings.

Similarly, parents may also be the beneficiaries of parentification. In their analysis of the family dynamics of celebrities, Mitchell and Cronson (1987) discovered that the spouses of these individuals often turned to one of the children for companionship and help in maintaining the household, thus enabling their mates to pursue their careers unencumbered by family responsibilities. Of course, siblings and parents who benefit from the parentification of others in the family may also realize a cost—not infrequently in the form of distant, if not fully ruptured, family ties.

Duly crediting parentified individuals, for example, by acknowledging their contributions to the achievements of others in the family, helps to "balance the ledger sheet" (Boszormenyi-Nagy & Krasner, 1986) and to preserve family solidarity. An example of such acknowledgment can be found in the words of the popular song, "Wind Beneath My Wings" (Henley & Silbar, 1982). Unfortunately, this sentiment is oftentimes expressed only to one's partner. The children's role goes unnoticed.

In our clinical experiences with high-achieving, publicly visible individuals, we have recurrently uncovered evidence of marked parentification in their family histories. Of course, career success and notoriety are multiply determined phenomena rooted in a complex interplay of biological, psychological, social, and historical variables. However, the possible role of parentification in an individual's ascendance to the heights of his or her life's work has not been considered in the professional literature. The goal of this chapter is to explore this putative link, thus laying the groundwork for further theoretical and empirical study.

Specifically, guided by the research and clinical observations discussed earlier, two potential pathways along which parentification operates in the family systems of those who achieve prominence are considered. These pathways include career success that is purchased, in part, through either one's own or another family member's parentification. To illustrate these pathways, we draw examples from the lives of high-profile figures in American culture.

High Performance as an Extension of One's Own Childhood Parentification

One of the first places that we searched for high-profile examples of this first pathway was the presidency of the United States. What motivates an individual to pursue the penultimate "civil service" job—one that is regularly subject to the vicissitudes of public exposure and opinion as well as disparate and often incompatible constituencies? To the extent that occupational pursuits are continuous with family role activities in childhood, it seemed plausible that the memoirs and biographies of some of the former U.S. presidents would yield evidence of parentification. However, we quickly discovered that much of the literature in this area, particularly of an autobiographical nature, presents an idealized and personally unrevealing picture of these individuals and their families of origin (e.g., a rags-to-riches ascendance from a happy childhood). Obviously, our presidents and their biographers have an investment in putting an auspicious "spin" on such material. Nevertheless, we found one political biography, Doris Kearns Goodwin's (1991) portrait of Lyndon Baines Johnson, to be particularly incisive and supported by numerous direct quotes. In Goodwin's role as Johnson's personal confidante, Johnson disclosed himself to her in a refreshingly unguarded manner.

Lyndon Baines Johnson

The son and grandson of politicians on both his mother's and father's sides of the family, Lyndon Baines Johnson served as the 36th president of the United States. He was an indefatigable champion of the people fighting for their civil rights and for governmental measures designed to improve the quality of their lives. During his 32 years of public service as a Democrat in the U.S. House of Representatives, the Senate, and finally the presidency, Johnson amassed legendary political capital. Although he clearly enjoyed power, power for him did not appear to be only an end in itself but also a means by which to give others what they could not give themselves.

Indeed, Johnson's presidency was distinguished by such accomplishments as an $11.5 billion tax cut, his renown "war on poverty," and his wide-reaching initiative, referred to as the "Great Society," designed to ensure that "no one should be deprived of the essentials of a decent life" (Goodwin, 1991, p. 215). Programs and laws that are still extant, such as Medicare, the federal Department of Housing and Urban Development, and voting and open-housing rights, originated in Johnson's Great Society. Of his 252 legislative recommendations, Congress enacted 226, marking one of the most productive legislative periods in U.S. history (Sidey, 1994).

Johnson's political undoing, however, was his management of foreign affairs. In particular, his escalation of the United States' involvement in the undeclared war in Vietnam drew widespread criticism. By failing to deal openly with the American people and with Congress about Vietnam, he further weakened his position to the point that he was viewed as a liability in many Democratic congressional campaigns (Sidey, 1994). His efforts, moreover, to pursue both his Great Society at home and victory abroad, to be "simultaneously first in peace and first in war" (Goodwin, 1991, p. 285), were unrealistic, if not grandiose. Facing intense opposition in the New Hampshire presidential primary in 1968 and wishing to restore harmony in his personal life and in the life of the nation, he announced in a televised speech on March 31, 1968, a unilateral deescalation of the Vietnam War and his decision not to run for another term as president.

Despite his shortcomings, it is apparent that Johnson was a tour de force politically. Goodwin (1991) aptly observed that one of the primary sources of his power and persuasiveness derived from his role as a caretaker—a role that he skillfully played not only in national politics but also in family politics as the eldest child of five growing up in a home plagued by marital dissatisfaction and unrealized parental aspirations. Johnson himself drew a connection between these two arenas in one of his discussions with Goodwin, justifying the United States' military assistance to the South Vietnamese.

> There is a great responsibility on the strong. The oldest member of the family has got to look after the smaller ones and protect them when the wolf comes to the door. (quoted in Goodwin, 1991, p. 56)

Parentified Role Activities

LBJ's parents charged him with the responsibility of "head of the household" during his father's absences from home. His instrumental duties included delegating chores to his brothers and sisters and resolving their problems. He recalled,

> On weekends they would run off to the city and rack up enormous bills. Mother would ask me to fix things up. I resented it every time, but I always did what she asked. For she would tell me over and over that the strong *must* care for the weak. (quoted in Goodwin, 1991, p. 55)

Characteristic of parentifying parents, Johnson's mother labeled him as special, as the "strongest" of his siblings with the most "ambition," "self-discipline," and ability to succeed, qualities that he internalized.

His parentified role at home was not restricted to the instrumental sphere but also included extensive and taxing emotional caretaking, particularly of his unhappy and unfulfilled mother. Probably reflecting her own loneliness, she never wanted him to be alone as a youngster. "She kept me constantly amused," Johnson remembered (quoted in Goodwin, 1991, p. 24). When her husband was away, she would invite her oldest son to share her bed at night.

Johnson recalled numerous instances as a child when he astutely discerned his mother's unhappiness or happened upon her when she was crying and provided comfort, promising her that he would always "protect" her. A refined woman who valued education and culture, she confided in him her dissatisfaction with his father.

> My mother soon discovered that my daddy was not a man to discuss higher things. To her mind his life was vulgar and ignorant. His idea of pleasure was to sit up half the night with his friends, drinking beer, telling stories, and playing dominoes. She felt very much alone. The first year of her marriage was the worst year of her life. Then I came along and suddenly everything was all right again. I could do all the things she never did. (quoted in Goodwin, 1991, p. 22)

Consequences

Emotional–social functioning. As a result of their parentified role, children develop an exquisite ability to read and to respond to the feelings, needs, and expectations of others. Johnson put this ability to good use in his career. He was the consummate politician. Through his constant scrutiny of people, capacity to please and form relationships with others, particularly older successful and powerful men, loyalty to friends and associates, and mastery of the realpolitik of government, he excelled in his career (Goodwin, 1991).

Characteristic of many adults with a history of parentification, Johnson was also adept in handling crises. This perhaps was most evident when he transitioned from his post as vice president to the presidency following President Kennedy's assassination in late 1963. He effectively shepherded the country through this traumatic period and was rewarded by the Democratic party with the presidential nomination the following year.

The downside of Johnson's extreme sociability and responsiveness was a fear of confrontation. In their efforts to keep the peace, parentified individuals often avoid conflict. Paradoxically, Johnson's reticence to confront others contributed to his many successes as a politician (Goodwin, 1991). To avoid conflict, he resolved it—typically behind the scenes—through bargaining, negotiation, and mediation. In fact, he was so skilled at privately resolving conflict while leader of the Senate that Paul Douglas and other senators criticized him for abolishing debate. Ultimately, his avoidance of open dis-

cord with the citizenry and Congress over Vietnam contributed to
his political demise.

Power seeking. Parentified children typically feel needed by
their parents, which confers enormous power on them and may
contribute to their power seeking and leadership style as adults
(Erikson, 1969). This certainly seemed to be case for Johnson. Referring to his mother, he said,

> I knew how much she needed me, that she needed me to take
> care of her. I liked that. It made me feel big and important. It
> made me believe I could do anything in the whole world. (quoted
> in Goodwin, 1991, pp. 24–25)

The child, however, often experiences the power associated with
parentification as illegitimate, particularly if his or her parentified
role is part of an unhealthy familial triangle designed to detour or
modulate marital conflict. Johnson recalled feeling "absolute ter-
ror" as a youngster while sleeping one night with his mother. Awak-
ened by the opening of the bedroom door, he feared that it was his
father. Instead, it was one of his sisters (Goodwin, 1991, p. 26).
Goodwin surmised that questions about the legitimacy of his power
may have plagued Johnson as an adult—questions perhaps reinforced by the fact that he assumed three of his political positions,
including the presidency initially, through the deaths of others.

There was another side to Johnson's relationship with his mother,
one that many emotionally parentified children experience. Namely,
she seemed to value him for what he did rather than for who he
was. Her love was conditional on his performance, particularly
performance of activities that compensated for her own unrealized
desires. Once when he refused to continue the violin and dancing
lessons that she had arranged for him, she withheld her affection.
"For days after I quit those lessons she walked around that house
pretending that I was dead," Johnson told Goodwin (1991, p. 25).

Evidence of her conditional love can also be found in a letter
that she wrote her son after his marriage to Claudia Alta ("Lady
Bird") Taylor.

> Now that you have the love and companionship of the one and
> only girl I am sure you will go far. You are fortunate in finding
> and winning the girl you love and I am sure your love for each
> other will be an *incentive to you to do all the great things of
> which you are capable.* Sweet son, I am loving you and *count-*

ing on you as never before [italics added]. (quoted in Goodwin, pp. 82–83)

The maternal love that Johnson experienced not only motivated but also demanded performance. Accordingly, he worked constantly, which doubtlessly protected him from untoward feelings and memories. Sleeping little, his adult life was marked by "endless activity and conquest" (Goodwin, 1991, p. 52). The label *workaholism* (Robinson, 1998) is probably apropos. It is also plausible that Johnson's tremendous fear of elections, prompting him to threaten to withdraw from many races in his political career, stemmed from the unbearable rejection and shame that he anticipated experiencing if he lost. For Johnson, votes appeared to represent love and affirmation of his adequacy as a person (Goodwin, 1991). They also fulfilled the needs of his mother. Following his election to Congress at the age of 29, Johnson's mother wrote to him,

> To me your election . . . it compensates for the heartache and disappointment I experienced as a child when my dear father lost the race you have just won . . . you have always justified my expectations, my hopes, my dreams. (quoted in Goodwin, 1991, pp. 88–89)

Fortunately, Johnson's ties with his paternal grandfather and father appeared to provide important buffers in his enmeshed relationship with his mother. As a young child, he spent countless hours at his grandfather's small farmhouse on the Pedernales in central Texas, enjoying his romanticized stories about the frontier and the Populist Party and, more importantly, the unconditional regard of his grandfather. Johnson's identification with this man influenced his conduct as a congressman.

> I thought about my Populist grandfather and promised myself that I'd always be the people's Congressman, representing all the people, not just the ones with money and power. (quoted in Goodwin, 1991, p. 91)

After his grandfather's death, LBJ grew closer to his father, a local politician and farmer. As an adolescent, he adopted patterns of behavior modeled by his father (e.g., drinking, distrust of ideas and intellectuals) that his mother despised. Later in his years as a politician he believed that the intellectuals hated him, a belief that was arguably buttressed by fears that his mother might feel the same. Yet, perhaps as a defiant expression of his independence from her, like the activist antagonist in Hesse's (1943/1949) novel, *Magister Ludi*, he steadfastly favored action over contemplation. Despite his mother's jaundiced view of her husband, he modeled for young Lyndon more than a bawdy masculinity. He also fought the Ku Klux Klan in his community and was a staunch defender of civil liberties.

Identity development and leaving home. In a dramatic display of autonomy, after completing high school at the age of 15 Johnson left for California with some friends without permission and did not return until 2 years later. He was not prepared to abide by his mother's wish that he attend college or to face her disappointment and abandonment if he discontinued his studies (Goodwin, 1991). In an effort to escape the prison of their childhood, many parentified youngsters precipitously leave home (Jurkovic, 1997). In Johnson's case, he most likely drew ego strength to do so from his relationship with his father and earlier his grandfather. These relationships may have also fostered his capacity for independent action later in his career as a politician.

The time away allowed Johnson to resolve his identity crisis. During his trip home, he thought to himself,

> I still believed . . . I would become a political figure. Daddy would like that. He would consider it a manly thing to be. But that would be just the beginning. I was going to reach beyond my father. I would finish college; mother would like that. I would succeed where her own father had failed, I would go to the Capitol and talk about big ideas. She would never be disappointed in me again. (quoted in Goodwin, 1991, p. 44)

Johnson's career choice represents a creative, although not fully autonomous, resolution of the conflicting demands of his parents. In keeping with his parentified role, he found an ingenious way to avoid conflict and to remain loyal to both parents.

Destructive entitlement. Referring to the public's loss of confidence in his leadership in the late 1960s, Johnson asked Goodwin (1991, p. xi): "How is it possible that all these people could be ungrateful to me after I had given them so much?" Although a question probably asked by many, if not most, U.S. presidents, it is also a common refrain of individuals with a history of destructive parentification. It is likely that his family of origin did not duly credit him for his contributions to their welfare, causing him to look elsewhere for acknowledgment and appreciation (namely, to the American people)—a process referred to by Boszormenyi-Nagy (1987) as "destructive entitlement."

Relatedly, Johnson was a demanding giver in extrafamilial relationships. Although exceedingly generous, the degree of gratitude and loyalty that he exacted in return inevitably led to disappointment. Like his mother, he tended to withdraw (referred to as the "Johnson freeze-out") when others did not live up to his expectations (Goodwin, 1991).

Discussion

We discovered other public figures whose writings and biographies echoed many of the same themes as Johnson. For example, Gloria Steinem, one of the founders of *Ms. Magazine* and a key figure in the modern feminist movement, was for much of her childhood and adolescence the primary caregiver for her psychologically fragile mother. In *Ruth's Song*, a tribute to her mother, Steinem (1983) wrote, "In many ways, our roles were reversed: I was the mother and she was the child" (pp. 140–141).

Like Johnson, Steinem (1983) also recalled in the same essay the unalloyed fear that she experienced at times in the course of fulfilling her parentified role.

> I remember a long Thanksgiving weekend spent hanging on to her with one hand and holding my eighth-grade assignment of *A Tale of Two Cities* in the other, because the war outside our house was so real to my mother that she had plunged her hand through the window, badly cutting her arm in an effort to help us escape. Only when she agreed to swallow the medicine could she sleep, and only then could I end the terrible calm that comes with crisis and admit to myself how afraid I had been. (pp. 142–143)

In one of her other works, Steinem (1992b, p. 190) again referred to the "panic of trying to be her [mother's] caretaker" before she was able to care for herself. Fear may be an inherent feature of extreme forms of destructive parentification. If so, it would help explain why Jurkovic and Martin (1999) discovered in a recent study that after controlling for multiple other sources of trauma, destructive parentification related to various symptoms of posttraumatic stress.

Steinem (1992a) further admitted to having used first school and then work to escape emotions that she did not want to experience. By focusing on the problems of others, she avoided the sadness and anxiety that come with introspection. Indeed, she, in part, saw her feminist activities as a way of indirectly helping her mother, whom she regarded as a victim of a male-dominated society, and as an "anesthetic to buried childhood emotions" (p. x). Steinem (1992b) observed that, as an adult, it "took me much longer to give up my image of myself as someone who helped other people through crises but never had any of my own" (p. 6).

In her insightful biography of Steinem, Heilbrun (1995) suggested that Steinem's early experiences, albeit costly, may have also bolstered her feelings of self-efficacy (see Hetherington, 1999).

> Because of her responsibilities for the household with her disturbed mother, she tended to think of herself in the active role: she saw herself as the successful last resort for people almost beyond saving. (p. 30)

Indeed, this may be the case. Steinem, like Johnson, appeared to gain from the experience a strong belief in her own power and capacities, an intense desire to help others, and strong skills as a mediator, as well as a tendency to overfunction and overcommit. If there were a need, such as the need of women in the United States for liberation, she felt responsible for satisfying it (Heilbrun, 1995).

It is also apparent that Johnson and Steinem owed their career successes, in part, to supportive relationships with intra- and extrafamilial individuals. Recall the nurturing role of Johnson's paternal grandfather. Steinem's older sister persuaded their father, who had left the family years earlier, to take care of their mother so that Gloria could attend college (Heilbrun, 1995).

In cases of nondestructive parentification, the parents themselves, despite their reliance on their children for help, are often a trustworthy source of support and affection. This was the experience of Jocelyn Elders, MD, the first African American surgeon general of the United States. The oldest child of a large economically impoverished family living in rural Arkansas, she credits not only her parents and extended family but also her teachers. She wrote, "Our teachers taught us that black people were people of great courage and accomplishment, that they could raise themselves up" (Elders & Chanoff, 1997, p. 54).

Other forces often fuel the ambitions and achievements of parentified individuals as well. Out of loyalty many of them fulfill the personal demands and wishes (e.g., for education, for national recognition) of their parents—serving as their "delegates" (Stierlin, 1974). Jones and Wells (1996) referred to this process as "narcissistic parentification," which represents one form of emotional parentification from our perspective. Narcissistically parentified children, such as Lyndon Johnson, internalize the projected ego ideal of parental figures, thus compromising their own self-actualization to realize parental expectations, hopes, and dreams. Parents of these children use their children "to live out unlived adult lives" (Steinem, 1992b, p. 70).

On a more positive level, parentified individuals who achieve prominence, particularly those who use their status and endowments for the betterment of humankind, may be especially committed to the transgenerational mandate to improve the quality of life of the next generation (Boszormenyi-Nagy & Krasner, 1986). According to Boszormenyi-Nagy and Krasner, the survival of the human species depends on the commitment of all of us to posterity. Genuine concern along these lines is clearly evident in the lives of Johnson, Steinem, and Elders. For example, in the epilogue of her autobiography, Elders wrote about the values underlying her groundbreaking course to the highest medical office in the United States.

> Family values mean nurturing our nuclear and extended families. Everybody's family doesn't have to look like mine. We can have single-parent families. We can have same-sex families. But we must have families that support each other, take care of each other, protect each other, and respect each other. And we have to have public programs and policies that help them to do that. Because sooner or later a nation that does not take care of its youngest, eldest, and weakest will truly self-destruct. (Elders & Chanoff, 1997, pp. 338–339)

High Performance at the Expense of Another Family Member's Parentification

In contrast to the first pathway, examples of the second pathway along which parentification operates in the family systems of those who achieve prominence were much more difficult to find in the biographies and autobiographies of high-performing individuals. Considering research and clinical observations noted earlier, our hunch is that many of them did benefit from the parentification of family members but failed to give them due credit. The lives of the legendary actress, Marlene Dietrich, and her only child, Maria, vividly exemplifies this second pathway.

Marlene's career as an actress and entertainer began in Germany. In 1929 she was discovered by Josep von Sternberg and soon had six film contracts with Paramount Studios in the United States, including *The Blue Angel* and *Morocco*. She went on not only to star in numerous movies, stage productions, and concerts but also to become a popular performer for the USO during World War II. Marlene often accompanied General George Patton at the front. For her support of the Allies, the United States, French, and Israeli governments honored her with medals (Streif, 1997). Maria's in-depth account (Riva, 1992) of her renowned mother illustrates the role that children may play in their parents' career success.

Marlene Dietrich

Maria Magdalene ("Marlene") Dietrich was born on December, 27, 1901, to Lieutenant Louis Erich Otto Dietrich and Wilhelmina Elisabeth Felsing in Schoneberg, Germany. The younger of two daughters, Maria stood apart from others at an early age.

> Maria Magdalene was special—everyone knew it without reasoning, accepting its truth. Lena, as she was known, knew it too. She felt different from those around her. She was sure all the beautiful things in the world had been created just to please her. (Riva, 1992, p. 7)

According to family lore, Maria's power was not lost on her older sister, who became her "happy handmaiden." At the age of 13, Maria's father was killed in World War I. Her mother remarried not long after his death to a man who suffered the same fate. By the end of the war, Maria Magdalena had changed her name to Marlene.

In her early 20s, Marlene began acting in Europe and married Rudolph Sieber. Within 7 months of marrying, she gave birth to her only daughter, Maria. Marlene's proprietary feelings toward her child soon surfaced.

> By the time she had given birth, she had convinced herself that her child was her own creation. Nothing so vulgar as male sperm had anything to do with it. She and she alone had made her child in her own image. The child was hers, by right of immaculate conception. (Riva, 1992, p. 53)

Accordingly, it is not surprising that she named her daughter after herself. Further signs that the boundaries between mother and daughter were abnormally blurred, setting the stage for a particularly pernicious form of parentification, can be found in an entry in Marlene's diary when Maria was 2 years old,

> Nobody understands that I am so attached to the child because nobody knows that apart from that I have nothing. I, myself, experience nothing as a woman—nothing as a person. The child is incredible, strangers who belong to the family love her and miss her. The child is the essence of my life. I think I will die young. (quoted in Riva, 1992, p. 54)

Parentified Role Activities

Like Lyndon Johnson, Maria acted as both an emotional and instrumental provider for her mother. Maria was astutely aware of her mother's emotional needs, which she dutifully attempted to meet. Contributing to the destructiveness of Maria's parentification, many of her efforts involved sacrifices that went unstated and unnoticed. For instance, reflecting on an enjoyable experience from her childhood with her father, Maria wrote,

> Why did I never rush to tell my mother of those special moments? It would have been such a natural thing to do for a three-year-old, to wish to share joy, at least, proclaim it. I have often wondered what made me choose not to, at such an early age. Maybe I knew even then, that my mother would resent my receiving joy from anyone but herself. So I kept quiet and never questioned why my father never mentioned it either, just felt somehow relieved that he didn't. (Riva, 1992, p. 55)

Indeed, Maria's father colluded with Marlene in destructively parentifying their daughter by failing to interdict the process. Apparently, he viewed Maria's role as necessary, if not normal (Miller, 1981). Writing about the passivity of her own father, Miller, the analyst referred to earlier, stated that she had been pathologically parentified for years by her mother "because no one close to me, not even my kind and wise father, was capable of noticing or challenging this form of child abuse" (p. viii).

Maria's burdens as an emotional caregiver increased at the age of 7 when her mother entered a state of a depressive withdrawal.

> This was the first time I experienced this type of withdrawal, a
> form of mourning that was to be such a well known behavior
> of Dietrich for the rest of her life. . . . In her hand she held one
> of my notes. I had written her one of my little love notes. She
> treasured them, as they seemed to lift her moods, I wrote them
> often, slipping my crayoned epistles under her bedroom door.
> I had felt that, after von Sternberg's departure, one of my notes
> was definitely needed, it read: Oh, Mutti! You are sad, I miss
> you and I love you. (Riva, 1992, p. 157)

The research of Zahn-Waxler and her colleagues (see Zahn-Waxler &
Robinson, 1995) has shown that parental mood disorders are a powerful inducement to parentified role behavior on the part of children.

In addition to her emotional parentification, Maria also discharged
various instrumental duties. Beginning as early as 8 years of age,
Maria played a key role in her mother's work. She held many positions both in the work environment of the studios as well as in the
home. For example, Maria would frequently arise at 3 in the morning to help her mother conduct research for a movie. She would
also tuck her mother into her bed, tell her goodnight, and turn out
the light at whatever time of the night her mother arrived home.

Consequences

Loss. Because of the imbalance of give-and-take in the destructively parentified child's relationship with his or her parents, perhaps one of the most devastating effects of this childhood role is
the psychological loss of parents. Maria's realization of this loss
dawned on her as early as the age of 3 when she "knew" that she
"did not have a mother" but instead "belonged to a queen." It was
not until later that she began to "yearn for a real mother, like real
people had" (Riva, 1992, p. 56).

As with Lyndon Johnson and his mother, the relationship between
Maria and Marlene was conditional. When Maria gave her mother
what she wanted, they were close. Otherwise, Marlene would ignore or cut herself off from her daughter. Maria provides a poignant
example of this dynamic when she was 10 years of age.

> My mother was ignoring me. I was told by a maid to stay at
> home. I did what was expected of me and tried to think what I
> had done or said that could have angered her. Usually, I was
> able to identify my mistake almost immediately, but this time I
> drew a blank. So I stayed in Bel Air, was particularly careful,

and hoped my mother's displeasure would wear itself out. (Riva, 1992, p. 342)

It turned out that Maria was being punished because Marlene felt that one of her male lovers was paying too much attention to her daughter.

Maria's sense of loss extended to her father and relatives as well. After the birth of Maria, the relationship between Marlene and her husband became more that of friends and associates than spouses. Leading separate lives, rarely did they live under the same roof. Yet, Rudolph provided emotional and professional support to Marlene in times of crisis. In the interest of his wife's career, he also maintained the facade of the happy couple for the press. The distance between the two, however, was so great and Marlene's bond to her daughter so strong that Maria wrote,

> Until I was twelve I wasn't sure who my real father was either, granted the one I called Papi seemed to be the best candidate, but . . . I didn't churn about all this confusion. My mother had told me so often that I was hers and hers alone, that whoever was my biological father wouldn't have had a chance in my life anyway. (Riva, 1992, p. 53)

Driven by loyalty to her mother, Maria also did not openly express feelings of love or connection with her grandparents, which greatly aggrieved her. Maria had the following thoughts while burying her mother next to her maternal grandmother:

> I stand by my grandmother's grave and tears choke me. I have so much to tell her, and childhood words are not enough, to say it all—let her know I have brought her child, that was given me so long ago, back to her to love again—perhaps even forgive for the hurting of those who needed her so. I only whisper be good to her and I cry for all the lost love so unretrievable and leave them to make their way together. (Riva, 1992, p. 790)

Academic and social functioning. Reflecting Maria's extraordinary enmeshment with her mother, she did not attend school until she was old enough to enter high school. Even then, her schooling was constantly interrupted by phone calls from her mother or by extended periods of absence because her mother needed her help. After describing her friendship with a schoolmate to her mother, Maria immediately became apprehensive.

> I had feared she might decide to remove me from my new school. I never said another word about my new world, reverted to being engrossed in hers, and assured once again of my exclusive devotion, my mother stopped feeling threatened and was content. (Riva, 1992, p. 423)

Friends or companions (including pets) who competed with Marlene for her daughter's attention were summarily dismissed. After Maria's bodyguard was fired, she realized, "That must be it! I let my liking for my kind bodyguard show and lost him his job. That was awful! I must be more careful in the future" (Riva, 1992, p. 325). In keeping with her parentified role, Maria assumed blame for her mother's actions. To test the theory that her mother removed those close to her, Maria excessively praised a dog that she disliked. Within 1 week, the dog was replaced with another one.

Upon understanding that she was imprisoned by her destructively parentified role, Maria had a daunting feeling.

> I suddenly felt cold inside. There seemed to be no one. Not a single person I could trust to do something very important for me, without my omnipotent mother being informed of it. I remember feeling utterly alone and being frightened by that reality. As these unrelated moments in childhood have a way of doing, it marked me. (Riva, 1992, p. 348)

Fortunately, Maria had one person with whom she was able to maintain a trusting relationship throughout her childhood years: her father's live-in lover.

> I could talk to Tami, even cry. She never preached bravery; *she believed in feeling things, not pretending* [italics added]. So I told her of my sorrow, and she held me, comforted me, let me mourn without rhetoric. (Riva, 1992, p. 102)

The ability to express one's true rather than false self, that is, not to pretend, is born of trust (Winnicott, 1965). It is inimical to denying one's own feelings to attend only to those of others. Tami appeared to serve the buffering function that we discussed earlier, providing some relief for Maria from her role as well as giving her an opportunity to process her pain.

Identity development and leaving home. Because of their submission to the needs of their families, destructively parentified children are unable to explore and to solidify their own identities. They are at risk of internalizing the parentified role and of becoming compulsive caregivers (Bowlby, 1979; Jurkovic, 1997). Maria's identity was that of being the daughter of Marlene Dietrich.

> There was a time in my childhood when I actually believed that was my name. I remember writing a thank-you note for some gift I had received and signing "Sincerely Yours, Maria Daughter of Marlene Dietrich." My mother, on checking it over, declared my note "perfect" and sent it off. The memory still embarrasses me. (Riva, 1992, p. 280)

In a disturbing passage, Maria discusses the consequences of her lack of self-reference when she was older.

> In some ways, I was trained for rape. Always obedient, always trying to please those in charge of me, pliable, an owned object, conditioned to usage. If you don't have an identity and someone helps themselves to you, you respond more passively, you're so unaccustomed to the right to question. Oh, I ran. In my own way I ran, but I had nowhere to go, no one to listen and be kind—even if I could have found the right words. [I hid] it—let it fester, become my private hell. Becoming damaged through the instigated negligence of the one nature and society recognize as your "loving" parent begets a special hell. (Riva, 1992, p. 500)

Indeed, destructive parentification that begins early in the lives of youngsters leaves them susceptible to intra- and extrafamilial exploitation, including sexual abuse. Furthermore, as Maria painfully reveals, once violated they lack the social and personal resources to work through their trauma. In a recent study, we discovered that the traumatizing effects of sexual abuse may be potentiated by a history of destructive parentification (Jurkovic & Martin, 1999).

Related to their difficulty in forming an identity, destructively parentified children often struggle with the developmental process of leaving home. To leave is to be disloyal. Like Maria, many attempt to extricate themselves from their families through marriage.

> I found someone who was willing to marry me and thought salvation was at hand. . . . Of course, this desperate attempt at escape, this pathetic self-delusion of normalcy, was doomed

from the start. The so-called marriage was finished before it ever began. (Riva, 1992, p. 527)

The escape route for others often includes substance abuse and promiscuity. Maria abused alcohol and became mired in depression.

For me, life lost its color. Became a sameness. Meaningless hours—to meaningless days that ended in empty weeks that became meaningless hours on their way to infinity. (Riva, 1992, p. 543)

Even after successfully establishing a separate residence, parentified children qua adults may continue to discharge their emotional and instrumental responsibilities to their families of origin. Their families, moreover, may continue to recruit them to do so. After Maria remarried and had children, her mother attempted to maintain her desperate hold on her. When that failed, she told her grandson how his mother had abused him in an effort to co-opt him and indirectly to retain possession of her daughter.

Discussion

Maria Riva's story graphically illustrates how one family member's high performance and career achievements can be leveraged by the parentification of others in the family. Because of her daughter's stabilizing influence, Marlene Dietrich was able to sustain her long and productive career as a performing artist. As she stated, without Maria she was "nothing." Maria was her raison d'être. In other cases, the spouses of high-performing family members may call on one of the children to fill the void in their marriages (Mitchell & Cronson, 1987).

Just as LBJ was destructively parentified in his family, so was Maria but in a different way. As discussed earlier, LBJ's parentification had, to a significant degree, a narcissistic quality. He was charged by his mother to gratify her unfulfilled dreams; Maria was primarily parentified in a masochistic (self-defeating) fashion by being conscripted to satisfy her mother's needs for emotional and physical caretaking (Jones & Wells, 1996). Rather than compelling her to achieve great things, her masochistic parentification was designed to ensure her mother's success.

Nevertheless, LBJ and Maria experienced many of the same consequences as a result of their varying forms of destructive parentification. For example, both struggled with identity concerns and more basic questions about self-worth. As their stories reflect, the destructively parentified child is treated as a part object whose value fluctuates depending on whether the parentifying party's needs are gratified. Such conditional regard and associated distrust form the matrix for a variety of personal and relational problems.

Yet, LBJ and Maria's resilience supported by buffering figures (e.g., Tami, the lover of Maria's father) mollified the destructiveness of their parentification. For example, at 6 years of age, Maria changed her name to "Heidede" in an effort to differentiate herself from her mother. Johnson left home at the age of 15 to escape the oppressive influence of his mother. Both became increasingly aware of the emotional entrapment of their parentified role. Even though many of their behaviors and adaptations appeared pathological on the surface, they also reflected their valiant attempts, however misguided, to give voice to their true selves while at the same time remaining loyal to their families. However, as seen in the cases of LBJ and Maria, the sacrifices and selfhood of the destructively parentified child are seldom acknowledged.

The contributions of parentified family members in earlier generations to the accomplishments of their successors are also often overlooked. Indeed, we found some evidence that the beneficiaries of parentification in high-performing families may be more than one generation removed. For example, before former President Jimmy Carter was born, his paternal grandfather, William Carter, was killed in an altercation in 1903. Alton ("Buddy") Carter, William's eldest son and Jimmy's uncle, assumed full control of the family at the age of 16. Within a short period of time he moved his mother, sisters, and brother, James Earl Carter (Jimmy's father) to Plains, Georgia (Morris, 1996).

Relieved of his older brother's parental responsibilities, James Earl or Earl, as he was called, was able to continue his schooling rather than quit as soon as he was old enough to work like the other Carter offspring. He proceeded after a brief stint as a cowboy in Texas and a member of the armed forces to become a successful businessman and farmer in southwest Georgia (Morris, 1996). He, in turn, was capable of providing his family, including Jimmy, his oldest son, opportunities that helped them to realize their aspirations in life. It can be argued that the earlier parentification of Uncle Buddy contributed, however indirectly, to Jimmy Carter's accomplishments. More systematic research tracing the intergenerational effects, both positive and negative, of parentification in families would enrich our understanding in this area.

Clinical Implications

The case material presented in this chapter points to a number of issues that therapists should consider in their clinical work with high-profile individuals and their families. Our discussion of these issues is informed primarily by the complementary emphases of Boszormenyi-Nagy (Boszormenyi-Nagy & Krasner, 1986) and Bowen (1978; Kerr & Bowen, 1988) on relational ethics and differentiation, respectively (see also Jurkovic, 1997).

1. It is important in therapy of high-profile individuals and their families to entertain the possibility that parentification plays a direct or indirect role in both their strength and their distress. Parentification in families may follow different pathways. As we have illustrated, two prominent ones in the families of high-profile individuals include (a) the progression from a high-performing parentified childhood to a high-performing adulthood and (b) the parentification of a child to support the high performance of a parental figure.

   In attempting to uncover parentification, the therapist should not underestimate the parentified individual's loyalty to his or her family of origin (Boszormenyi-Nagy & Spark, 1973). Indeed, therapists who are hoodwinked by their parentified clients' conforming presentation and well-varnished descriptions of their families often miss destructive forms of this process. Along these lines, Miller (1981) sardonically observed, I had completed two analyses as part of my psychoanalytic training, but both analysts had been unable to question my version of the happy childhood I supposedly had enjoyed (p. viii).

   One frequently overlooked clue of destructive parentification is excessively compliant and helpful behavior on the part of a child. This dynamic has been referred to as the "well sibling" in the family therapy literature (Boszormenyi-Nagy & Spark, 1973; Framo, 1965; Friedman, 1964). Speaking from personal experience, Maria Riva (1992) observed, "I am always suspicious of perfectly behaved children and their self-satisfied parents. I search: Somewhere behind that ideal exterior, there may be a real child, crying to get out" (p. 181).

2. In the interest of preserving the public image of the high-profile member or members, everyone in the family may collude to mask the truth. The therapist's ability to acknowledge each family member's contributions, particularly those parentified

in current and past generations, to the well-being and success of the family can be a powerful entrée into the family's emotional system. It can also lay the groundwork for encouraging family members to credit one another, fostering their sense of familial and personal solidarity. Ultimately, as a critical self-differentiating step, the parentified individual can be helped to credit himself or herself.

Relatedly, credit should also be extended to intra- and extrafamilial figures who supported the destructively parentified family member and encouraged him or her to express his or her true self. Recall Maria Riva's childhood relationship with Tami. It may be helpful to encourage the destructively parentified client to reconnect with these individuals. By doing so, they often quickly regain a sense of hope and reactivate a dormant part of themselves.

A complementary aspect of acknowledgment is recognition of family members' unmet entitlements, including those of the parentifiers. Typically, parentifying activities are motivated by the parentifiers' attempts to redress their own privations and abuses as children. Capturing the essence of this dynamic, Steinem (1992b) stated that the "needy child of yesterday *inside the parent* is dominating the child of today" (p. 71).

3. Yet, just as all deserving persons should be acknowledged, so should everyone, including the nonparentifying parent, be held accountable. For example, although Maria Riva's father did not overtly parentify his daughter, he contributed to her painful subjugation at the hands of her mother through his inaction. The goal is not to blame but rather to help family members assume responsibility for their behavior and to make appropriate reparations. Placing their actions in an intergenerational context, that is, explaining them in light of dynamic patterns originating in earlier generations, can facilitate this process. It can also help the parentified victims to exonerate their parentifiers even if the latter are unable to address their errant child rearing.

4. It is also important not to focus exclusively on the negative outcomes of destructive parentification. As we saw in the examples reviewed earlier, this process often has auspicious results, which may figure critically in an individual's career success. Recognition of this fact can help parentified individuals

to find meaning in their hurtful experiences as a child. Moreover, even the apparently negative sequelae of destructive parentification may represent the individual's fight for self-definition and authenticity. The therapist who sees all symptoms in absolutistic terms, that is, as either good or bad, will miss countless opportunities to help his or her clients catch healing glimpses of their true selves.

5. Not all parentification is destructive. In many instances, children's caregiving activities are appropriately supported and reciprocated within the family and are part of a culturally prescriptive process (Jurkovic, 1997). This was true in Jocelyn Elders' case, for example. Therapists who are not sensitive to cultural features that help determine whether parentification is adaptive or maladaptive risk inappropriately pathologizing all forms of parentification.

6. High achievers who are dutifully fulfilling their parents' dreams and caregivers who are compulsively playing their parentified role in extrafamilial as well as intrafamilial settings must be helped to differentiate sufficiently from their family of origin and their parentified role to decide for themselves their life course. Are the roles that they are enacting as adults—roles that may bring them considerable attention, praise, and notoriety—the products of their own self-differentiated choices? Answering such a question requires that they also reexamine their overweening loyalty to their families. The balancing of self-definition and sociofamilial obligation is a formidable challenge for individuals with a history of destructive parentification. Helping these individuals simply entertain the question of whether a better balance is desirable can have a salutary effect.

7. In the process of "de-roling," as it were, parentified individuals typically confront the loss of parental nurturance and protection that they experienced growing up. Gloria Steinem (1992b) realized in a therapy session, "For the first time, I would have to admit just how much I had missed having a mother" (p. 190). The seemingly inexplicable dysphoria that many parentified clients report is often part of an unidentified and complicated grief reaction. By labeling it as such, the therapist facilitates the client's ability to mourn openly and completely. Grief work with parentified individuals is frequently a

necessary stepping stone in their journey to a more solid sense of self and healthier relationships with others.

Conclusion

We continue to be impressed with the pervasiveness of parentification in families from every walk of life. In addition to having elucidated the dynamics of this process in families generally and high-profile ones specifically, it is hoped that the present chapter has raised questions warranting further investigation and has highlighted key issues in the therapy of high-profile persons and their families. Because of space limitations, we could not expound on all the ways in which the parentification process played out in the high-profile individuals considered. The reader is encouraged to peruse the source material for this chapter to appreciate more fully the implications of the lives of these individuals for theory, research, and practice in the area of parentification.

References

Boszormenyi-Nagy, I. (1987). *Foundations of contextual therapy*. Philadelphia: Brunner/Mazel.

Boszormenyi-Nagy, I., & Krasner, B. R. (1986). *Between give and take: A clinical guide to contextual therapy*. Philadelphia: Brunner/Mazel.

Boszormenyi-Nagy, I., & Spark, G. M. (1973). *Invisible loyalties: Reciprocity in intergenerational family therapy*. Hagerstown, MD: Harper & Row.

Bowen, M. (1978). *Family therapy in clinical practice*. New York: Aronson.

Bowlby, J. (1979). *The making and breaking of affectional bonds*. London: Tavistock.

Chase, N. D. (Ed.). (1999). *Burdened children: Theory, research, and treatment of parentification*. Thousands Oaks, CA: Sage.

Dart, B. (1999, June 27). The growing power of Maria Echaveste. *The Atlanta Journal-Constitution*, pp. M1, M3.

Elders, J., & Chanoff, D. (1997). *Jocelyn Elders, MD: From sharecropper's daughter to surgeon general of the United States of America*. New York: Avon Books.

Erikson, E. (1969). *Gandhi's truth: On the origins of militant nonviolence*. New York: Norton.

Framo, J. L. (1965). Systemic research on family dynamics. In I. Boszormenyi-Nagy & J. L. Framo (Eds.), *Intensive family therapy: Theoretical and practical aspects* (pp. 407–462). New York: Harper & Row.

Friedman, A. S. (1964). The "well" sibling in the sick family: A contradiction. *International Journal of Social Psychiatry, 2,* 47–53.

Ginzberg, L. (1956). *Legends of the bible.* Philadelphia: Jewish Publication Society of America.

Goodwin, D. K. (1991). *Lyndon Johnson and the American dream.* New York: St. Martin's Griffin.

Heilbrun, C. G. (1995). *The education of a woman: The life of Gloria Steinem.* New York: Ballantine Books.

Henley, L., & Silbar, J. (1982). Wind beneath my wings [Recorded by Bette Midler]. On *Beaches* [record]. New York: Atlantic Records. (1990)

Hesse, H. (1949). *Magister Ludi* (M. Savill, Trans.). New York: Ungar. (Original work published 1943)

Hetherington, E. M. (1999). Should we stay together for the sake of the children? In E. M. Hetherington (Ed.), *Coping with divorce, single parenting, and remarriage: A risk and resiliency perspective.* Mahwah, NJ: Erlbaum.

Jones, R., & Wells, M. (1996). An empirical study of parentification and personality. *American Journal of Family Therapy, 24,* 145–152.

Jung, C. G. (1966). *The practice of psychotherapy* (2nd ed., R.R.C Hull, Trans.). Princeton, NJ: Princeton University Press.

Jurkovic, G. J. (1997). *Lost childhoods: The plight of the parentified child.* Philadelphia: Brunner/Mazel.

Jurkovic, G. J. (1998). Destructive parentification in families: Causes and consequences. In L. L'Abate (Ed.), *Family psychopathology: The relational roots of dysfunctional behavior* (pp. 237–255). New York: Guilford Press.

Jurkovic, G. J., Kuperminc, G. P., Perilla, J., Murphy, A. D., Ibanez, G., & Casey, S. (2000). *The role of parentification and cultural–ecological processes in school and social adjustment of immigrant Latino adolescents.* Manuscript submitted for publication.

Jurkovic, G. J., & Martin, J. (1999, April). *Parentification, sexual abuse, and posttraumatic stress.* Poster presented at the meeting of the American Association of Marriage and Family Therapy, Chicago.

Jurkovic, G. J., Morrell, R., & Thirkield, A. (1999). Assessment of childhood parentification: Guidelines for researchers and clinicians. In N. Chase (Ed.), *Burdened children: Theory, research, and treatment of parentification* (pp. 92–113). Thousand Oaks, CA: Sage.

Kerr, M. E., & Bowen, M. (1988). *Family evaluation.* New York: Norton.

Lackie, B. (1983). The families of origin of social workers. *Clinical Social Work Journal, 11,* 309–322.

Miller, A. (1981). *Prisoners of childhood: The drama of the gifted child and the search for the true self.* New York: Basic Books.

Mitchell, G., & Cronson, H. (1987). The celebrity family: A clinical perspective. *American Journal of Family Therapy, 15,* 235–241.

Morris, K. E. (1996). *Jimmy Carter: American moralist.* Athens: University of Georgia Press.

Riva, M. (1992). *Marlene Dietrich.* New York: Knopf.

Robinson, B. E. (1998). *Chained to the desk: A guidebook for workaholics, their partners and children, and the clinicians who treat them.* New York: New York University Press.

Searles, H. F. (1971). Pathological symbiosis and autism. In B. Landis & E. S. Touber (Eds.), *In the name of life: Essays in honor of Erich Fromm.* New York: Holt, Rinehart, & Winston.

Sessions, M. (1986.) *Influence of parentification, professional role choice and interpersonal style. Dissertation Abstracts International, 47,* 5066. (University Microfilms No. 87-06815)

Sidey, H. S. (1994). *Johnson, Lyndon Baines.* New York: Funk & Wagnalls.

Steinem, G. (1983). *Outrageous acts and everyday rebellions* (2nd ed.). New York: Henry Holt.

Steinem, G. (1992a). Foreword. In B. E. Robinson, *Overdoing it* (pp. ix–xv). Deerfield Beach, FL: Health Communications.

Steinem, G. (1992b). *Revolution from within: A book of self-esteem.* Boston: Little, Brown.

Stierlin, H. (1974). *Separating parents and adolescents: A perspective on running away, schizophrenia, and waywardness.* New York: Quadrangle.

Streif, M. (1997). *Marlene: Meik's tribute to the goddess of the century* [On-Line]. Available: www.ivnet.co.at/streif/biograph.htm.

Winnicott, D. W. (1965). *Maturational processes and the facilitating environment: Studies in the theory of emotional development.* New York: International Universities Press.

Zahn-Waxler, C., & Robinson, J. (1995). Empathy and guilt: Early origins of feelings of responsibility. In J. P. Tangney & K. W. Fischer (Eds.), *Self-conscious emotions: The psychology of shame, guilt, embarrassment, and pride* (pp. 143–173). New York: Guilford Press.

■ ■ ■

7

Parentified Children Grow Up: Dual Patterns of High and Low Functioning

Nancy D. Chase, PhD, MSW

In J. D. Salinger's (1953) short story, *Teddy*, a precocious 10-year-old boy, caught between wealthy and bickering parents, offers insight and wise counsel to surrounding adults. In a moment of intimate revelation, Teddy describes his family.

> I have a very strong affinity for them. They're my parents, I mean, and we're all part of each other's harmony and everything. . . . I want them to have a nice time while they're alive, because they like having a nice time. . . . But they don't love me and Booper—that's my sister—that way. I mean they don't seem able to love us just the way we are. They don't seem able to love us unless they can keep changing us a little bit. They love their reasons for loving us as much as they love us, and most of the time more. It's not so good, that way. (p. 187)

At the end of the story Teddy dies, apparently by suicide in a swimming pool on an ocean liner cruise, although details of his death are left to speculation. Nowhere is there a more apt description of the parentified child's dilemma: useful and overfunctioning in his precocity, yet invisible in terms of his true nature, needs, and selfhood.

Self-inflicted annihilation of this character only makes tangible the identity he has lost as a child, drowning, so to speak, in a sea of adult projections and expectations.

Let us suppose that this story's outcome was different: Teddy perseveres and endures his serious and adultlike childhood. What kind of adult life would follow his foreclosed childhood? Would he be angry and disappointed in a marriage like his parents? Would he enjoy pleasures of wealth and ambition? As a bright and over-functioning child, would he be destined as an adult to great successes, achievements, and contributions to humanity? Embedded in Salinger's story is the intricate and paradoxical relationship between high-functioning behavior and one's deterioration, or demise, especially for children who are called to function beyond their years in achievement-oriented or caretaking ways. In families in which compulsive work habits and high performance are valued to the exclusion of positive connection, well-being, and intimacy in family relations, children are at risk for becoming as pseudomature, stressed, and overfunctioning as Teddy—at risk for becoming parentified as children (see chapters 5 and 6 of this monograph). Moreover, like Teddy, these children learn that in their parents' eyes love and nurturance are awarded according to an ethos of accomplishment, loyalty, and duty to overperform.

Recently, a National Public Radio (Weiss, 1999) feature on the life of baseball great, Joe DiMaggio, revealed an interesting and sad irony: DiMaggio's heir, an adult son, lived a reclusive life housed in a trailer in an isolated western mountain region, imprisoned by the shadow of his father's fame. How did it happen that the offspring of such a talented and legendary hero became in his own life so apparently devoid of success? Literature, biography, and media are filled with stories of ambitious and highly accomplished parents whose children are flunking out of school or drifting aimlessly through life without motivation, commitment, achievement, and contentment (Coles, 1977; Johnson, 1993; Maraniss, 1999; Pittman, 1985). Metaphorically speaking, there is evidence to say that the cobbler's kids indeed have no shoes. Yet, the question remains: How can such hard-working and well-intentioned parents raise so many directionless, uninspired children or, equally disturbing, raise children who are driven self-destructively by a need to achieve at any cost?

This chapter proposes some answers to these questions by examining adult legacies of *childhood parentification* wherein parentified children relinquish many of the normal, appropriate activities and emotional needs of childhood. They construct a "false self" that is consonant with the wishes, needs, and vulnerabilities of the parent and wear a cloak of maturity and vigilance long before they are ready psychologically or physically for such responsibility, or worse, before they are able to protect themselves from such enmeshment (Miller, 1981).

Two hypotheses, both supported by empirical and qualitative research on families, serve as the theoretical foundation for this chapter: parentification in severe form is inherently an overfunctioning role for children that yields long-term deleterious effects; and of further relevance to the topic of this monograph, children in compulsively high-performing, workaholic families are at risk for parentification and its long-term adult consequences (Chase, 1999; Jurkovic, 1997, 1998; Robinson, 1998a, 1998b). On the basis of these assumptions, this chapter examines dual patterns of high and low functioning in the lives of adults who were parentified as children, particularly those from high-performance families. By illustrating the paradoxical high and low functioning often seen in adults who were parentified, I hope to extend discussions about positive and negative legacies of childhood parentification with speculation about its etiological connection to family workaholism. Noted outcomes of childhood parentification such as enmeshment with others, codependency, and an undifferentiated sense of self make it difficult, if not impossible, for parentified individuals to live adult lives in balanced and productive, yet healthy ways. This discussion identifies characteristics and consequences of parentification and its effects in high-performing families specifically, and it argues that parentification in these families can be as prevalent and deleterious as in alcoholic or abusive families. Suggestions are made for counselors working with adult clients who are attempting to break the long-standing, perpetuating, and painful paradoxical cycles of confusing imbalances in relationships and work that mark the lives of adults with parentification history.

What Is Childhood Parentification?

A growing body of empirical investigations and anecdotal observations define and describe parentification (Chase, 1999). The conditions for destructive parentification occur in families when imbalances in the relationships between parents and their children persist and place excessive emotional or logistical demands on children or adolescents to function prematurely as if they were adults. Parentifying children, that is, elevating them to an adultlike position of power and responsibility, is sometimes the solution families seek when adults are distracted or absent from ongoing participation in family life as is often found in workaholic or high-performing families, or when adults are incapacitated by illness, or when they are unable to resolve disappointments in career or relationship areas of their lives (see chapters 5 and 6 of this monograph). This solution, although usually effective in keeping the family running smoothly, comes at a long-term psychological expense to children (Chase, 1999; Jurkovic, 1997, 1998).

When parentification is a *chronic, unspoken, and excessive* family dynamic, children and adolescents assume pseudomature functioning too early in their own development while adults abdicate parental functioning in areas such as nurturing, guiding, comforting, and protecting their offspring. As children are elevated to positions of emotional or logistical power in the family, in turn, adult abdication of functioning often reduces the parent to childlike helplessness or indulgences in irresponsible behavior or emotion. Parentification of children has been associated with dynamics existing in alcoholic families (Bekir, McLellan, Childress, & Gariti, 1993; Chase, Deming, & Wells, 1998; Goglia, Jurkovic, Burt, & Burge-Callaway, 1992; Robinson & Rhoden, 1998; West & Prinz, 1987), families with intense marital discord and disappointment (Buchanan, Maccoby, & Dornbusch, 1991; Cummings, Zahn-Waxler, & Radke-Yarrow, 1984; Hetherington, 1988; Howes & Markman, 1989; Johnston, 1990; Mahler & Rabinovitch, 1956; Wiess, 1999), work-addicted families (Carroll & Robinson, in press; Robinson, 1998a, 1998b; Robinson, Carroll, & Flowers, in press; Robinson & Post, 1995), and families in which a parent dies, suffers a prolonged mental or physical illness, or in some way is incapacitated in adult functioning (Downey & Coyne, 1990; Main & Hesse, 1990; Morris & Gould, 1963; Zahn-Waxler, Cummings, Iannotti, & Radke-Yarrow, 1984; Zahn-Waxler, Kochanska, Krupnick, & McKnew, 1990). The parentified child is typically described as a child who is keenly attuned to the emotional and logistical needs of the family and behaves in ways that "help" keep the family operating. The role of "hero child" prevalent in the literature on family alcoholism is akin to the parentified role but does not encompass the full range of behavioral and emotional experiences assumed by the child who is parentified. Whereas overachievement is the hallmark of hero children who keep the family looking good, the parentified child may or may not display personal high achievements or successes depending on the nature of caretaking the family requires. A parentified child may be so bound by the needs of others that no time or energy remains for his or her own accomplishments to blossom (Karpel, 1976).

All families to some degree, and on occasion, place overfunctioning demands on their children, especially in times of crisis and stress. Jurkovic (1997) distinguished *destructive or pathological* from *adaptive* parentification. The former requires long-term, unacknowledged, and age-inappropriate contributions from the child (e.g., mediating ongoing parental marital conflict), whereas the latter asks of the child to contribute to the family's well-being in ways that are time-limited, acknowledged, and clarified directly and do not overtax the child emotionally or physically (e.g., missing baseball practice to help with younger siblings during a parent's short hospitalization). Because of the denial system operative in families plagued by addiction, it is likely that parentification in high-performing families would remain unacknowledged and chronic, and thus potentially destructive to the child's well-being. Just as there is a necessary distinction between *healthy* high performers and *compulsive* high performers, not all parentifying experiences are pathological. Such distinctions are important in making these constructs viable areas for research as well as practically valuable to clinicians (Jurkovic, 1997).

Parentified children respond to the spoken or unspoken expectation that they fill the adult parental void in numerous ways (Boszormenyi-Nagy & Spark, 1973; Coale, 1999; Jones & Wells, 1996; Miller, 1981; Robinson, 1999; Wells & Jones, 1998). They may behave as overly responsible and serious children, in essence, raising themselves and in some cases their younger siblings. They may behave as pseudosophisticated children and relate in peerlike fashion to adults, advising and comforting their unhappy, distressed parents or teasing and entertaining their parents in a peerlike or spouselike fashion. Parentified children may also display excessive worry about their parents or siblings and engage in nurturing behaviors, such as caring for ailing parents, tracking their moods and needs, coddling them, soothing them, or ensuring that other children in the household are attended to so as not to disturb the stressed, ill, or preoccupied adults (Boszormenyi-Nagy & Spark, 1973; Karpel, 1976; Lamorey, 1999). Oddly enough, a child's need to be what his or her parents need, in some cases, also induces infantilized, overly dependent, or developmentally incompetent, acting-out behaviors in children if it serves to enhance the parental functioning of the adult. For example, a child's school failure can draw the attention of a busy father, a temper tantrum can rally a depressed mother from her bed, or a troubled adolescent can distract parents from the unresolved conflicts in their marriage (Boszormenyi-Nagy & Spark, 1973; Bowen, 1978; Coale, 1999; Jones & Wells, 1996).

It is possible, thus, to conceptualize parentification as an effort by all family members to correct functional or emotional imbalances in the family within and across generations. The parentified child provides what is needed and sometimes *overfunctions* (even in some cases as "the baby" to appease indulgent parents) as compensation for the adults' deficits or *underfunctioning* (Boszormenyi-Nagy & Spark, 1973). Whatever the specific manifestations of a parentified role, children pay the price by learning that their own needs to be vulnerable, attended to, and parented as children— cornerstones of a child's development of a valued sense of self— are overridden by the more powerful, dominating deficits and preoccupations of adults. Inherent in the parentification dynamic, thus, is a dialectic of overfunctioning and underfunctioning in the family as a whole, and it carries a legacy across generations of imbalanced functioning into the lives of all individuals caught in these relational patterns (Boszormenyi-Nagy & Spark, 1973; Bowen, 1978).

Parentification in High-Performing Families

Numerous theoretical explanations, research descriptions, and clinical issues related to parentification and its immediate and long-term effects are found in books (Chase, 1999; Jurkovic, 1997, 1998; Robinson, 1998a) and journal articles (Barnett & Parker, 1998; Carroll & Robinson, in press; Fullinwider-Bush & Jacobvitz, 1993; Valleau, Bergner, & Horton, 1995; Wells & Jones, 1998; West & Keller, 1991) and have been mentioned in previous chapters of this monograph. Publications since the 1970s and earlier have made initial observations and have developed definitions of parentification that contributed to the theoretical foundation and clinical documentation for understanding these phenomena and have inspired many empirical investigations over several decades (Boszormenyi-Nagy & Spark, 1973; Bowen, 1978; Karpel, 1976; Minuchin, Montalvo, Guerney, Rosman, & Schumer, 1967; Schmideberg, 1948).

Investigations of parentification as it appears in families of career-focused, high-achieving professionals have been few but are quite noteworthy in the insights they offer (Carroll & Robinson, in press; Keele, 1984; Mitchell & Cronson, 1987). According to these studies, it is characteristic of some "professional families" to organize in ways that support high performance and achievement for one member, usually the one capable of producing the greatest income and recognition. Such "support" for career pursuits excuses this member, traditionally the father, from direct participation in home life, or even in maintaining intimate connection with the spouse and children. Thus, Dad's overfunctioning outside the family allows him to underfunction in his relationships at home, and the stage is then set for further imbalances to emerge (Robinson, 1998a). Lacking spousal involvement, Mom may become overly involved with her children and actually designate one child as surrogate for her absent adult partner, soliciting the child's excessive input and attention in family affairs. It is not unusual for children in such families to willingly sacrifice their own goals and endeavors in compliance to expectations that they too "help" Dad by supporting Mom. Not only are children at risk for becoming parentified, but in such a dynamic, which requires their overfunctioning at home, they may unwittingly function less outside the home in activities that are rewarding and enhance growth. In fact, Karpel (1976, p. 365) cited that one of the great losses endured by children who are parentified is that they become "bound to the constellation of the home" emotionally, if not also physically, and miss out on many important aspects of childhood experienced with peers and in activities beyond the family.

Mitchell and Cronson (1987) described a career-focused family in which the father was a "celebrity" professional athlete. The full energies of all the family members revolved around the development of the father's career, which meant long absences from the household and, subsequently, a marriage empty of emotional and logistical support. As predicted, the oldest boy "filled-in" as the mother's confidante and helper. Problems did not arise in this arrangement until the "spousified" child reached adolescence and became indifferent to his mother's needs as well as angry and confused by his father's episodic interventions. Ingrained with a privileged and pseudomature role assumed for years, this young man began to simply ignore all efforts at parental structure. The crisis of adolescent rebellion prompted the family to seek professional help and reevaluate the overt and covert expectations imposed by the father's primary relationship to his career. Keele (1984) had previously documented similar patterns of imbalanced functioning in families of highly successful business executives.

The following descriptions of Randy and Stephanie present two other profiles of how parentification manifests in high-performing, overworking families. With the increase of dual-career families in the past two decades and the economic challenges often faced by single-parent homes, such stereotypical family roles as described by Mitchell and Cronson (1987) do not provide the only template for parentification in workaholic families.

The Case of Randy

Randy, a university student on academic suspension, described his mother's reaction to his academic failure.

> My mother has no idea and doesn't understand why I can't get it together and just do it [college]. She's a nurse, works in a hospital and runs her own private care business on the side. She works all the time, and makes money. She loves her work. She's real organized. She tells me to get more disciplined and I can do anything. I help out around the house. I'm the oldest— three children. And I'm expected to go to med school—and yeah—I wanta go to med school. But I don't really talk to my mother much about it . . . you see why?

At a later time, Randy told of how his mother used to "bail me out" when he faced challenges or unmet deadlines in his early years of schooling. Although a bright and capable boy, Randy described that sometimes he would not do his homework simply because he knew that his mother, frustrated and in a rush, would do it for him. Randy's mother blamed his teachers or the school "atmosphere" when Randy expressed disinterest or low motivation in academics, and she provided little supervision or structure to help Randy accomplish many of the school and social tasks children face. Yet, Randy, who presented himself as poised, intelligent, and articulate, also learned that he could please his mother by setting high, distant goals and expressing career ambitions in the medical field, especially because his younger brother and sister showed little inclination in this direction. Because of the lack of sufficient support from other adults, it seemed that the mother's focus on her own stressful career while raising three children made it easier, expedient, and possibly less embarrassing to rescue Randy rather than help structure and parent him. In turn, Randy was elevated to the status of "man of the house," assisted with the care of his younger siblings, cooked regularly, contributed to the family budget with odd jobs, was congenial, and stayed out of any "serious" trouble. By all appearances, Randy cooperated with his mother's wish that the family excel. Rather than consider a change of major or explore other career possibilities, he persistently held to dreams and high aspirations for future accomplishment, like medical school, despite repeated failure in undergraduate science courses.

The Case of Stephanie

Stephanie was the 15-year-old daughter of dual-career parents. Her father was a corporate attorney and her mother a private-practice physician. Stephanie and her younger sister, Elizabeth, were inundated with the accolades of affluence afforded by the professional successes of their parents. In addition to their enrollment in an elite and rigorous private school where they both demonstrated high achievements in academics and sports, these children had been sent to camps and on travel expeditions worldwide, and had been indulged since a very young age with seemingly all their material wishes from extravagant clothes to toys, computers, sound and video systems, and sporting equipment. At 15, Stephanie was miserably depressed and confused. The girls had been "trained" since elementary school to conduct their daily lives in much the same highly scheduled and accomplishment-focused way as their parents, with calendars, beepers, schedules, appointments, and production goals. In a sense, even as young children and now teenagers, they conducted themselves as "little professionals"—orderly, self-sufficient, and cooperative. In Stephanie's words, echoing the despair of adolescent characters in J. D. Salinger's (1953) fiction, "all my parents talk about is what I do or what they do . . . how I have improved in something or wrote a great term paper, how Elizabeth won a swim meet, or how Dad performed in a trial . . . that's all we ever talk about and all they care about." Stephanie's observation appeared validated when 9 weeks passed without the entire family even having an overnight at home together because of fluctuating vacations, sports camps, consulting trips, and work-related travel. During 3 of these weeks, the children stayed at home with a hired au-pair who transported and supervised the kids in the execution of their usual routines while the parents were in Europe at an international professional conference. Communication was conducted via electronic mail and voice mail, and Stephanie acknowledged that she knew her mother *did* worry about Elizabeth and her because sometimes her mother "was there" for them. Stephanie presented herself as a haggard, yet driven, and unhappy faux-40-year-old with normal 15-year-old needs, angers, and fears brewing beneath the facade of competent sophistication. The void Stephanie described was understandable; these children were virtually operating as their parents colleagues or proteges and were, to a great extent, left on their own emotionally despite their parents' genuine concern and good intentions. They got needed compassion and intimacy from each other and their peers, but their development into adolescents became rife with complications and confusions without close, trusting relationships with supportive adults.

Case Analyses

Although in very different family circumstances, Stephanie and Randy both showed signs of struggling with being parentified. Neither demonstrate the traditional profile of parentified child caring for an ill or depressed, underfunctioning parent. On the contrary, the parents in these scenarios fit generic definitions of high-functioning, career-successful individuals, and thus these cases provide examples of the ways parentification emerges in high-performing families. Most definitions of parentification entail two fundamental components: (a) the adult's abdication of parenting (nurturance, guidance, comfort, mirroring, structure, protection, resources) and (b) the child's compensatory efforts, which exceed developmental appropriateness in response to parental abdication (Jurkovic, 1997; Karpel, 1976). Both Randy and Stephanie are missing out on some important aspects of being parented, and both are demonstrating long-standing efforts on their part to "self-parent" at ages when they are still in need of structure, guidance, and emotional comfort from adults. Furthermore, it can be construed that Randy and Stephanie are, in-fact, "caretaking" their busy, career-oriented parents by being such competent, nontroublesome children. They have made it easier for their parents to pursue high-demand careers by being children who required low-demand parenting. Yet, as these scenarios reveal, the price of their parentification eventually becomes evident in some form of the child's distress, a price that surfaced emotionally for Stephanie and academically for Randy.

The specific characteristics of the parentified behaviors exhibited by Randy and Stephanie are another distinguishing factor. Randy's parentification was primarily instrumental (performing tangible caregiving tasks) with some emotional aspects related to "looking good" for normalizing the family. Stephanie's parentification was largely emotional (mirroring the values and ambitions of her parents) and entailed an acceleration of her emotional world in addition to an exaggerated emphasis on high achievement as the family standard.

In later sections of this chapter, adult legacies according to the quality of parentification experience are discussed. It is evident that

Randy may be a candidate for self-defeating, caretaking patterns and related low functioning as is already appearing in his confusion about his education. Stephanie, in contrast and despite her current depression, might find her adult life driven and measured by her accomplishments, giving her an appearance of high functioning that in actuality may be the facade covering an emotional void and lack of connectedness to herself and others, a facade analogous to the pseudosophistication she now presents.

Research on Parentification and Young Adults

Robinson and Post (1995) conducted the only study to date on the impact of work addiction on the entire family (see chapter 1). They found that workaholism was associated with dysfunctional family interaction patterns. In a separate study, young adults who self-reported having work-addicted parents showed higher scores on a parentification measure and depression measure than young adult offspring from alcoholic homes (Carroll & Robinson, in press). In other words, children and adolescents of high-performing, overworked, successful, but highly stressed parents may be, as a variety of studies support, at greater risk for depression, anxiety, an external locus of control, and parentification (Carroll & Robinson, in press; Robinson & Kelley, 1998; Robinson & Post, 1995). Chase et al. (1998) found that young adults with lower S.A.T. scores and high school grade point averages also reported that they carried excessive emotional and logistical burdens at home, scored higher than controls on a parentification measure, and thus, theoretically, were at risk for underfunctioning outside the home (e.g., at school).

Others have documented the long-term effects of having functioned as a parentified child as these children transition into adulthood, especially as found in studies on college-age populations (Burt, 1992; Chase et al., 1998; Fullinwider-Bush & Jacobvitz, 1993; Goglia et al., 1992; Jones & Wells, 1996; Wells & Jones, 1998; Wolkin, 1984). Despite having exhibited overly competent and responsible behaviors as children, many parentified children struggle with becoming independent, productive adults, and the transition from adolescence to young adulthood can be particularly rocky for these children, who have built their psychological world around the needs and reactions of their parents. It can be difficult to pursue relationships outside the family, academics, and career interests if one is continuing to fulfill a parentified role in one's family of origin (Berman & Sperling, 1991; Bloom, 1987; Held & Bellows, 1983).

Fullinwider-Bush and Jacobvitz (1993) found that parentification affected later relationship and career decisions for young women. When parentification alliances existed with the mother, the daughters were likely to simply follow a path of identity that reflected their parents' values and expectations regarding relationships and career without questioning or exploring new or different directions from those prescribed by the parents. When the parentification occurred as a father–daughter alliance, even greater dysfunction was indicated in young women's efforts to develop an independent identity. Daughters who had served as surrogate spouses (companion and confidante) to their fathers showed an especially low level of commitment to any career and relationship pursuits (Fullinwider-Bush & Jacobvitz, 1993; Jacobvitz, Riggs, & Johnson, 1999). In this sense, "Daddy's little girl" often remains a lost and dependent "little girl." Jacobvitz and Bush (1996) found father–daughter parentification alliances to be associated with depression, anxiety, and low self-esteem in young women, and mother–daughter alliances to be associated with higher anxiety for daughters.

Again, these findings beg the question: How is it that one who fulfills an inherently overfunctioning family role may also exhibit underfunctioning in various ways? Principles of systems theory tell us that if too much energy, worry, and attention are focused in one direction, then less energy and attention are left for other pursuits; that is, imbalances in one area affect all other aspects of the system (Boszormenyi-Nagy, 1987; Bowen, 1978; L'Abate, 1998). Furthermore, individuals, at least to some degree, participate in and absorb qualities of behaviors exhibited by all members of the system. This notion contributes to understanding the sometimes puzzling, uncanny intergenerational transmission of negative emotional and behavioral family dynamics; for example, adult perpetrators frequently have childhood histories of traumatic victimization, and adults who were parentified as children are at risk for becoming excessively needy or controlling in relationships with their own children (Boszormenyi-Nagy & Spark, 1973; Jacobvitz, Morgan, Kretchmar, & Morgan, 1991; Jacobvitz et al., 1999). Parentified children and adolescents caught in an entire family dialectic of high and low functioning are also likely, therefore, to internalize and play out both patterns, subsequently manifesting behavioral extremes and imbalances in adult relationships, work, and parenting. Chase (1999) described parentification as learned and perpetuated cycles of abdication.

When adults abdicate parental responsibility, children face abdication, by default, of their childhood status and the range of developmental needs, pleasures, struggles, and opportunities childhood rightly entails. Children thus learn first to give up their childhood, and then, with a cycle of abdicating needs and responsibilities well-grooved, they become candidates for later abdicating adult responsibilities. (p. 6)

Inverted cycles of giving up one's needs and giving up one's responsibilities is a hallmark of losing one's childhood to premature adult functioning. (p. 24)

Parentified Children as Adults: Paradoxical Patterns of Functioning

The experience of childhood parentification is predicated, in part, on the child's temperament and capacities to be attuned to the needs of the parent and family circumstance. Alice Miller (1981) referred to those children who were capable of responding to narcissistic parents as "gifted" in their ability to relinquish their authentic needs and construct a "false self" in service to their inadequate and needy parents. The perceptiveness and compassionate sensitivity of such children can be remarkable. Thus, the irony for the parentified child is that the context of deprivation elicits greater rather than lesser functioning from the child and is as much a display of his or her strengths and resourcefulness as it is a foreboding of future stress and deficit. The notion of *resiliency* in children who endure trauma and hardship underscores this assertion (Robinson & Fields, 1983; Rubin, 1996; Werner, 1986). Many studies have documented that adults with parentification histories bring valued insight, compassion, skills of negotiating, adaptability, creativity, and resilience in crisis to their personal and professional relationships (see chapter 6 of this volume). Some of these strengths are shown in Figure 7.1.

At the same time, empirical research and case studies reveal that being parentified as a child, especially when the ingredients for destructive parentification have characterized the child's experience, does have long-term consequences that compromise healthy adult functioning. Studies investigating adult legacies of child and adolescent parentification can be grouped into three categories according to impact on adult functioning in work, relationships, and parenting.

Work

Many studies have documented that individuals who fulfilled parentification roles in their families of origin often enter the "helping

FIGURE 7.1
Strengths and Positive Characteristics of
Adults Who Were Parentified

- Adaptable
- Flexible
- Able to "take charge" and know tacitly how to respond to crisis
- Resourceful
- Competent
- Empathic; others feel a genuine sense of being cared for
- Independent
- Initiating
- Tenacious
- Tolerant and able to persevere in the face of challenges
- Aware of the importance of reciprocity, balance, and imbalances in relationships
- Aware of the importance of justice and fairness
- Able to use their own experience to act compassionately and respectfully toward others
- Perspective and insightful

professions." They are drawn to and excel at work that requires them to exercise the same skills of healing, helping, guiding, mediating, and nurturing that they used as parentified children. Psychology, social work, counseling, teaching, the clergy, nursing, and many areas of medicine are careers that seem to attract high representations of individuals who report having parentification experiences as children (Friedman, 1985; Glickauf-Hughes & Mehlman, 1995; Lackie, 1983; Robinson, 1998a; Sessions, 1986). Sessions (1986) compared the extent of childhood parentification experiences reported by two groups of graduate students, one group working on degrees in psychology and the other on degrees in engineering. The psychology graduate students produced higher scores than their engineering cohorts on objective parentification measures.

In a study using a large sample of 1,577 social workers, Lackie (1982) found that more than two thirds of his respondents had childhood histories of "caretaking" or "go-between" roles in their families. Lackie argued that advantages exist in choosing a career that taps skills cultivated in childhood but cautioned that the legacy of parentification can be a setup for overextending and setting unrealistic standards that then feed a sense of ineffectiveness, leading to eventual burnout in the social worker. Clinicians who have not acknowledged and attempted to resolve personal issues related to their own childhood parentification history risk perpetuating overly caretaking and self-serving relationships with their clients. They are vulnerable to a range of professional problems, such as difficulties setting limits and boundaries, feeling a sense of failure or personal inadequacy when clients do not improve, demonstrating inadequate self-care and access to personal support, and showing the tendency to overextend emotionally and logistically in their work (Blumenstein, 1986; Glickauf-Hughes & Mehlman, 1995, Jurkovic, 1997). Although not yet documented, it is also possible that therapists with unresolved parentification history may tend to overly focus on client deficits rather than strengths given that their family role exacted a vigilance for detecting distress and problems to fix. Nevertheless, Jurkovic (1997) listed as many strengths as liabilities that psychotherapists with parentification history bring to their practice. These strengths include a great capacity for empathy and "humanness," creativity, and a constructive tolerance for working with severely disturbed clients. In fact, as Jurkovic pointed out, it can be an inspiration and source of hope for clients when they learn that their therapist has actually experienced and worked through the grief, pain, and various adult struggles that accompany the recognition of a childhood sacrificed to parentification.

Observing the relationship between career and family role, Bernstein (1985) wrote, "Although we may not realize it, or want to admit it, many of us bring our personal lives, with childhood's emotional baggage, to work with us, with far greater intensity than we bring work home at night" (p. 9). Others, too, have examined the significant, but often unconscious, connection among career choice, work distress, burnout, and family-of-origin experience (Friedman, 1985). The following case example illustrates how insidious such a connection can be, and how childhood experience cultivates "talents" that are useful, even rewarded, in the workplace in spite of the personal toll paid by the individual in such a dilemma.

The Case of Deborah. Deborah, a 27-year-old PhD candidate in education, taught in a federally funded program for economically disadvantaged adolescents. In an effort to assign faculty to teaching "teams" or units, program administrators asked each teacher to submit in writing the names of three other teachers with whom they were willing to work in close alliance. Later, Deborah was commended that she was the only faculty member that everyone put on their lists of names—everyone was willing to work on a team with

Deborah. When units were formed, Deborah was assigned to a group with two other members who happened to be individuals least frequently listed by colleagues as a choice of teammate. Because of her apparent capacity to work well with everyone, to smooth the rough edges in difficult working relations, to function well "in the middle" of less adaptable personalities, Deborah spent a stressful and exhausting year carrying an excessive amount of responsibility in the unit to which she had been assigned with partners who were well known as "difficult" colleagues. Not surprisingly, Deborah's family history had entailed her playing negotiator between hostile and conflicting parents. As an adolescent, she was often brought into her parents' arguments where she developed great acumen into how to avoid taking sides by identifying with everyone's perspective, and in doing so, "talking her parents' down" when their disputes were most acute. She could voice their grievances to each other better than they could, and not only did this establish her connection with each parent, it reserved her place in a triangle of anxious and agitated relating.

Relationships

Because the parentified role requires the child to focus on and orient his or her world around the needs of others—a parent, siblings, or the entire family—many parentified children operate reactively and as overfunctioners or caretakers in their adult relationships. Consequently, it is not unusual for adults with histories of parentification to find themselves in relationships with partners who have many problems, who are needy, or who require a lot of accommodating. From a Bowenian theoretical perspective, overfunctioners attract underfunctioners and vice versa until one partner decides to operate in a nonreactive, self-defining way in relation to the other, and thus begins a process of self-differentiation leading to the possibility of more balanced, reciprocal relating to others (Bowen, 1978). Many case studies and empirical investigations have described problematic adult relationships, "addictive" relationships, "compulsive care-giving" relationships, and the "caretaker syndrome" as patterns associated with unresolved childhood parentification (Betchen, 1996; Olson & Gariti, 1993; Valleau et al., 1995; West & Keller, 1991), and as a legacy of parentified children in workaholic families specifically (Robinson, 1998a). In this sense, the role of caretaker, fixer, family healer, confidante, or whatever service is rendered the family by the parentified child is not simply a role but becomes an internalized sense of self-defined by what he or she does for others. To relate, then, means to do for others rather than *be with* others in a more egalitarian give-and-take fashion.

This historical template overlaying friendships and intimate partnerships is actually a complex phenomenon with seemingly contradictory aspects for the adult parentified child. Overfunctioning through excessive caretaking is a familiar, and thus safe, way of assuring closeness to others just as it secured the child's closeness to an underfunctioning parent. With close proximity established, overfunctioning provides an illusion of control and power in relation to others ("I'll fix, advise, and rescue you"), and in doing so the adult parentified child avoids having to address his or her own fears of inadequacy or pain by directing energy to the distress and needs of others. Furthermore, overfunctioning in relationships keeps one's own vulnerabilities hidden, something that parentified children learn readily to do as they devote themselves to "not needing or wanting much" as children. For a parentified child to be childish—goofy, needy, dependent, and demanding—was to risk rejection by the parent, a threat to survival. As stated, when overfunctioners direct their energy to caretaking, nurturing, responding to, fixing, comforting, and otherwise "doing for" the significant other, the needs, issues and problems of their own lives often are left unattended. Threads of their own low functioning and self-neglect are thus woven into the psychic fabric of the adult parentified child's excessive "caring" for others in this pattern of imbalanced relating. A man in his early 50s, the oldest son of a volatile alcoholic father and codependent mother, became so obsessed with monitoring and "fixing" his unhappy wife that he remained completely oblivious to his own pain and dire circumstance regarding loss of employment during a corporate downsizing. Although unable to provide financially for his wife and children, he resisted job hunting or even discussing their dwindling savings account, and instead argued with his wife about her unwillingness to attend church with him and her increasing irritability in their marriage.

Adult relationships for the individual who was parentified as a child often recapitulate patterns of disappointments, burdens, and the feelings of despair associated with early family experience. Work with couples in which one or both members have family histories of parentification indicates that partners tend to solicit or display parental behavior with each other in attempts to make up for losses and unmet needs endured as parentified children with their parents (Olson & Gariti, 1993). Adult relating is "symbolic" relating and serves as an effort to resolve grievances or simply express that which is familiar from family-of-origin experience. This dynamic is not inherently problematic unless roles become reified with one partner polarized as high functioner and the other as low functioner (Betchen, 1996; Jurkovic, 1997). Such polarization reveals itself also in workaholic families (Robinson et al., in press), suggesting that the adults parentified as children are indeed familiar with such disparate functioning.

Jones and Wells (1996) and Wells and Jones (1998) investigated adult personality development and childhood parentification experiences. In several empirical studies, they found that patterns of masochistic, self-defeating, and narcissistic grandiose adult personality tendencies were associated with certain kinds of parentification experience (see chapter 5 of this volume). In some cases, children who are parentified may be expected as part of their role to achieve for the parent, and in other cases, care for and validate the parent. The adult legacy, then becomes either one of *worth through achievement* (narcissistic pattern) or *worth through caretaking* (masochistic pattern) if the parentification was severe enough to be internalized as the individual's sense of self in relation to others. In either case, the individual who has internalized the parentified role is compelled in adulthood to "earn" his or her sense of worth to others and to self (Wells, 1999).

When driven to establish worth by whatever route most familiar, the adult who was parentified as a child may appear as depressed or grandiose, high or low functioning, competent or burdened. Given the paradoxical nature of the parentification experience, it is arguable that adults who struggle with this legacy will demonstrate tendencies in both dimensions discussed.

Many adults and young adults who describe childhood experiences of caretaking their parents and family also describe feeling shortchanged in their adult lives. They entered adulthood sometimes already quite weary and disillusioned from having lived as pseudoadults while still very young and lacking mature adult resources. Even when material comforts and social and educational opportunities are available, as is usually evident in high-performing families, the parentification experience of childhood and adolescence can render young adults drained and disappointed about adulthood.

The Case of Matt. Matt was in his late 20s. He carried a profound and pervasive cynicism and despair about work, relationships, and mostly, about himself. Matt was the oldest son in an affluent family. His father was a physician, and his mother had been a homemaker while the family was intact, and, after his parents' divorce, became a businesswoman. By his late 20s, Matt was in recovery for alcoholism and "white-collar" heroin addiction, and he had returned to college to finish his undergraduate degree, majoring in counseling psychology. During childhood and early adolescence, Matt had played three caretaking roles in his troubled, yet high-status family. Matt aligned with his mother and served as her confidante and surrogate husband after his parents' bitter divorce. In addition, he also lived out a role of warrior, challenging and fighting his father, "the enemy," and at the same time protecting and reassuring his younger brother, who was terribly frightened when the parents fought. Matt described his father as "emotionally and physically unavailable and shut down." Matt reported that as an 11- or 12-year-old boy when he would get particularly anxious himself he would "clean the house" and that would soothe him. By age 14, Matt was drinking and using marijuana regularly, and in his own words, "entered my fuck-up phase," which followed him through boarding school, military service, college expulsion, and finally, alcohol and drug treatment. Today he continues to struggle to understand many paradoxical feelings and behaviors. He describes being burdened with feeling responsible for "everything" and, at the same time, feeling incompetent and not good at "anything" in work and in his relationship with his girlfriend. Matt would report frustration that his contributions at work were undervalued and unrecognized, although he also reported being highly competent at work according to supervisors. Similarly, Matt was both overly tolerant and overly reactive to criticism and grievances from his girlfriend, as if every word of complaint from her carried absolute truth and was an immediate call to action and reform on his part—to fix or change himself or the circumstance in some fashion. "What's me and what's not me?" he would ask repeatedly, or "When is it ever my turn to complain?" or "Why don't others do for me what I do for them?"

Matt struggled with beginning his adulthood literally exhausted and shortchanged by his childhood and disguised this "chronic fatigue" of sorts with fluctuating patterns of competency, organization, and activation and of depression, cynicism, overextension, and enmeshed reactivity in close relationships. With time and the support of psychotherapy, Matt learned to set limits with his overinvolved mother, cultivate a relationship as an adult with his father, and stand up for himself more with his girlfriend by talking directly about his feelings and desires.

Parenting

Adults who were parentified as children are at risk of perpetuating similar patterns of relating to their own children in direct and unconscious ways. Parentification as an intergenerational family dynamic is well elucidated in the history of family therapy literature as well as in current research investigating attachment patterns and generational boundary dissolutions across multiple generations within families (Boszormenyi-Nagy & Spark, 1973; Jacobvitz & Bush, 1996; Jacobvitz et al., 1991). In this sense, the parentification of a child involves relational imbalances in responsible parenting that spans at least three generations. Adults who parentify their children are seeking to fill deficits experienced in relation to their childhood experience, and often specifically related to having been parentified themselves as children. Again, underscoring the theme of relationships as dialectics and yielding paradoxical experiences on the individual and systemic levels, Jacobvitz et al. (1999) described the intergenerational transmission of parentification.

> Because participants in close relationships learn both roles of a relationship pattern, a dialectic dynamic results in which one can play either role of a dyadic pattern. This switching between one of two complementary roles can occur over time within one relationship or between generations. A woman who was parentified as a child may, with her own child, take on the role of needy adult and thereby replicate the relationship that she experienced as a child, this time assuming her mother's role. (p. 41)

As indicated in the previous section, adults with parentification histories have difficulties in forming reciprocal, egalitarian, and mutually satisfying adult partnerships and marriages. The prevalence of marital discord, disappointment, and an alienation from supportive adult-to-adult connections has been shown to be a key ingredient in prompting adults to seek inordinate satisfaction—becoming dependent, too involved, and controlling—in relationship to their children (Jacobvitz & Bush, 1996; Karpel, 1976).

Another factor in perpetuating a cycle of parentification is illustrated in the following case example.

The Case of Joyce. Agnes, Joyce's aging but healthy mother, divorced her husband after 34 years of marriage when she was in her late 50s. Agnes's former husband, a business executive, had provided well financially for his wife and two children but had been distant from marital and parenting responsibilities and was suspected to have "affairs" outside the marriage. After Joyce and her brother grew up and left home, Agnes no longer tolerated her husband's philandering and absence. She filed for divorce and received a substantial settlement and alimony agreement. Now living comfortably in a condominium, Agnes stays in daily contact with her daughter, Joyce, who lives nearby with her husband and children. Joyce runs errands to the grocery, takes her mother on weekly outings, invites her mother to dinner, returns her mother's advice-seeking phone calls, and frequently offers to drive her mother places despite Agnes's ability to drive herself. Joyce has always insisted that Agnes also join her and her family on out-of-town vacation trips. Joyce is reluctant to say no to any of her mother's requests or demands even though sometimes she would express her frustration that her mother "always needs so much." Joyce believes that saying no at times would be "rude" or stir things up, and maintains that it is "easier" to cater to her mom's wishes instead of setting limits. Joyce has three children, a husband, and works full time; she holds herself to exceedingly high standards as a mother, wife, and employee—and as her mother's only daughter. She has set a routine for her days that begins before dawn and sometimes does not end until after midnight. As long as her routine is not disrupted, Joyce seems to "manage." Yet, when her children "get too messy," as she says, or when her husband becomes inattentive, Joyce says she "snaps." "I can't take care of everything and everybody around here—so get it together—and now!" Her oldest son, already showing stressful signs of his own parentification, can be "counted on," according to Joyce, to be the first to rally in response to his mother's angry and frantic plea. Joyce admits, "Sometimes I'm so tired I could sob, but everyone's depending on me—and there are just never enough hours in the day." Once her husband said to her, "Must we always think of your mother first—why can't it sometimes just be you, me, and the kids?" Joyce felt frustrated and unsupported by her husband. After all, she retorts, "I'm all my mother's got—what would she do if it weren't for me—and us!"

Case Analyses

In most cases, the enmeshed nature of parent–child relating does not simply end when the child reaches adulthood. In fact, when the parentified child reaches adulthood, further complications may emerge as children are born, new families established, and the parent ages and requires necessary care. Observations of three generations of mothers and their children have documented ongoing patterns of over- and underinvolvement, further evidence that parentification predisposes the individual to carry confusions about boundaries, responsibilities, and mutuality in relating across the life span. Women who reported that their mothers had been excessively involved and controlling also demonstrated excessive control and intrusion into the lives of their now elderly mothers, as well as with their own children (Jacobvitz & Bush, 1996). Deborah, Matt, and Joyce represent different aspects of parentification consequences on adult functioning. Deborah's vulnerability to being triangulated represents not only her strengths at negotiating but also her Achilles' heel at finding herself caught in the middle and overly stressed by divided loyalties. Parentified children often feel quite powerful in their family role. Deborah provides a good illustration of how a boundless sense of power and capacity to "cope" with anything can promote a person professionally, and yet plant seeds for unraveling tendencies to overextend.

Matt's sense of life as perpetual burden points to the extent to which he still functions reactively, feeling overly responsible for others and carrying the exhausted vigilance and self-doubt characteristic of his parentification experience. His ambiguity about his role and commitment in relationships and career echoes the findings of Fullinwider-Bush and Jacobvitz's (1993) study of young women in parentified roles with their fathers (i.e., opposite-sex parent–child alliances). Matt's experience elucidates the gnawing and subtle difficulty young adults face in claiming identity and purpose when significant adults have been absent or overly needy. Matt's father's devotion to his medical career, and the bitterness and demise of his parents' marriage, left both parents insensitive to the protection, parenting, and guidance Matt and his younger brother deserved in formative years. In this light, Matt's alcohol and drug use can be understood as an effort, inadvertently, to abandon his overextended family responsibility. "Fucking-up" meant a twisted sense of freedom from obligation and worry.

Joyce provides an example of intergenerational patterns of imbalance in what is expected and given between parents and children. Joyce has structured her adult life, and even her relationship with her husband and children, around doing for her mother. The care she offers her mother is given as obligation and duty and is elicited without the freedom to regulate, to say no, or to set limits. Such a dynamic has been described as "destructive entitlement" by family therapists (Boszormenyi-Nagy & Krasner, 1986; Boszormenyi-Nagy & Spark, 1973). It is likely that the enmeshed relationship with her mother is long-standing and predicated on Agnes's conflict with her husband during their marriage (related also to Agnes's family-of-origin history). If Joyce were required to "fill in" in her father's absence or take sides with her mother, her role as her mother's caretaker was established early on, and it has simply continued. The price Joyce pays is the stress and compulsivity of overdoing, which, moreover, is evident in the disappointments and breech of intimacy she and her husband express. Her son has also learned the family's pattern of reactivity and caretaking, and no doubt is also sensitive to his parents marital stress.

Figure 7.2 summarizes the liabilities that often are sources of confusion, pain, and struggle for adults with parentification history.

FIGURE 7.2
Liabilities and At-Risk Characteristics of
Adults Who Were Parentified

- "Compulsive caregiving" and/or addictive relating
- Stress-related physical symptoms
- Burnout (negativity, irritability, fatigue, isolation, despair, desire for escape)
- Haunted by feelings of inadequacy and self-doubt
- Chronic worrying, anxiety, and feeling overwhelmed
- Addictions (alcohol, food, work)
- Inability to set limits, overextends
- Can't say no without feeling guilty
- Inappropriate boundaries and limits with others (clients, students, coworkers, personal relations)
- Divided energies and loyalties—feels caught in the middle and unable to remove self from triangulated relating
- Exhaustion, inadequate self-care
- Overly serious, difficulty relaxing, difficulty experiencing pleasure and enjoyment
- Pleasing-others orientation
- Difficulty asking for help or support
- Denies own needs and vulnerabilities
- Self-defeating personality traits and behaviors
- Depression, resentment, bitterness

Suggestions for Clinical Practice

Although the picture of adulthood for those who endured parentified childhoods seems filled with obstacles, it is important that clinicians remember the paradox inherent in parentification. In the context of being deprived of parental nurturance, these children displayed, in some manifestation, greater rather than lesser functioning. Parentified children are resilient and resourceful, and in most cases, become resilient and resourceful adults. In fact, they often show great tenacity and motivation in their psychotherapeutic process.

The circumstances that bring adults with parentification history into treatment vary greatly. In some cases, the themes and issues related to their parentification are easily discernible, and in other cases, they are hidden beneath pressing crises or simply disguised. One therapist described working with a female client who was experiencing symptoms of posttraumatic stress disorder after a gunpoint robbery, only to uncover months later that many of the distressful symptoms persisting were tapping into exploitative experiences of childhood parentification (Hickman, 1998). Figure 7.3 lists some of the symptoms, behaviors, and issues of adults with histories of childhood parentification, and Figure 7.4 lists treatment themes in working with these parentified clients.

The first challenge that clinicians face in working with adults with parentification history is identifying it, especially when other issues or crises appear as presenting problems. Treatment of parentification in individual adults usually emerges as an underlying theme or unspoken story beneath overt complaints and symptoms ranging from stress, anxiety, and depression to relationship difficulties and addictive and obsessive–compulsive behaviors. Broadly speaking, clinical work with individuals struggling with the array of distress related to historical parentification entails three interrelated therapeutic categories, as follows.

Developing Self-Care and Self-Expression

Helping clients differentiate from imbalanced and enmeshed relationships by developing greater self-care, self-awareness, and expression of their needs, wants, and perspectives to others is essential for overcoming patterns of compulsive overdoing and caretaking. Such differentiation of self also begins to clarify dual patterns of under- and overfunctioning operating and allows clients to reevaluate where their energies are directed, what priorities they value, and what is and what is not their responsibility. Adults with parent-

FIGURE 7.3
Symptoms, Behaviors, and Issues Characteristic of
Adults With Histories of Childhood Parentification

Symptoms
- Depression
- Anxiety
- Chronic posttraumatic stress disorder
- Dissociation
- Stress-related physical symptoms
- Anger
- Addictions
- Exhaustion
- Sadness
- Loneliness
- Confusion and divided energies
- Sense of being overwhelmed, self-doubt, sense of inadequacy or failure

Behaviors
- Fears others' reactions
- Difficulty with decisions
- Overly compliant
- Overly controlling
- Overly involved with parents or children
- Overly responsible
- Enmeshed, undifferentiated relationships
- Compulsive caretaking
- Problems with intimacy (safety/vulnerability)
- Difficulty setting limits
- Inadequate self-care and self-soothing
- Discounts self
- Puts the needs and opinions of others first
- Excessive anger when reciprocity does not exist
- Excessively high or low expectations of others
- Empathic toward others or causes
- Perceives own vulnerability as weakness
- Uncomfortable with or denies vulnerabilities or needs in self

Issues
- Leaving home
- Separations
- Work/career
- Relationships
- Addictions
- Parenting
- Abuse/trauma

Figure 7.4
Treatment Themes in Working With Adults
With Histories of Childhood Parentification

- Developing relationship with self
- Expressing feelings and opinions in appropriate ways
- Learning to set limits
- Removing self from parentified role with others
- Grief, mourning
- Identifying hurt and sadness beneath anger
- Self-care
- Developing reciprocal relationships with others
- Identifying and reducing distortions of responsibility in relating to others
- Developing capacity to play; lightheartedness, fun, pleasure
- Addressing addictive behaviors
- Developing capacity for self-validation
- Developing openness to support

ification history are often blind to the degree to which they guide themselves according to others' needs and wishes, and likewise remain unaware of the extent to which they ignore or discount their own personal needs and signals of distress either on a physical or emotional level. They may need encouragement in expressing genuine wants, making requests of others, and overcoming feelings of guilt especially in situations in which others are making contrary demands or requests. "I don't want to be selfish" and "I don't want to be needy like my mother" are worries that clients carry as they begin to directly acknowledge their own limits and vulnerabilities. Learning to remove oneself and avoid getting "caught in the middle" or triangulated in conflicted relationships are skills for clients to identify and develop with practice. Again, divided loyalties and triangulated relational dynamics are sometimes so much a part of the parentification experience that clients may report feeling "torn" and frustrated without recognizing an unfair or impossible position. Similarly, because parentification is a distortion of responsibility for self and others, and results in profound insecurities and confusions about intimate attachment, trust, interdependency, and balanced reciprocity in relating, clients may need support in knowing reasonable expectations of others as well as themselves. Cultivating balance and an egalitarian, nondemanding sense of giving and receiving in relationships, in work, and in all areas of living is new territory for most parentified adults. Clients may report that any effort at giving in relationships feels like a burdening sacrifice, and in the same vein, they may have difficulty appreciating and accepting what is offered them by others. Both of these challenges to genuine intimacy and healthy reciprocity are rooted at least to some extent in exploitative, disappointing, or manipulative aspects of a parentified role in relation to others.

Mourning Loss of Childhood

Loss and grief are fundamental themes for those adults who missed being parented as children and may surface in all its stages as clients acknowledge and tell their stories. Journaling feelings and experiences and experiencing safety, acknowledgment, and support from the therapeutic relationship are important for helping clients explore, express, and accept the major loss that is inherent in being parentified as a child. As discussed at the beginning of this chapter, parentified children often feel invisible regarding their true nature and feelings in spite of overfunctioning. Listening to, validating, and having their experiences and feelings heard and valued provide corrective emotional experiences for adults who were parentified. Groups and opportunities to share with other adults who have had similar experiences are also beneficial and encourage parentified adults to seek and be open to receiving as well as giving support.

Overcoming Feelings of Guilt and Shame, and Tolerating One's Own Vulnerability

Related to parentified adults' overextended sense of responsibility and its ensuing sense of guilt are also pervasive feelings of failure and inadequacy—"No matter how much I do, it's never enough." Because many parentified children never actually "righted" the wrongs and sufferings in their families (nor could they), many are haunted in adulthood with shame regarding vulnerability, a lingering sense of inadequacy and failure, or fear that who they are somehow falls short of who they should be. Helping clients recognize, accept, and enjoy their humanness is part of the healing for parentified adults. Identifying the inordinate expectations and experiences parentified children fulfilled and endured is important for helping them realize the intensity and mercilessness with which they, as adults, scrutinize and judge themselves. In addition to learning that their needs and vulnerabilities are a normal part of being human and do not need to be discounted or hidden, adults who experienced parentified childhoods sometimes need to be encouraged to play, to find joy and pleasure in ways that are purely fun. Similarly, helping clients to develop a self-care plan that identifies ways to rest and replenish themselves when fatigued and to cultivate healthy forms of self-soothing and relaxation is also a component of encouraging balance and self-awareness.

Other chapters in this monograph offer additional recommendations for treatment of parentification issues in adults (see chapters 5 and 6) and in families as it is related to family dynamics surrounding workaholism (see chapter 1).

Conclusion

The question remains as to whether parentification in high-performing or workaholic families carries distinct characteristics differing from its etiology and symptoms in other family conditions, for example, abuse and violence, alcoholism, and chronic mental or physical illness. Until further empirical and qualitative investigation of this question is undertaken, responses remain speculative, based in case examples and anecdotal reports, and gleaned from the few newly conducted studies examining family consequences of workaholism. To date, one study documents self-reported parentification experiences in a sample of adult children of workaholics to be of greater degree than self-reported parentification experiences in a sample of adult children of alcoholics (Carroll & Robinson, in press).

Because workaholism is described as "the best-dressed addiction" (Robinson, 1998a), it is possible that in high-performing families the parentification of their children remains also well-clothed under garments of achievement and affluence, as Stephanie's case example illustrated. Damage to intimacy, emotional unavailability, marital estrangement, and systems of enabling denial—characteristic of families of workaholics—are all variables that have been observed and documented in other family constellations as contributing to destructive parentification of children (Boszormenyi-Nagy & Spark, 1973; Jurkovic, 1997; Karpel, 1976; Robinson et al., in press). Further research is needed to determine if long-term consequences of childhood parentification are mediated by the strengths and resources often available in high-performing families or if such conditions actually exacerbate or disguise parentifying dynamics.

The paradoxes, comingling strengths and liabilities, of adults who were parentified children are presented in this chapter. For the cobbler's children to remain shoeless is now explainable in the context of high-performing families, but it remains an unjust and tragic price to pay for a parent's devotion to work. In connection to high-performing families and the successes and failures of their offspring, parentification might be the form in which such payments are made and such losses rendered.

References

Barnett, B., & Parker, G. (1998). The parentified child: Early competence or childhood deprivation? *Child Psychology and Psychiatry Review, 3,* 146–155.

Bekir, P., McLellan, T., Childress, A. R., & Gariti, P. (1993). Role reversals in families of substance abusers: A transgenerational phenomenon. *International Journal of the Addictions, 28,* 613–630.

Berman, W. H., & Sperling, M. B. (1991). Parental attachment and emotional distress in the transition to college. *Journal of Youth and Adolescence, 20,* 427–440.

Bernstein, P. (1985). *Family ties, corporate bonds.* New York: Henry Holt.

Betchen, S. J. (1996). Parentified pursuers and childlike distancers in marital therapy. *Family Journal: Counseling and Therapy for Couples and Families, 4,* 100–108.

Bloom, M. V. (1987). Leaving home: A family transition. In J. Bloom-Feshbach & S. Bloom-Feshbach (Eds.), *The psychology of separation and loss* (pp. 227–245). San Francisco: Jossey-Bass.

Blumenstein, H. (1986). Maintaining a family focus: Underlying issues and challenges. *Clinical Social Work Journal, 14,* 238–249.

Boszormenyi-Nagy, I. (1987). *Foundations of contextual therapy.* New York: Brunner/Mazel.

Boszormenyi-Nagy, I., & Krasner, B. R. (1986). *Between give and take: A clinical guide to contextual therapy.* New York: Brunner/Mazel.

Boszormenyi-Nagy, I., & Spark, G. (1973). *Invisible loyalties: Reciprocity in intergenerational family therapy.* New York: Harper & Row.

Bowen, M. (1978). *Family therapy in clinical practice.* Northvale, NJ: Jason Aronson.

Buchanan, C. M., Maccoby, E. E., & Dornbusch, S. M. (1991). Caught between parents: Adolescents' experience in divorced homes. *Child Development, 62,* 1008–1029.

Burt, A. (1992). *Generation boundary distortion: Implications for object relations development.* Unpublished doctoral dissertation, Georgia State University.

Carroll, J. J., & Robinson, B. E. (in press). Depression and parentification among adults as related to parental workaholism and alcoholism. *The Family Journal.*

Chase, N. D. (Ed.). (1999) *Burdened children: Theory, research, and treatment of parentification.* Thousand Oaks, CA: Sage.

Chase, N. D., Deming, M. P., & Wells, M. C. (1998). Parentification, parental alcoholism, and academic status among young adults. *American Journal of Family Therapy, 26,* 105–114.

Coale, H. W. (1999). Therapeutic rituals and rites of passage: Helping parentified children and their families. In N. Chase (Ed.), *Burdened children: Theory, research, and treatment of parentification* (pp. 132–140). Thousand Oaks, CA: Sage.

Coles, R. (1977). *Children of crisis: Privileged ones.* Boston: Little Brown.

Cummings, E. M., Zahn-Waxler, C., & Radke-Yarrow, M. (1984). Developmental changes in children's reaction to anger in the same family. *Developmental Psychology, 21,* 747–760.

Downey, G., & Coyne, J. C. (1990). Children of depressed parents: An integrative review. *Psychological Bulletin, 108,* 50–76.

Friedman, E. H. (1985). *Generation to generation: Family process in church and synagogue.* New York: Guilford Press.

Fullinwider-Bush, N., & Jacobvitz, D. B. (1993). The transition to young adulthood: Generational boundary dissolution and female identity development. *Family Process, 32,* 87–103.

Glickauf-Hughes, C., & Mehlman, E. (1995). Narcissistic issues in therapists: Diagnostic and treatment considerations. *Psychotherapy, 32,* 213–220.

Goglia, L. R., Jurkovic, G., Burt, A., & Burge-Callaway, K. (1992). Generational boundary distortions by adult children of alcoholics: Child-as-parent and child-as-mate. *American Journal of Family Therapy, 20,* 291–299.

Held, B., & Bellows, D. (1983). A family systems approach to crisis reactions in college students. *Journal of Marital and Family Therapy, 9,* 363–373.

Hetherington, E. M. (1988). Parents, children, and siblings 6 years after divorce. In R. A. Hinde & J. Stevenson-Hinde (Eds.), *Relations within families: Mutual influences* (pp. 311–331). New York: Oxford University Press.

Hickman, N. (1998, April 17). *Parentification: A case study in PTSD.* Paper presented at the Atlanta Area Child Guidance Clinic, Atlanta, GA.

Howes, P., & Markman, H. J. (1989). Marital quality and child functioning: A longitudinal investigation. *Child Development, 60,* 1044–1051.

Jacobvitz, D. B., & Bush, N. (1996). Reconstructions of family relationships: Parent–child alliances, personal distress, and self-esteem. *Developmental Psychology, 32,* 732–743.

Jacobvitz, D. B., Morgan, E., Kretchmar, M., & Morgan, Y. (1991). The transmission of mother–child boundary disturbances across three generations. *Development and Psychopathology, 3,* 513–527.

Jacobvitz, D. B., Riggs, S., & Johnson, E. (1999). Cross-sex and same-sex family alliances: Immediate and long-term effects on sons and daughters. In N. Chase (Ed.), *Burdened children: Theory, research, and treatment of parentification* (pp. 34–55). Thousand Oaks, CA: Sage.

Johnson, S. (1993). Structural elements in Franz Kafka's *The Metamorphosis. Journal of Marital and Family Therapy, 19,* 149–157.

Johnston, J. R. (1990). Role diffusion and role reversal: Structural variations in divorced families and children's functioning. *Family Relations, 39*, 405–413.

Jones, R., & Wells, M. C. (1996). An empirical study of parentification and personality. *American Journal of Family Therapy, 24*, 145–152.

Jurkovic, G. J. (1997). *Lost childhoods: The plight of the parentified child.* New York: Brunner-Mazel.

Jurkovic, G. J. (1998). Destructive parentification in families: Causes and consequences. In L. L'Abate (Ed.), *Family psychopathology: The relational roots of dysfunctional behavior* (pp. 237–255). New York: Guilford Press.

Karpel, M. A. (1976). Intrapsychic and interpersonal processes in the parentification of children (Doctoral dissertation, University of Massachusetts). *Dissertation Abstracts International, 38*, 365. (University Microfilms No. 77–15090)

Keele, R. L. (1984). Executive families: From pitfalls to payoffs. In N. M. Hoopes, F. L. Fisher, & S. H. Barlow (Eds.), *Structured family facilitation programs: Enrichment, education, and treatment* (pp. 209–229). Rockville, MD: Aspen System.

L'Abate, L. (Ed.). (1998). *Family psychopathology: The relational roots of dysfunctional behavior.* New York: Guilford Press.

Lackie, B. (1982). *Family correlates of career achievement in social work.* Unpublished doctoral dissertation, Rutgers University. (University Microfilm No. 8221687)

Lackie, B. (1983). The families of origin of social workers. *Clinical Social Work Journal, 11*, 309–322.

Lamorey, S. (1999). Parentification of siblings of children with disability or chronic disease. In N. Chase (Ed.), *Burdened children: Theory, research, and treatment of parentification* (pp. 75–91). Thousand Oaks, CA: Sage.

Mahler, M. S., & Rabinovitch, R. (1956). The effects of marital conflict on child development. In V. E. Eisenstein (Ed.), *Neurotic interaction in marriage* (pp. 44–56). New York: Basic Books.

Main, M., & Hesse, E. (1990). Parents' unresolved traumatic experiences are related to infant disorganized attachment status: Is frightened and/or frightening parental behavior the linking mechanism? In M. Greenberg, D. Cicchetti, & M. Cummings (Eds.), *Attachment in the preschool years* (pp. 161–182). Chicago: University of Chicago Press.

Maraniss, D. (1999). *When pride still mattered: A life of Vince Lombardi.* New York: Simon & Schuster.

Miller, A. (1981). *Prisoners of childhood: The drama of the gifted child and the search for the true self.* New York: Basic Books.

Minuchin, S., Montalvo, B., Guerney, B.G., Rosman, B., & Schumer, F. (1967). *Families of the slums: An exploration of their structure and treatment.* New York: Basic Books.

Mitchell, G., & Cronson H. (1987). The celebrity family: A clinical perspective. *American Journal of Family Therapy, 15*, 235–241.

Morris, M. G., & Gould, R. W. (1963). Role reversal: A necessary concept in dealing with the battered child syndrome. *American Journal of Orthopsychiatry, 33*, 298–299.

Olson, M., & Gariti, P. (1993). Symbolic loss in horizontal relating: Defining the role of parentification in addictive/destructive relationships. *Contemporary Family Journal, 15*, 197–208.

Pittman, F. S. (1985). Children of the rich. *Family Process, 24* 461–472.

Robinson, B.E. (1998a). *Chained to the desk: A guidebook for workaholics, their partners and children, and the clinicians who treat them.* New York: New York University Press.

Robinson, B. E. (1998b). The workaholic family: A clinical perspective. *American Journal of Family Therapy, 26*, 63–73.

Robinson, B. E. (1999). Workaholic children: One method of fulfilling the parentification role. In N. Chase (Ed.), *Burdened children: Theory, research, and treatment* (pp. 56–74). Thousand Oaks, CA: Sage.

Robinson, B. E., Carroll, J. J., & Flowers, C. (in press). Marital estrangement, positive affect, and locus of control among spouses of workaholics and spouses of nonworkaholics: A national study. *American Journal of Family Therapy.*

Robinson, B. E., & Fields, N. (1983). Casework with invulnerable children. *Social Work, 28*, 63–65.

Robinson, B. E., & Kelley, L. (1998). Adult children of workaholics: Self-concept, anxiety, depression, and locus of control. *American Journal of Family Therapy, 26*, 35–50.

Robinson, B. E., & Post, P. (1995). Work addiction as a function of family of origin and its influence on current family functioning. *Family Journal, 3*, 200–206.

Robinson, B. E., & Rhoden, L. (1998). *Working with children of alcoholics: The practitioner's handbook* (2nd ed.). Thousand Oaks, CA: Sage.

Rubin, L. (1996). *The transcendent child: Tales of triumph over the past.* New York: Basic Books.

Salinger, J. D. (1953). *Nine stories.* Boston: Little, Brown.

Schmideberg, M. (1948). Parents as children. *Psychiatric Quarterly Supplement, 22*, 207–218.

Sessions, M. W. (1986). *Influence of parentification on professional role choice and interpersonal style* (Doctoral dissertation, Georgia State University). *Dissertation Abstracts International, 47*, 5066. (University Microfilms No. 87-06815)

Valleau, M. P., Bergner, R. M., & Horton, C. B. (1995). Parentification and caretaker syndrome: An empirical investigation. *Family Therapy, 22*, 157–164.

Wells, M. (1999, September). *Three forms of parentification.* Paper presented at Charis Books, Atlanta, GA.

Wells, M., & Jones, R. (1998). The relationship between parentification, splitting, and dissociation: Preliminary findings. *American Journal of Family Therapy, 26*, 331–339.

Weiss, E. (Executive Producer). (1999, March 8). *All things considered.* Washington, DC: National Public Radio.

Werner, E. E. (1986). Resilient offspring of alcoholics: A longitudinal study from birth to age 18. *Journal of Studies on Alcohol, 47,* 34–40.

West, M. L., & Keller, A. E. R. (1991). Parentification of the child: A case study of Bowlby's compulsive caregiving attachment pattern. *American Journal of Psychotherapy, 45,* 425–431.

West, M. O., & Prinz, R. J. (1987). Parental alcoholism and childhood psychopathology. *Psychological Bulletin, 102,* 204–218.

Wolkin, J. (1984). Childhood parentification: An exploration of long-term effects (Doctoral dissertation, Georgia State University). *Dissertation Abstracts International, 45,* 2702-B.

Zahn-Waxler, C., Cummings, E. M., Iannotti, R. M., & Radke-Yarrow, M. (1984). Young offspring of depressed parents: A population at risk for affective problems. In D. Cicchetti & K. Schneider-Rosen (Eds.), *New directions for child development: No. 26. Childhood depression* (pp. 81–105). San Francisco: Jossey-Bass.

Zahn-Waxler, C., Kochanska, G., Krupnick, J., & McKnew, D. (1990). Patterns of guilt in children of depressed and well mothers. *Developmental Psychology, 26,* 51–59.

■ ■ ■

High performing families :
causes, consequences, and
clinical solutions